Appellate Justice in England and the United States: A Comparative Analysis

by **Robert J. Martineau**
Distinguished Research Professor of Law
University of Cincinnati

William S. Hein & Co., Inc.
Buffalo, New York
1990

Library of Congress Catalog Card Number 90-84310
ISBN 0-89941-733-7

Copyright © 1990 William S. Hein & Co., Inc.
All rights reserved.

Printed in the United States of America

This volume is printed on acid-free paper by
William S. Hein & Co., Inc.

Table of Contents

Introduction xi
Acknowledgements xvii
Comparative Glossary of Terms xxi

Chapter 1	Structure and Function of Appellate Courts	1

A. England 1
  1. Historical Development 1
  2. Purpose and Function of
     Appellate Review 5
  3. Principles of Appellate Review 13
    a. The Right to Appeal 13
    b. What Can Be Appealed 15
    c. Who Can Appeal 17
    d. Standard of Review 18
    e. Reversible Error 18
    f. Issues That Can Be Raised 19
  4. Criminal Division of Court of Appeal 19
  5. Civil Appeals in Scotland 21

B. United States 23
  1. Historical Development 23
  2. Relationship Between State
     and Federal Court Systems 26
  3. Purpose and Function of Appellate Review . . 27
  4. Principles of Appellate Review 32
    a. The Right to Appeal 32
    b. What Can Be Appealed 33

   c. Who Can Appeal 34
   d. Standard of Review 35
   e. Reversible Error 36
   f. Issues That Can Be Raised 37
 C. Comparison 37
  1. Historical Development 37
  2. Purpose and Function of Appellate Review . . 40
  3. Principles of Appellate Review 42
   a. The Right to Appeal 42
   b. What Can Be Appealed 46
   c. Who Can Appeal 47
   d. Standard of Review 48
   e. Reversible Error 48
   f. Issues That Can Be Raised 48
Endnotes 50

Chapter 2	The Personnel of Appellate Review	57

 A. England 57
  1. The Lawyers 57
   a. Barristers 57
   b. Solicitors 62
  2. The Judges 64
  3. The Staff 67
  4. Reform of the Legal Profession 69
 B. United States 79
  1. The Lawyers 80
  2. The Judges 82
  3. The Staff 84
 C. Comparison 86
  1. The Lawyers 86
  2. The Judges 89
  3. The Staff 91
Endnotes 94

Chapter 3	The Written Tradition and the Oral Tradition	101

A. The Oral Tradition in England 101
   1. Arguments of Counsel 101
   2. Judgments 104

B. The Written Tradition in the United States ... 108
   1. The Brief 108
   2. Opinions 110

C. Comparison 115
   1. Reasons for Development of Different Tradition 115
   2. Accountability 118
   3. Efficiency 120
   4. Effectiveness 123
   5. Judgments and Opinions 133

Endnotes 140

Chapter 4	Coping with Increased Caseloads	149

A. Caseload Growth and Responses 149
   1. England 149
      a. Caseload Growth 149
      b. Responses 150
   2. United States 155
      a. Caseload Growth 155
      b. Responses 156

B. Efficiency 161
   1. England 161
   2. United States 162

C. Comparison 167

Endnotes 172

The Civil Appeals Process	175

- A. England 175
  1. The Appealable Order 175
  2. Parties 175
  3. Initiating and Perfecting the Appeal 176
     - a. The Notice Of Appeal 176
     - b. Respondent's Notice 180
  4. Relief Pending Appeal 180
  5. Bundles 181
  6. Application Practice 183
  7. Briefs and Appendices 184
  8. Case Management and Internal Operating Procedures 184
     - a. Case Processing 184
     - b. The Disposition Process 188
  9. Order 194
  10. Appeal to the House of Lords 194
- B. United States 195
  1. The Appealable Judgment 195
  2. Parties 196
  3. Initiating and Perfecting the Appeal 197
     - a. The Notice of Appeal 197
     - b. Cross Appeals 200
     - c. Perfecting the Appeal 200
  4. Relief Pending Appeal 201
  5. Record on Appeal 202
  6. Motion Practice 205
  7. Briefs and Appendix 206
     - a. Briefs 206
     - b. Appendix 209
  8. Case Management and Internal Operating Procedures 210
     - a. Case Processing 210
     - b. The Disposition Process 213

		i. Submission on Briefs	213
		ii. Submission After Oral Argument	214
	9.	Reconsideration	216
	10.	Seeking Review in a Supreme Cou	217
	11.	Issuance of Mandate	219
C.	Comparison		219
	1.	The Appealable Judgment or Order	219
	2.	Parties	220
	3.	Initiating and Perfecting the Appeal	221
		a. The Notice of Appeal	221
		b. Cross Appeal and Respondent's Notice	226
	4.	Relief Pending Appeal	226
	5.	Records and Bundles	227
	6.	Application and Motion Practice	229
	7.	Briefs and Appendices	230
	8.	Case Management and Internal Operating Procedures	230
		a. Philosophy of Case Management	230
		b. Case Processing	230
		c. The Disposition Process	232
	9.	Mandate and Order	232
	10.	Reconsideration	233
	11.	Seeking Review in the Supreme Court of the House of Lords	233
Endnotes			235

Chapter 6	The Future of Appellate Justice in England and the United States	239

A.	Summary of Similarities and Differences	239
	1. Structure and Function	239
	2. Personnel	240
	3. The Oral and Written Traditions	242
	4. Caseload Growth and Responses to It	243
	5. The Civil Appeals Process	244

B. The Future of Appellate Justice 245
　1. England 245
　2. United States 248
Endnotes 252

Appendix A	Summary of Recommendations	253

　1. England 253
　2. United States 256

Appendix B	The Oral Tradition in Practice — 5 Case Studies	259

Introduction 259
Re "C" A Minor 261
　Facts and Procedural History 261
　Oral Hearing 266
　Judgments 267
　Observations 271
Bray v. Best 272
　Facts and Procedural History 272
　Oral Hearing 276
　Judgments 278
　Observations 282
The Queen v. Secretary of State for the
　Home Department: Ex Parte Zalike Huseyin . 284
　Facts and Procedural History 284
　Oral Hearing 287
　Judgments 289
　Observations 291
Slazengers Ltd. v. Seaspeed Ferries
　International Ltd. 293
　Facts and Procedural History 293
　Oral Hearing 297
　Judgments 298

　　　　　Observations 301
Harrods Limited v.
　　　Schwartz--Sachin & Co. Ltd. 303
　　　　　Facts and Procedural History 303
　　　　　Oral Hearing 309
　　　　　Judgments 311
　　　　　Observations 316

Appendix C   319

Introduction to March 19, 1989
　　　Practice Direction 319
March 19, 1989 Practice Direction 325

Index   333

INTRODUCTION

The idea of doing a comparative study of the English and American civil appellate systems grew out of my studies of the American appellate process and in particular the changing role of oral argument in that process. At the same time that I was concluding that the declining importance of oral argument was justified because its cost outweighed the benefits and not simply as an expedient to help courts cope with a crisis of volume, other knowledgeable persons were advocating an increased reliance on oral argument and a concomitant decrease in the reliance on written briefs. The latter position was in large part based on conclusions drawn from a study of the Criminal Division of the English Court of Appeal by Professor Daniel Meador. His book, *Criminal Appeals: English Practices and American Reform,* was published in 1973 and was based upon work done in 1971. His principal proposals were later incorporated into recommendations of the American Bar Association's Action Commission to Reduce Court Costs and Delay in its 1984 report *Attacking Litigation Costs and Delay*. My questions about these proposals were twofold: first, were the English procedures used as the model, which were designed for a criminal appellate process, suitable for a civil appellate process and second, was the oral nature of the proceedings dependent upon unique qualities of English judges and barristers not present in their American counterparts?

The first step that had to be taken was to conduct a study of the procedures and processes of the civil appeals system in England. An analysis could then be made of whether these procedures and processes were efficient and effective; if so, what were the key factors that made them so; and finally, whether those key factors existed in the United States or could be established there.

A decision was to concentrate on the Civil Division of the Court of Appeal. This decision was based on several factors. First, in the United States, the civil, not the criminal, appellate process is the norm. The same is true in England. The large majority of cases decided by appellate courts, English and American, are civil. Further, in all but a few jurisdictions in the United States appellate courts hear both civil and criminal appeals following the same procedures. If there are differences, they are made for criminal appeals, not civil. Second, it is the final court for most civil appeals, only a small percentage going on to the House of Lords. Sir Jack Jacob, in his 1986 Hamlyn lecture, characterized the Civil Division as the "centrepiece in the hierarchy of the civil judicial structure." Third, the Civil Division and the Criminal Division are for all practical purposes, two separate courts with separate procedures, presiding officers, staffs, and functions. Fourth, no study by either a British or American legal scholar had ever been made of the Civil Division. The Appellate Committee of the House of Lords has been the focus of three relatively recent books--L. Blom-Cooper & G. Drewry, *Final Appeal* (1972), R. Stevens, *Law and Politics* (1976), and A. Paterson, *The Law Lords* (1982)--but none gives any attention to the Court of Appeal. In 1962, Dehmar Karlen published *Appellate Courts in the United States and England* but this book was a more generalized and essentially descriptive treatment of appellate courts in the two countries. In any event the nature of the appellate process and of appellate courts in both countries has changed so dramatically in the intervening quarter century that the book is out of date.

The study began with the principal goal of ascertaining what American appellate courts could learn from the English system. My working hypotheses were that (1) the English system was efficient and effective, (2) it was the oral tradition and the unique qualities of the English barrister and English judge that made it so, but (3) the oral tradition could not be adopted in the United States because the training and experience of American lawyers and judges did not equip them to perform effectively in a system that was primarily oral rather than written.

The study, however, turned into something quite different than I had originally envisioned. Very early on it became apparent that the Civil Division of the Court of Appeal was facing caseload and backlog problems of major proportions. Various changes that had been implemented since 1982 as well as the addition of new judges had little effect on the backlog or the time it took for appeals to move through the system. It soon became apparent that the Court of Appeal was confronting problems substantially similar to those faced by American appellate courts going back to the 1960's and continuing through the 1980's. It thus became necessary to compare the two systems, beginning with their historical development and underlying premises and extending to how appeals moved from one step to the next throughout the entire appellate process. Because American appellate courts had faced the crisis of volume much earlier than the English Court of Appeal, the focus became much more on whether the English could learn from the American experience. Essentially, the study focused on the relative merits of the English oral tradition and the American written tradition as a means for providing appellate justice effectively and efficiently.

The methodology used in the study was one I developed in the early 1970's in conducting studies of several American appellate courts for the Institute of Judicial Administration, which is affiliated with the New York University Law School. It involves the development of a description of how a case moves step by step through the appellate process, beginning with the rendition of judgment in the trial court through the publication of the opinion of the appellate court. It also involves an understanding of the role of each participant in the process--litigant, lawyer, judge, court staff, court reporter--as well as the development of statistical data. All of this is accomplished by the traditional means of the study of statutes, rules, and available data and literature, plus observation of court proceedings, interviews with persons involved in the system and interested observers, and the collection of statistics.

Because of my experience with the American system, observations and interviews concerning it were not necessary, but they were for the English system. To this end, access to English judges, courtrooms, clerk's office, court staff, and counsel was essential. This was arranged by first having the study adopted as a project of the Institute of Judicial Administration and subsequently co-sponsored by the Appellate Judges Conference of the American Bar Association. Margaret Shaw, the director of IJA, then wrote to Lord (then Sir John) Donaldson, who as Master of the Rolls was the president or chief judge of the Civil Division, requesting his approval of the study and the provision of an office in the Royal Courts of Justice for the period of the study. Lord Donaldson, the Master of the Rolls, graciously agreed to both requests after obtaining the approval of the Lord Chancellor. An academic affiliation was also arranged at the University of Birmingham at the invitation of the dean of its Faculty of Law, Professor Ian Scott. This affiliation was especially appropriate because the British Institute of Judicial Administration is a part of the Faculty of Law at Birmingham. The Institute has a long term interest in civil justice and publishes the Civil Justice Quarterly.

The on-site portion of the study began in mid-September, 1987, and was completed in mid-December. In addition to studying the Civil Division of the Court of Appeal, two days were spent at the House of Lords observing its Appellate Committee and three days were spent in Edinburgh studying the Inner House of the Court of Session, Scotland's counterpart to the Court of Appeal. I also spent several days observing the Criminal Division of the Court of Appeal and discussing its procedures with its staff.

In view of the nature of the study, I have written this book with several different audiences on both sides of the Atlantic in mind.

First and foremost are those who are responsible for the efficient and effective operation of the two appellate systems and who have the authority to make changes in it. These include judges, legislators, executive branch officers and employees, court staff, and rule makers. A broader audience, but one almost as important, is the lawyers who appear in appellate courts or handle the paperwork connected with appeals. Cooperation of the legal profession, or at least of its leadership, is always necessary for any substantial court reform. Most lawyers in either system have little knowledge of their own appellate system, and virtually none of the other system. What knowledge they do have of the other system is usually based on vague impressions rather than on careful study. These same persons should find the book useful in understanding how their own system operates so that they can practice more effectively in it. In view of the dearth of material written about the Court of Appeal and how it functions, the book should be particularly helpful to barristers and solicitors involved in appeals. For the same reason, the book should be beneficial to law students who wish to prepare for a career in litigation. Few academics in England or the United States have any knowledge or understanding of the appellate process in their own system, much less than of its trans-Atlantic counterpart. They, and particularly those who are interested in comparative studies of legal institutions, should find the book informative.

When I was about to make my first trip to London to begin this study, Ian Scott gave me a crucial piece of advice: "Remember, when American and English lawyers get together and talk about their own legal systems, they lie. American lawyers make their system sound much worse than it is while the English lawyers make their system sound much better than it is." I hope that this book is a balanced treatment of each system.

It should be noted that I had originally planned to complete this manuscript in early 1989 with publication later that year. I had, in fact, completed an earlier draft when three developments in England required me to make substantial revisions in it. These three were the Lord Chancellor's proposals for reform of the legal profession and the reaction to them; the revisions in the vocational training of those seeking admission to the bar; and the March, 1989, Practice Direction concerning procedures in the Court of Appeal. The potential effect of each of these developments was such that I considered it necessary to include a discussion of each of them.

Robert J. Martineau
April 15, 1990

ACKNOWLEDGMENTS

It is customary for authors to acknowledge those who assisted in bringing a book from a vague idea to publication. In this case it is mandatory because the support and cooperation of so many people were essential to this particular book. First and foremost are Lord Donaldson, the Master of the Rolls, and Professor Ian Scott, the dean of the Faculty of Law at the University of Birmingham. Without the support and cooperation of Lord Donaldson, the study and this book would not have been possible. No matter what request I made, Lord Donaldson always saw to it that directives were issued or contacts made that resulted in my obtaining what I asked for. Perhaps even more important is his total commitment to improving the processes and procedures of the Court of Appeals so that the court can perform its judicial functions in the most efficient and effective way possible. His cooperation did not flow from mere courtesy, although he could not have been more so, but from an intense desire to learn as much as possible from someone from an entirely different legal background. The only limitation on his cooperation was not to tell me what he thought the problems of the Civil Division were or the solutions to them. Whatever conclusions I came to, he wanted me to reach them on my own.

Professor Scott's contribution was of a somewhat different nature, but of similar importance. In addition to providing me with an academic home, his vast knowledge of both the civil justice system and the players in it gave me an understanding of how the system really works that few others would have been able to provide. Particularly refreshing was his perspective gained not only from his Australian upbringing and eduction but his familiarity with civil justice systems in the

Commonwealth countries and the United States.

Special mention should also be made of Professor Michael Zander, the convenor (dean) of the Law Faculty at the London School of Economics and Political Science, for his advice, interest, and support. His American legal education and special knowledge of the English legal system and its legal profession were extremely helpful.

Others who also made significant contributions to the study were Lord Griffiths, a Lord of Appeal in Ordinary; Lord Justice of Appeal Michael Kerr; Lord McCluskey of the Court of Session of Scotland and the members and staff of that court; the members and staff of the Faculty of Law of the University of Birmingham; John Adams, Registrar of the Civil Division; Steve Orchard, Administrator of the Royal Courts of Justice; Robert Angel, Chief Clerk of the Civil Division and his staff; Stuart Cole, Librarian of the Supreme Court; Rear Admiral Richard Hill, Under Treasurer of the Middle Temple Inn of Court; C. R. Martin of the Association of Official Shorthandwriters Ltd.; Judge Joseph Sneed of the U.S. Court of Appeals for the Ninth Circuit; Judge Joseph Weis, Jr. of the U.S. Court of Appeals for the Third Circuit; Margaret Shaw, Director of the Institute of Judicial Administration (U.S.); and Mary Ellen Donaghy, Staff Director of the American Bar Association Appellate Judges Conference. In addition, there were many other persons too numerous to mention individually including judges, barristers, and solicitors, who were kind enough to consent to be interviewed by me or who reviewed the first draft of the manuscript. Special thanks are due to my colleague Michael Solimini and Professor Ralph Towne of Temple University. Any errors are of course, solely mine.

My wife Connie made a contribution to this book different from that to my other books. The disruption to her normal life was substantial. To the extent that there were inconveniences in living temporarily in an English village, she had to bear them much more than I and she did so with her usual good cheer and adaptability.

The actual writing of this book was greatly aided by my

student research assistants Bonnie Camden and Jeffrey Dehner and by the efficient typing of Lynn Clark and Connie Miller of the Word Processing Center at the University of Cincinnati College of Law. Financial support by the University of Cincinati College of Law is also gratefully acknowledged.

Comparative Glossary of Terms

Any comparative study of legal systems, even two as closely related as the English and American, that is intended to be read in each country is confronted with the problem of differences in terminoloy and what terminology to use. The terminology of one or the other can be used in the entire study, or the terminology of one system can be used when refering to that system, and vice versa. The latter choice has been made for this book. For this reason, set forth below are the principal differences and the appropriate term in each system.

United States	England
U.S. Supreme Court or state supreme court	Appellate Committee of the House of Lords (House of Lords or law lords)
U.S. Court of Appeals, state court of appeal or intermediate appellate court	Court of Appeal, Civil Division
Chief Justice of a supreme court	Lord Chancellor
Justice of a supreme	Lord of Appeal in Ordinary (law lord)
Chief Judge of a federal or state court of appeals	Lord Chief Justice Master of the Rolls

United States	England
U.S. circuit judge or judge of a state court of appeal	Lord Justice of Appeal (Judge)
attorney (litigation)	barrister or counsel
attorney (office)	solicitor
admission	call to the bar (barrister) admission (solicitor)
court reporter	official shorthand writer
appellee	respondent
judgment (trial court)	order
opinion	judgment (Court of Appeal) speech (House of Lords)
record	bundle
file	lodge
motion or petition	application
mandate (appellate court)	order
oral argument	hearing
cross appeal	respondent's notice
affirm	deny the appeal
reverse	allow the appeal
clerk's office	Civil Appeals Office (Court of Appeal) Judicial office (House of Lords)

Chapter 1   Structure and Function of Appellate Courts

A. ENGLAND

1. Historical Development

Appellate review in England[1] developed over a long period of time, accompanying the development of a central legal system.[2] The Norman Conquest in 1066 greatly enhanced royal power. A significant part of that power was judicial, exercised personally by the King and by his officers. A separate judicial power resided in the ecclesiastical courts of the Roman Catholic Church.

The administration of the King's justice was divided between the common law courts and the Chancellor. The Chancellor's role was to give justice if a writ in a common law court was not available. This power became known as equity and was vested in the Court of Chancery.[3]

Two different appellate systems developed, one for the common law courts and one for equity.[4] Originally at common law the judge was the defendant when his decision was contested. By the time of Edward I, however, the prevailing party rather than the judge was required to defend the judgment. During this same period it was established that the lower court developed the record, the jury was the finder of fact, and the judge discovered and applied the law to those facts.

By the beginning of the Eighteenth Century there were two principal procedures for appellate review, writ of error for common law and appeal for equity. Other procedures included review of trials at circuit by the common law courts sitting *en banc* and certiorari to remove a cause pending before an inferior court to a superior court of common law. The writ of error was a common law writ that grew out of the earlier procedure under which the losing party filed suit against the judge. As it existed in the 1700's, a writ of error could be obtained in the King's Bench to review decisions of the Common Pleas court, and in the Exchequer Chamber to review decisions of the King's Bench and the Exchequer.

The writ initiated a new law suit with the parties known as plaintiff in error (the losing party in the lower court) and defendant in error (the winning party in the lower court). Obtainable as a matter of right, the writ operated as a supersedeas, that is it stayed the enforcement of the lower court judgment if bond were posted to secure the amount of the judgment and any costs or damages for delaying execution. The plaintiff in error arranged for a copy of the record in the lower court to be sent to the reviewing court. The record consisted of the writ of error, the pleadings, the recital of the trial, the verdict, the proceedings after the verdict, and the judgment.

To raise in the appellate court any matter not included in the ordinary record, the plaintiff in error had to prepare a bill of exceptions. An exception to an adverse ruling that would not otherwise be shown on the record had to be made and recorded in writing by the judge at the time of the ruling. At the end of the trial all exceptions were put together to constitute the bill of exceptions. The bill of exceptions, when approved by the trial judge, was then appended to the record. If there were no record, the bill contained all the items that would otherwise be contained in the record.

After the record and bill of exceptions were transmitted to the appellate court, the plaintiff in error filed an assignment of errors in the appellate court. It served the same function as a declaration or complaint in the trial court. The defendant in error then filed a plea in response to the assignment of errors. Review was limited to errors of law. Some errors referred to as errors of fact could be reviewed, but they concerned the status of the parties or capacity to sue. They were not consequently issues of fact as determined at trial. In the King's Bench oral argument was heard at the request of either side, with copies of the record being given to each of the judges.[5] Further review could be had in the House of Lords on a writ of error, but this was seldom done.[6]

In equity, review of the Court of Chancery was in the House of Lords, in a procedure designated as an appeal.[7] The appellant filed with the House a petition and appeal that recited the proceedings below and presented the grounds for appeal. The appellant was also required to file a bond of 200 pounds for costs. The appellee was ordered to file an answer, have the papers printed, and participate in an oral argument held in the House. The House could review any matter in the case whether or not it was in the record and could render any judgment it thought appropriate. New evidence could not, however, be taken. A separate Court of Appeal in Chancery was established in 1851 as an intermediate appellate court between the Court of Chancery and the House of Lords.[8]

During the Nineteenth Century, a series of major reforms were made culminating in the Judicature Acts of 1873 and 1875[9] that became effective in November, 1875. Under these acts a Supreme Court of Judicature was created with jurisdiction co-extensive with that of the previously existing superior courts of law and equity. The county courts remained as inferior courts. The Supreme Court was divided into the High Court of Justice and the Court of Appeal. The High Court, originally five divisions, has had three divisions since 1880: Queen's Bench, Chancery and Family (formerly Probate, Divorce, and Admiralty). These three divisions are the heirs of the three historical jurisdictions: common law, equity, and ecclesiastical.

The Court of Appeal was established as a separate appellate court with only civil jurisdiction. It was modeled after the Court of Appeal in Chancery, which was created in 1851 with permanent judges to hear appeals from the vice-chancellors and the Master of the Rolls. It was also given the jurisdiction of the Court of Exchequer Chamber, which was the court of error for the three common law courts. The Exchequer Chamber did not, however, have separate judges. For any given case it was composed of judges from the two common law courts other than the one from which the appeal was taken. In 1934, the Court of Appeal was given jurisdiction over appeals from county courts and in 1966 over criminal appeals, at which time the Criminal Division of the Court of Appeal was established. It succeeded the Court of Criminal Appeal, created in 1907.

As it exists today, the Civil Division of the Court of Appeal has jurisdiction over virtually all civil appeals from the High Court and the county courts. The only major exception to its jurisdiction is appeals from magistrates' courts. These go to the divisional court of the Queen's Bench Division, but the Court of Appeal has jurisdiction over appeals from that court. It is also possible for an appeal to go directly from the High Court to the House of Lords in the discretion of the House.

Review of a decision of the Court of Appeal may be sought in the House of Lords. The judicial power of the House of Lords goes back to the fourteenth century. The appellate role of the House of Lords extended both to common law and equity.[10] Until 1844 it was possible for a lay member of the House of Lords to sit on an appeal. In 1876, when the Appellate Jurisdiction Act created salaried life peers formally called Lords of Appeal in Ordinary but commonly referred to as law lords, were created to sit on appeals and the convention against participation by lay peers was accepted. With that Act, the jurisdiction of the House of Lords over the decisions of the Court of Appeal was fixed and has remained so to the present time.

The territorial jurisdiction of the High Court and the Court of Appeal is limited to England and Wales. Scotland and Northern Ireland, the other constituent parts of Great Britain, have their own separate legal and judicial systems and appellate courts. The House of Lords jurisdiction is not limited, however, to decisions of the Court of Appeal. It also hears appeals from the Inner House of The Court of Session, Scotland's highest court, and from the Court of Appeal of Northern

Ireland. The House of Lords, or more properly the Appellate Committee of the House of Lords, is the supreme court of Great Britain. The law lords also sit as the Judicial Committee of the Privy Council, which hears appeals from those commonwealth nations that choose to submit to its jurisdiction. A panel of five constitutes the Judicial Committee for any given appeal.

Although the House of Lords, when it exercises its judicial function, is the highest judicial body in England, its principal status is a legislative body. This is reflected in a number of ways. When it hears an appeal, it is formally designated as the Appellate Committee of the House of Lords, and not as a court. It is composed of five members. The five members who sit can include not only any of the ten law lords but also the Lord Chancellor and any member of the House of Lords who has held high judicial office. The panel hears arguments in a House committee room, not a courtroom, and while sitting the members of the panel do not wear judicial robes. Their opinions are referred to as speeches in support of a motion by the senior member of the panel whether to allow or disallow the appeal. The House of Lords issues an order based on its decision, but before it can be enforced it must be made an order of the High Court.[11]

The changes made by the Judicature Acts of 1873 and 1875 went as much to substance as to form. In addition to setting up a true appellate court with permanent judges (the Court of Appeal in Chancery was the first to be so constituted twenty-four years earlier) the nature of the review applicable to both law and equity was based on the appeal in equity rather than the common law writ of error. The effect of these changes on the functions of appellate courts in England is discussed in the next section.

2. Purpose and Function of Appellate Review

One of the principal purposes of the Judicature Acts of 1873 and 1875 was to do away with the restrictions on appellate review as they had developed under the common law writ of error and to adopt those of the equity appeal. The contrast between the two could not have been greater. The former was limited to errors of law reflected in the record and the bill of exceptions. This meant that the only purpose of appellate review was to ascertain whether the judge made a mistake in a legal ruling. Appellate review had nothing to do with whether justice was done, that is whether the right party, as demonstrated by the evidence, won. If the judge made a mistake, then a new trial was necessary. This meant, of course, that the issue on which the writ of error was based had to have been presented to the trial judge and the fact of the presentation and the judge's ruling had to be in the record. The facts, having been presented to the jury and decided by it, were not subject to review, both because this would be a denial of the right to a jury trial and because there was no record of the evidence presented to the jury.[12]

In equity, the purpose of the appeal was quite different. Equity was, by its nature, not tied to the technicalities of writ procedure or the factual findings of a jury. It was, rather, the doing of justice as determined by the conscience of the King or his *alter ego,* the Chancellor. An equity proceeding was a request for the exercise of discretion by the decision maker, unrestrained by rules of law or the content of the record. If the original decision maker did not grant the relief requested, then the same request was made to a higher ranking person or body to exercise its independent authority in favor of the petitioning party. The request was based on the relative equities between the parties, not whether the first person from whom relief was sought had made an error. The higher authority was as free as the lower one to grant or deny relief, or to grant some other relief, even to the opposing party. Although the proceeding before the higher authority was termed an appeal, it was in fact a *de novo* proceeding in which what had transpired in the initial proceeding was not relevant (except in the House of Lords which was bound by the record).[13] When the Court of Appeal in Chancery was established in 1851, appeal by way of rehearing was the procedure that was followed.[14]

When a formal appellate review process was established in

the Judicature Acts of 1873-75, the Court of Appeal was given jurisdiction over both common law and equity proceedings. A choice had to be made whether to continue the two different types of review, writ of error for common law and appeal for equity, or apply one or the other to both. The choice was made to apply the equity appeal to both types of proceedings. This was consistent with the entire philosophy of the Acts to do away with the procedural niceties of the common law and to replace it with a simple procedure that enabled the judges to reach the merits of the case. This philosophy was as applicable to the appellate process as to proceedings in the courts of original jurisdiction.

The most significant aspect of the decision to follow the equity appeal model for appellate review goes to the nature the authority of the Court of Appeal when it hears an appeal. The nature of the appeal is characterized as "by way of rehearing." Specifically the Court of Appeal has all the authority, powers, and jurisdiction of the court from which the appeal is taken. It has the power to examine witnesses and to receive new evidence in any form. It can draw inferences of fact and substitute its findings for that of the judge or jury. The Court can enter any order that should have been entered in the lower court, and can substitute its order on liability, damages, or costs for that of the lower court. It may allow amendments to the pleadings so that it can decide a new issue of fact and it is not limited to considering those issues raised on appeal by the parties. It can even bring in new parties. The ultimate purpose of the Court is to decide the merits of the real dispute between the parties. If all else fails it can order a new trial, a power not possessed by the High Court.[15]

In theory, then, the purpose of the Court of Appeal is simply to do justice between the parties by whatever means are necessary, without being confined to what occurred in the lower court. This is in perfect accord with the philosophy of the drafters of the 1873 and 1875 Judicature Acts in electing to adopt the equity model for appellate review. In practice, however, the nature of the review performed by the Court of Appeal is much more restrictive.

On questions of law, the subject of most appeals, the Court limits itself to the issues raised by the parties. Further, a party may not raise on appeal an issue not presented to the trial court. The Court will, however, consider a new point if all the facts necessary to rule on the issue have been developed at trial.[16] On issues of fact, the Court again limits itself to the review of findings challenged in the notice of appeal. Most importantly, the Court will not overturn a finding of a direct or basic fact made by a judge or jury, in large part because of the trier of fact's opportunity to observe the demeanor of the witnesses giving testimony. The Court is, however, not bound by the inferences drawn from the facts found by the judge or jury. These inferences go to the legal conclusions drawn from the facts, for example, whether particular facts constitute negligence or a breach of contract. These conclusions are sometimes referred to as ultimate facts or a mixed question of law and fact. In reality they involve the application of legal rules or principles to known facts. In a case tried before a jury (now common only in libel actions), if the jury returns a general verdict that does not distinguish between direct findings of fact and inferential findings, the Court of Appeal will overturn it only if the verdict is not supported by the evidence or is one that a reasonable jury could not have reached.

In reviewing the exercise of discretion by a judge, the Court of Appeal will not reverse simply because it would have decided the matter differently. Before it will substitute its own discretion for that of the trial judge it must find that the trial judge made a mistake of law, a mistake of fact, took into consideration an irrelevant matter, failed to consider a relevant matter, or exercised his discretion in a way that no reasonable judge would have done. In the area of damages, if awarded by a jury the Court will interfere only if it finds the damages so large or small that no reasonable jury would have awarded them. In such a case, however, the Court of Appeal cannot make the award it thinks proper. It can only order a new trial, absent consent of the parties. If the damages were awarded by a judge, the review is limited to whether the judge acted under an incorrect rule or principle of law or whether the amount of the damages is out of line with the damages allowed in similar cases. One authority has suggested that as a practical matter the Court of Appeal will not interfere unless the disparity exceeds 20 to 25 percent. The circumstances under which the Court may order a new trial are carefully regulated by Order 59 which contains the procedural rules that govern appeals.

The power of the Court of Appeal to receive new evidence is the most dramatic illustration that the proceedings before it are a rehearing rather than simply an appellate review. In fact, the Court seldom uses the power, and only in sharply limited circumstances. Three conditions must be met. The evidence must:

(1) not have been available with due diligence for use at trial;

(2) probably have an important influence on the result of the case; and,

(3) apparently be credible.

Given these restrictions, it is not surprising that the Court of Appeal seldom receives new evidence and when it does the evidence is by affidavit.[17]

The foregoing description of the restrictions, self imposed or otherwise, on the manner in which the Court of Appeal exercises its powers makes it abundantly clear that, while in theory an appeal to the Court of Appeal is a *de novo* rehearing, in practice the review is a search for error by the trial court. This fact was acknowledged in the 1983 annual review of the Master of the Rolls in which he stated: "The function of the Court of Appeal is to correct errors, not to provide a second stage in the trial of an action." This self imposed limitation on the Court's power is an accommodation to reality, given the public resources available for the judicial process. Even more important, it recognizes the essential unfairness to the winning party who, after a full trial on the merits before an impartial tribunal, could be forced to retry the entire matter before another court simply on the request of the losing party.

Whether it be the restrictions against raising an issue on appeal that was not raised in the trial court or against introducing new evidence that could have been presented to the trial court, the Court of Appeal has obviously recognized that it could not perform its function of appellate review unless it restricted that review to a search for error in the trial court. Absent that, the order of the trial court must stand. Sir Jack Jacob has referred to the principle underlying these restrictions as the principle of finality.[18]

The extent to which an English appellate court exercises the function of law development varies greatly depending upon whether changing prior precedent or establishing law where none previously existed is being considered. The doctrine of precedent in English law has a very high priority.[19] The principles of the common law were thought not to be made by judges, but existed independent of judicial decisions. The law was there, and it was simply the task of the judge to discover it so that it could be applied to the facts of the case. This theory has now been acknowledged not to be correct, at least in cases of first impression. The doctrine of precedent, when precedent exists, however, is still of primary significance.

Under the doctrine of precedent, a court is bound to follow the decisions of a higher court and its own prior decisions, at least insofar as those decisions declare or establish legal principles of general application and how those principles are applied to particular factual situations. The benefits of the doctrine of precedent, or *stare decisis,* are certainty, precision, and flexibility.[20]

In applying these principles to the Court of Appeal, it must first be understood that even though the Court of Appeal sits in panels of two or three judges each panel when it sits, is considered to be the court thus the decision of one panel is binding upon subsequent panels. The Court has recognized, however, three situations in which a prior decision of a panel is not binding. These are when there are two conflicting prior decisions, when a prior decision is in conflict with, but not expressly overruled by, a subsequent decision of the House of

Lords, and when the prior decision of the Court of Appeal is characterized as *per incuriam*, i.e. a decision that was reached "through lack of care" because some relevant statute or precedent had not been brought to the court's attention. In reality, all of these rules mean only that the Court of Appeal must follow binding precedent or authority, and the fact that it failed to do so on an earlier occasion is no basis for not doing so on a subsequent occasion.

The doctrine of precedent is so strong that it was not until 1966 that the House of Lords asserted authority to overturn its own decisions. Prior to that time the House took the position that it was bound by prior decisions which could be changed only by Parliament. In 1966 the Lord Chancellor issued a statement on behalf of all of the law lords that in the future they would ignore prior precedent when they felt it "right" to do so.[21] The House of Lords has exercised this new found power, but not to any substantial extent. Under no circumstances could the House of Lords be described as an activist court looking for opportunities to mold the law to conform to the views of the current law lords.[22]

Both the Court of Appeal and the House of Lords are, of course, free to develop the law in the manner either thinks most appropriate when there is no binding precedent and the only relevant decisions are those of lower courts. In this circumstance, the Court of Appeal has a much greater law development role simply because it decides so many more cases. Perhaps the most dramatic recent example of not only developing new law but an entire area of law is in judicial review of administrative action.[23]

Lord Denning, the Master of the Rolls for over two decades until 1982, made a concerted effort to establish for the Court of Appeal the power to change the law as declared in the Court's prior decisions. The House of Lords, however, has refused to approve this effort and until recently there have been no attempts in the Court of Appeal to this end. In 1989, however, the Court of Appeal decided not to follow a precedent of the House of Lords under which the Court could not consider a new issue of law in an appeal from a county court, even though it could do so in an appeal from the High Court. It did so on the basis that the rule, established in 1891, was now obsolete, and to do justice to the parties, it refused to follow the rule.[24]

Neither the Court of Appeal nor the House of Lords identifies "doing justice" as a function separate and independent of error correction and law development. In the largest sense, of course, the ultimate goal of any court is to attempt to do justice between the parties. But to do justice in a structured legal system with rules of procedure and evidence and the doctrine of precedent does not mean that a judge or a panel of judges is free to ignore the restrictions imposed on it by these rules, the record, or statutory or binding precedent to achieve a particular result. Such was the power of the Chancellor, acting for the King, to do equity between the parties when the law could not or would not achieve that result. It might be thought that when the Judicature Acts of 1873 and 1875 used the equity appeal for its model for appellate review, made the appeal proceeding a *de novo* rehearing and gave the Court of Appeal the power to enter any order or judgment that the trial court might have done, that the judges of the Court of Appeal would feel free to "do justice" without regard to anything except their own sense of where justice lay between the parties. As was seen earlier in the discussion of the error correction function of the Court, it exercises its powers under a substantial number of restrictions, imposed by itself, the House of Lords, or statute. As a consequence, the justice that results from the decisions of the Court of Appeal is a justice based on the facts and legal issues as developed at trial, the issues properly raised by the parties on appeal, and the relevant legal authority, both statutory and judicial. The Court of Appeal, then, does not "do justice" in the sense of an *ad hoc* determination based on the sympathies of the judges, but justice in accordance with law, both substantive and procedural. Doing justice, then, is not a separate function of the Court of Appeal but a result of the Court, when it performs its error correction function, applying relevant legal authority to the facts of the particular case, and developing new law in the absence of binding precedent.[25]

The House of Lords has both error correction and law development functions. Its principal function is to review decisions of the Court of Appeal to ensure that the Court has properly applied House of Lords' decisions. It also reviews the Court of Appeal to give the correct interpretation to statutes of Parliament. It further develops law when the only precedent is that of the Court of Appeal. In such cases it is, of course, not bound by those decisions but is free to adopt the view of the law it thinks correct. Finally, and most dramatically, it develops law when it overrules its own precedents.

3. Principles of Appellate Review

a. The Right to Appeal

In examining the right of a party to appeal an adverse ruling of a court, several important distinctions must be made. Sometimes appeal rights are discussed in terms of the jurisdiction of the appellate court. If an appellate court is given jurisdiction to hear appeals of certain types of orders of an inferior court, it may be said that a party has the right to appeal that type of order. This is, technically, not correct. An appellate court's jurisdiction can be mandatory or discretionary. It is mandatory if a party can not only seek review of the order or judgment in the appellate court, but the appellate court must also decide the merits of the appeal. The jurisdiction is discretionary if the appellate court can make an initial determination not to hear the appeal, because the court does not think the attempted appeal has any merit, or the timing of the appeal is not appropriate, or for any other reason it considers proper.

This confusion may have arisen from the common law jurisdiction of the King's Bench to issue writs of error to review the orders of courts of local jurisdictions. Under the common law, this gave a party the right to request the issuance of the writ of error and once issued, the King's Bench was required to review the order that was the subject of the writ. The right to seek the writ of error is commonly characterized as a right to appeal. Whatever common law right to a writ of error once existed, today the only right of appeal is statutory.

Notwithstanding the technical difference between jurisdiction and right to appeal, in fact the basic right to appeal under English law is expressed in terms of the jurisdiction of the Court of Appeal. This is found in the 1981 Supreme Court Act, section 16(1), which states that "the Court of Appeal shall have jurisdiction to hear and determine appeals from any judgment or order of the High Court."[26] Other statutes give the Court of Appeal jurisdiction over decisions of the county court and certain administrative tribunals.[27] Again, these statutes are described as creating a right of appeal from the orders of those bodies to the Court of Appeal. When a statute seeks to make the hearing of the appeal discretionary in the Court of Appeal, it imposes the condition that a party must obtain leave to appeal. The principal orders that require leave to appeal are those:

(a) of a divisional court of the High Court;

(b) entered by consent of the parties;

(c) as to costs that are in the discretion of the court or tribunal;

(d) are interlocutory (with certain exceptions such as granting or denying an injunction, the liberty of a person is at issue or a decree *nisi* is awarded in a matrimonial cause); and

(e) of a county court that does not exceed one half the maximum monetary jurisdiction of the court.

The full list is much more extensive.[28] As to the last classification, orders of the county court, the Supreme Court Rules Committee is empowered by section 108(2) of the 1959 County Courts Act to enlarge the classes of orders of the county court that require leave to appeal. It could make every order of the county court subject to leave to appeal. In a few cases a statute has expressly provided that an order may not be appealed.

Five aspects of the application for leave to appeal are noteworthy. One, in most cases when leave is necessary it can be granted either by the trial judge or a single judge of the Court of Appeal and must first be sought from the former. Two, there is no appeal from the decision of the single judge of the Court of Appeal on whether or not to grant leave. Three, whether there is a right to appeal from county courts or leave must be granted is determined by rule and not by statute. Four, the application for leave to appeal in the Court of Appeal is filed *ex parte,* with no notice given to the prospective respondent unless a hearing on it is ordered. Fifth, there is an oral hearing on every application for leave to appeal if it is not dismissed *ex parte.*

The jurisdiction of the House of Lords extends to every order or judgment of the Court of Appeal and is entirely discretionary. Leave to appeal to the House of Lords can be granted either by the Court of Appeal or the House of Lords. The House of Lords also has discretion to accept jurisdiction over any matter that can be appealed to the Court of Appeal. There are a few appeals such as those from county courts in probate proceedings in which the decision of the Court of Appeal is final and no appeal can be taken to the House of Lords.[30]

b. What Can Be Appealed

As noted in the preceding section there is no longer a common law right of appeal; the right to appeal is now wholly statutory. These statutes determine not only the right to appeal, but also what it is that can be appealed. The two, in fact, are necessarily interrelated, because the right to appeal can exist only in relation to some action or non-action of an inferior court. The general statute creating the right to appeal, section 16(1) of the 1981 Supreme Court Act, specifies that the jurisdiction of the Court of Appeal extends to "any judgment or order" of the High Court. Read out of context, this would mean that any order, final or interlocutory, could be appealed as of right. This provision is limited, however, by section 18(1)(h) of the same act, which provides that leave to appeal is required to appeal any interlocutory order. The effect of these two provisions is that any action or non-action of a court or tribunal over which the Court of Appeal has jurisdiction can be appealed, the only distinction being between those matters that are appealable as of right and those that require leave to appeal. This distinction is, in effect, a final order rule.

Several aspects of this statutory arrangement are noteworthy. The first goes to the test for determining whether an order is final or interlocutory. It does not depend, as might be expected, upon the nature of order rendered by the court; rather, it depends upon what type of relief was sought from the court. The general definition of a final order is that it must finally determine the proceedings. A particular order can be classified as final, however, only if the proceedings would have been finally determined regardless of whether the application seeking relief was granted or denied. If granting the application would finally determine the proceedings but its denial would not, then the order is classified as interlocutory even though the application is granted, and vice-versa. Thus an order dismissing an action because it is frivolous, which certainly finally determines the proceeding, is still held to be interlocutory because if the court had refused to dismiss the action on a finding that the action was not frivolous, the proceedings would not have been finally determined and thus would have been interlocutory. On the other hand, if a trial or hearing is divided into two parts, one on liability and one on damages, and a separate order made as to each, each is considered a final order even though both are required before the proceedings are finally determined.[31] The confusion that can be generated by these efforts to apply the final order rule is obvious.

The second noteworthy aspect of the final-interlocutory distinction is that the Supreme Court Rules Committee has the authority to adopt rules of court that can classify an order as final or interlocutory.[32] Under this power, a rule can make that which is final interlocutory and that which is interlocutory final. In view of the fact that the classification of final or interlocutory determines whether there is a right to appeal or whether leave to appeal must be sought, the Rules Committee has, in effect, the power to determine the right to appeal.

It is also highly significant that there are no criteria in the statute, rule, or judicial decision on the granting of an application for leave to appeal. The matter is strictly in the discretion of the single judge who considers the application. The fact that it is heard by a single judge is one of the reasons there are no judicially developed criteria. The opinions of the single judge are usually not recorded or published. Even more significantly, there is no review of the decision of the single judge by a panel of the Court of Appeal,[33] so there is no opportunity for the Court to develop the criteria for the granting or denying of an application. The *ex parte* nature of the original application for leave to appeal is also significant. This means that the losing party may be seeking to overturn the order while the winning party is acting on the belief that the losing party is not planning to appeal.

Another aspect of the leave to appeal procedure is the power of a judge of the lower court to grant leave. In fact, an application for leave to appeal must be presented first to the trial court before it can be submitted to the Court of Appeal.[34] This places substantial control over the discretionary caseload of the Court of Appeal in the judges of the trial courts.

c. Who Can Appeal

The right to appeal or to seek leave to appeal depends upon a person having the status of a party in the trial court or having been treated as a party. Thus any party can appeal as can any other person who has been served with a notice of the judgment or order entered in the trial court. If a person could have been made a party, that person may also appeal, but only with leave of the Court of Appeal. A person who is not a party may also appeal if he is bound by the judgment or if leave to appeal is granted by the Court of Appeal.[35]

It is not stated expressly in a statute, rule, or judicial opinion that a person must be aggrieved by an order to have standing to appeal. A person is aggrieved in this context when its legal interests are adversely affected. To some degree the requirement of being aggrieved is implicit in the various provisions and cases concerning the right to appeal, but the more important requirement appears to be status as a party, actual or potential. A person can appeal, however, only against an order or judgment and not against the reasons given by the trial judge in support of the order.[36]

d. Standard of Review

There are four basic types of questions that can be presented to an appellate court--law, fact, discretion, and damages. In theory, because the proceedings in the Court of Appeal are considered to be a rehearing, all of the questions would be reviewed *de novo* and the Court of Appeal could freely substitute its judgment for that of the trial court on any questions presented. This is, in fact, not the case. While the Court of Appeal freely substitutes its judgment for that of the trial court on legal questions--that is, after all, the core function of an appellate court--its review of the other three types of issues is much more limited, as was discussed in section A 2, *supra*.

e. Reversible Error

The English appellate courts do not discuss the nature of their reviewing function in terms of reversible error. Once again, the rehearing nature of the proceeding in the Court of Appeal suggests that reversible error is not necessary to justify a reversal, but only that the Court of Appeal does not agree with the result or that it feels justice was not done. Once again this is not the case, as is evidenced by the standard of review exercised by the Court of Appeal, described in section A 2, *supra,* and by the grounds on which the Court of Appeal will order a new trial. Thus when a judgment is attacked because of misdirection (incorrect instructions to the jury), for error in the admission or exclusion of evidence, or the improper withdrawal of a question from the jury Rule 11(2) of Order 59 specifies that a new trial is not to be granted unless there has been "some substantial wrong or miscarriage of justice." Similarly, a new trial is ordered on the ground of misconduct by a participant in the trial or some other irregularity only if a party has been denied a fair trial. The appellant, consequently, must show not only that a mistake was made, but that the mistake resulted in substantial harm, a miscarriage of justice, or the denial of a fair trial. This is the equivalent of a reversible error requirement.

f. Issues That Can Be Raised

As discussed in section A 2, *supra,* one of the restrictions the Court of Appeal has imposed on its review of lower court orders is that it will not consider an issue not presented to the lower court unless the issue is one solely of law and does not require the development of additional facts. Under its authority to take new evidence and to exercise any power or grant any relief that the lower court could exercise or grant, it could consider any new issue it desired, but it has chosen not to do so.

4. Criminal Division of Court of Appeal[37]

As noted in the Introduction, the study on which this book is based was limited to the Civil Division of the Court of Appeal and did not include the Criminal Division. In addition to the reasons given there for this decision, another significant factor is that most of the appeals that come before it are challenges to sentences and thus not comparable to the usual fare for appellate courts in the United States.

The president or chief judge of the Criminal Division is the Lord Chief Justice, who is also the president or chief judge of the Queen's Bench Division. The Criminal Division has no judges permanently assigned to it. At any given time four Lord Justices of Appeal are designated for duty on the Criminal Division. This duty rotates among the Lord Justices, with each judge sitting for approximately a three week period. Each panel of the Criminal Division is usually composed of one Lord Justice and two High Court Judges. Four panels usually sit.

In 1985 the Criminal Division received approximately 7162 appeals and applications for leave to appeal. Leave to appeal was required in all but 70 cases. Of the 7162 appeals and applications, 5766 challenged only the sentence while 862 challenged the conviction only, and 534 attacked both the conviction and the sentence. Applications for leave to appeal are decided almost exclusively on written submissions. Of the 7022 filed, 2151 were granted, the remainder being refused or abandoned. A total of 2184 appeals were heard, 1655 on the sentence only, 372 on the conviction only, and 157 on both sentence and conviction. In 1136 cases the sentence was varied and in 167 cases the conviction was quashed.[38] A key provision in the Criminal Appeal Act gives the Criminal Division authority to quash a conviction if the judges think it is "unsafe and unsatisfatory"--without the necessity of showing any particular error.

The entire process up to the hearing is almost totally within the control of the Registrar of Criminal Appeals. He decides whether and how much of a transcript is to be ordered and he and his staff prepare summaries of the applications for leave to appeal. They similarly prepare summaries when an appeal is heard by a panel. The hearings on the appeals are usually short, less than an hour each. The principal document filed by the appellant is a "perfected grounds of appeal" which includes not only the grounds for appeal but the arguments in support of them, including references to the trancript of testimony. This is filed, however, only if the Registrar directs.

The process in the Criminal Division has been essentially the same for over 40 years, when the Court of Criminal Appeals had jurisdiction over criminal appeals. Not coincidentally the same person has been the Registrar of Criminal Appeals for the entire period. Both the judges and counsel are satisfied with the system as it operates. No one, however, has suggested that the system for criminal appeals has any relevance to the civil appeals system. The system is accepted for criminal appeals because they are just that -- criminal appeals. A similar system, or even major features of it, would not be accepted for civil appeals.

5. Civil Appeals in Scotland

As part of the author's study of the English civil appeals system, it was thought useful to examine briefly the appellate system in Scotland. The House of Lords is for Scotland the same as it is for England--the ultimate judicial authority in civil cases (but not in criminal cases).

There are differences of substance, court structure, procedure, and nomenclature between the legal systems of England and Scotland. Substantively, the law in Scotland is based on Roman law rather than the common law. Notwithstanding this, the House of Lords is still the final authority on these questions. To prevent serious aberrations, the tradition is that two law lords are always Scots, and at least one always sits on Scottish appeals. The highest court in Scotland is the Court of Session but it is divided between the Outer House, which is the equivalent of the High Court in England, and the Inner House, which is the Court of Appeal's counterpart. The Court of Session is composed of the Lord President, the Lord Justice-Clerk, and 18 Judges who are formally titled Senators of the College of Justice. The Inner House consists of two panels of four judges each, with the Lord President presiding over one and the Lord Justice-Clerk over the other. The other six Judges who sit on the Inner House are the senior Senators. The remaining 12 Senators sit individually as judges of the Outer House. Below the Outer House are over 60 full time judges called Sheriffs, who are the equivalent of the judges who sit on the county courts in England.

Appeals come to the Inner House from decisions of the Outer House judges and the sheriffs in the same manner as they do to the Civil Division of the Court of Appeal in England from the High Court and the county courts. The only major difference is that when the appeal is from the former it is labled a "reclaiming motion" while in the latter it is designated an "appeal." The number of civil appeals to the Inner House totaled only 143 in 1986, while during the same year the Inner House decided 96 appeals on the merits.[39] The judges of the Inner House also constitute the High Court of the Justiciary, which is the criminal appellate court.

Scotland has a divided legal profession between courtroom specialists called advocates and those who are primarily office lawyers who are called solicitors, as in England. Advocates have the exclusive right of audience in the Court of Session and are the only persons eligible to be appointed to that court. Both advocates and solicitors are appointed as sheriffs and can appear before them.[40]

In the trial court the initiating party is called the pursuer and the opponent the defender. Pleadings are used as a means of narrowing the issues in dispute until the trial can be held on very narrow issues of law or fact.

The appellate process is essentially the same in England and Scotland except that the oral tradition is even stronger in the latter. In the Inner House, the entire record from the trial court including all of the pleadings and the full transcript of testimony is read in open court by the appellant's advocate, even though each judge has a copy of the record. The justification given for this practice is that this is the only way that counsel can be sure the judges are exposed to the full record and understand its import.

The scheduling of the hearing of appeals is the same as in England--it is done at the initiative and at the convenience of counsel.

The result of the lengthy oral hearings and scheduling at the convenience of counsel has the inevitable result -- the delay in having appeals heard is substantial, often over a year. This delay is a cause of concern. One step taken to overcome it is for each panel to have what is in effect a docket call. A hearing is held on cases that have been pending for a substantial time to enquire of counsel when they plan on requesting that the appeal be set for hearing.

When an appeal is heard, judgments are rendered in writing rather than delivered extemporaneously. The decision appealed from is either "adhered to" or reversed.

B. United States

1. Historical Development

Appellate review in the United States has its origins in the American colonies in the 17th century.[41] Initially there were no appellate courts and relief from a decision of an inferior judicial officer was sought from whatever body was the repository of each colony's governmental authority. This could be the governor, the governor and council, or the legislature, depending upon the terms of the colony's charter or the commission of the governor. Further review could be had by the Privy Council in England, but in view of the time and expense involved this was seldom sought.

Appellate review in the colonies did not initially follow whatever formal procedure was then current for common law or equity proceedings in England. Those procedures themselves were still in a developmental stage. During the 18th century, however, formal judicial structures and review procedures were established in each colony. At the time of the revolution in 1776 each of the thirteen colonies adopted its own constitution and established its own judicial structure. In each state a system of courts was established with a supreme court to which appeals could be taken. As each new state was admitted to the federal union, it established its own judicial system with a supreme court. The appellate structure in most states has remained the same over the years except that in 37 states intermediate appellate courts have been created.

The federal appellate system came into existence in 1789 when the federal constitution was implemented. The only court established by the Constitution was the Supreme Court; it was left to Congress to create inferior courts. The Judiciary Act of 1789 established district courts with only original jurisdiction, circuit courts with both original jurisdiction and appellate jurisdiction over the district courts, and the Supreme Court as the ultimate reviewing court. The only major change in the structure of the federal court system occurred in 1891 when a court of appeals was established for each of the nine circuits into which the United States was then divided.

During the 19th century appellate review in both state and federal systems became bogged down in procedural technicalities and an excessive formalism. This situation arose from the application by Americans of the writ of error approach to appellate review to equity proceedings as well as those at law. The most complicated procedural requirements were those necessary to preserve an issue for appeal. This required six separate steps, the first four of which were taken in the trial court:

(1) making a timely objection;

(2) taking an exception to an adverse ruling;

(3) preserving the objection, ruling, and exception in the bill of exceptions;

(4) moving for a new trial;

(5) specifying the alleged error in the assignment of errors; and

(6) preparing and filing a written brief raising and arguing the alleged error.

If any of these steps was overlooked the appellate court would refuse to review the alleged error. In addition, review of the facts was very restricted whether the case arose at law or in equity. Essentially the appellate courts reviewed matters of law only and not questions of fact in either law or equity. Roscoe Pound has described the situation in the late 19th century as one in which "appellate procedure existed as a system of preventing the disposition of cases themselves upon their merits."[42]

This situation led to efforts at the beginning of the 20th century to simplify and streamline the appellate process. Reforms were designed to make appellate procedure simpler and less expensive and to allow the appellate court to review the merits of the appeal. Some of the major early reforms were:

(1) combining the two methods of appellate review, writ of error and appeal, into a single procedure designated appeal;

(2) reducing the time during which appellate review could be sought;

(3) using a simple notice of appeal to initiate the appellate process;

(4) abolishing the necessity for taking an exception in addition to an objection;

(5) eliminating or simplifying the bill of exceptions;

(6) simplifying the record; and

(7) abolishing the assignment of errors.[43]

The simplification of the appellate process combined with the litigation explosion of the early 1960's led to an enormous increase in the number of appeals in both the federal and state systems.[44] The response was not to limit the right to appeal but to expand the capacity of the appellate system to cope with the increased caseload by enlarging the number of intermediate appellate courts, adding more appellate judges, and a variety of other measures. These are discussed in Chapter 4.

Currently, in the federal system there is the United States Supreme Court, a separate United States court of appeals for each of the twelve geographical circuits into which the United States is divided, as well as a court of appeals that has nationwide jurisdiction over specific types of cases.

Each of the 50 states has its own supreme court. Texas and Oklahoma each have two separate supreme courts, one civil and one criminal. Only 13 of the 50 states now do not have intermediate courts of appeals. Intermediate appellate courts can be structured in several different ways. In some states there is a single court for the entire state while in other states there are separate courts of appeals for different geographical areas in the states. In most states the intermediate appellate courts have civil and criminal jurisdiction, but in a few states there are separate appellate courts for criminal cases. While supreme courts almost always sit *en banc,* that is with their entire membership, most of the courts of appeals sit in three judge panels. This is common to both the federal system and the state systems.

2. Relationship Between State and Federal Court System

As noted above, there is a separate judicial system for the federal government and for each of the 50 states with appellate courts in each of the 51 systems.[45] In most respects these 51 systems are completely separate. An appealable judgment or order in a case begun in a state court and involving only issues of state law is reviewed by the state intermediate appellate court and then by the state supreme court, the latter being the ultimate authority on questions of the law of that state. In the federal system a case begins in a federal district court, that systems trial court. An appealable judgment or order of the district court is subject to review by a federal court of appeals and, ultimately, by the United States Supreme Court.

There is, however, some overlap between the federal system and each state system. A case involving only state law issues or state and federal issues can be filed in or removed to a federal district court if the defendant is a resident of a different state than the plaintiff. This is called diversity jurisdiction. In such cases, the federal court decides the state issues as though it were a state court and the federal court is bound by the decisions of the state courts on the legal issues involved. In many states a procedure exists whereby a federal court, faced with a difficult question of state law, may ask a state supreme court to rule on the question if it has not previously ruled in a similar question in another case.[46] The federal court must then follow the ruling of the state court. If there is no such referral procedure, the federal court must decide the case in the way it thinks the state court would decide. On appeal the federal court of appeals and the Supreme Court give the same deference to the state court's interpretation of state law.

Similarly, cases involving solely questions of federal law or both federal and state law can be filed in the state court. Unless removed to a federal court, the state court decides the federal issues in accordance with the decisions of federal courts. Appeal is through the state system, but when the appeal procedures of the state system are exhausted, review of the federal issues can be sought in the United States Supreme Court. That Court, however, does not review the questions of state law and will review federal issues only if they are dispositive of the case.[47] Finally, a federal statute provides that the law of the several states, both statutory and judge made, are the rules of decision in civil actions in federal courts unless the Constitution or a federal statute otherwise requires.[48]

Each state system is completely independent of every other state. That is, a court of one state is not bound by the decision of a court in another state unless the same dispute between the same parties has been previously litigated.[49] The decision of a court of one state, however, is persuasive but not binding authority on a court of another state on a common legal question.

3. Purpose and Function of Appellate Review

It is generally recognized that the ultimate purpose of a system of appellate review in the United States is uniformity. Uniformity in this context means that in a particular jurisdiction individuals in substantially the same circumstances will have the law interpreted and applied in a consistent manner and in accordance with a similar procedure. To achieve uniformity, appellate courts are established within each separate judicial system. Judge John Parker stated this position in the following terms:

> The judicial function in its essence is the application of the rules and standards of organized society to the settlement of controversies, and for there to be any proper administration of justice these rules and standards must be applied, not only impartially, but also objectively and uniformly throughout the territory of the state. This requires that decisions of trial courts be subjected to review by a

panel of judges who are removed from the heat engendered by the trial and are consequently in a position to take a more objective view of the questions there raised to maintain uniformity of decisions throughout the territory.[50]

The goal of uniformity is pursued by having appellate courts perform two principal functions:

(1) error correction and

(2) law development.

Error correction, which is primarily for the benefit of the individual parties to a particular case, involves a review of the actions of the trial court to determine whether it failed to follow some previously established substantive or procedural legal rule, made an error as to facts, or abused its discretion so that reversal or modification of its judgment is required. Law development, which is also termed institutional review, is done for the benefit of society or the law in general and not primarily for the litigants in the particular case. Under this function the courts adopt or revise common law doctrines and interpret constitutional provisions, statutes, and formal rules adopted by administrative agencies and courts. The same law development function is carried on when a previously established judicial doctrine or interpretation is applied to a substantially different factual situation.[51] One of the principal concerns in the law development area is the doctrine of precedent or *stare decisis*. This doctrine binds courts by legal doctrines or interpretations established in earlier decisions of the same court. There are frequently great debates in the United States over whether a court is free to decide that an earlier doctrine or interpretation is incorrect or no longer meets the needs of society and thus should be changed. Implicit in this dispute is the question of whether judges make law or simply apply the law. The issue can be cast in either jurisprudential terms or political terms. Constitutional law theorists disagree over whether judges, when interpreting the constitution, are bound by the original intent of the drafters of the constitutional language or are free to redefine the words of the constitution in accordance with contemporary needs. It is now generally acknowledged in American legal circles that judges do indeed make the law. But the occasions on which they expressly overrule earlier decisions are relatively few. Precedent and *stare decisis* still remain the strongest influences in the appellate process.[52]

Another function that appellate courts sometimes are said to perform is that of "doing justice" between the parties. When a court states that it is "doing justice" independent of its error correction or law development function, it almost invariably means that the court ignores an applicable principle of substantive law or fails to enforce a procedural rule that would cause the appeal to be dismissed or deny a party the opportunity to raise an issue. Whether judges should be free to reach a result based on the relative equities of the parties to the dispute while ignoring either substantive law or procedural rules is a question on which there is substantial disagreement. Those who argue against such freedom are not suggesting that courts should do injustice. They argue, rather, that both substantive law and procedural rules exist for the benefit of both parties, and to ignore them to do justice for one party is to deny justice to the other party. The better approach is one that balances the desire of the judge to see that the litigants receive common sense justice against the discipline of legal doctrine or procedural rules and recognizes that the decision in the particular case will be precedent to future cases involving similar facts and issues. Judge Albert Tate, Jr. expressed the principle in the following terms:

> The result that seems 'just' for the present case must be a principled one that will afford just results in similar conflicts of interest. This judge has an initial human concern that the litigants receive common sense justice, but he also realizes that the discipline of legal doctrine governs his determination of the cause.[53]

There is a close relationship between the structure of the system of appellate review and its functions. Intermediate appellate courts primarily serve the function of error correction while supreme courts primarily serve the function of law development. The extent to which a supreme court will correct errors or an intermediate appellate court will engage in law development will depend in large part upon the caseload of the courts in a particular jurisdiction. In a relatively small state with a well developed jurisprudence, the supreme court has ample time to deal with all law development questions. As a result the intermediate appellate court may have little or no role in law development. In the federal system, in which the Supreme Court can decide on the merits less than 1% of the cases decided by the United States courts of appeals each year, these intermediate courts are forced to engage in substantial law development. A similar situation exists in any state with a large number of appeals and a large number of intermediate appellate judges. Even in these jurisdictions, however, a supreme court will occasionally engage in error correction. This is more likely to occur when it is exercising a "doing justice" function. In a state that has only a supreme court and no intermediate appellate court, of course, the supreme court must perform all of the functions.

Special problems of precedent arise in jurisdictions that have one or more intermediate appellate courts. Within a jurisdiction there may be one intermediate appellate court for the entire state even though the court has many judges that sit in three judge panels, with either fixed or rotating membership. Michigan and Pennsylvania have this type of court. The jurisdiction may also be divided into geographic districts with a separate court in each district, also sitting in fixed or rotating panels. The United States courts of appeals and the states of New York and California are examples of this structural arrangement. The question arises as to each separate court whether a decision of one panel of the court is binding precedent on other panels and if so whether there is any procedure within the court to engage in law development and ignore precedent or whether such a power resides only in the supreme court of the jurisdiction. The general rule is that every panel is bound by a prior decision of a panel of the same court. If the court has an *en banc* procedure, as do the federal courts of appeals, then an *en banc* court can overrule the precedent of a panel but not a prior *en banc* decision. If there is no *en banc* procedure, then only the supreme court can change the law. In jurisdictions that are divided into circuits or districts with separate courts, each court is free to establish its own precedents. This means that the law in one part of the jurisdiction may be different than in another part, and only the supreme court can resolve the conflicts. This is the federal system as well as that of many states. The problem in the federal system is that there are so many conflicts between the circuits that the Supreme Court cannot or will not resolve them all. Such conflicts have given rise to proposals to establish a court beneath the Supreme Court that would be able to resolve inter-circuit conflicts until the Supreme Court decides to resolve the issue. No such proposal has gained wide support, in part because some Supreme Court justices maintain that they are able to resolve all important conflicts. Similar problems exist in some states, particularly larger ones.

An even greater problem exists in those jurisdictions in which one panel is not bound by the earlier decision of another panel. Unless the supreme court is obligated to review any such decision, there should be some procedure within the intermediate court to resolve the conflict. An *en banc* procedure is the most common way to deal with the problem. *En banc* procedures, however, create their own problems. To require or permit an *en banc* request in every case is simply to build in another opportunity for the unsuccessful appellant to delay the ultimate day of reckoning. It would be far preferable to make the decision of the earlier panel binding precedent but to permit another panel faced with a precedent with which it disagrees to invoke the *en banc* procedure.

The size of the *en banc* court is also an issue that must be resolved. If the intermediate appellate court is no larger than nine, all of the judges can sit on the *en banc* court. If, however, the number is substantially larger, having all the judges sit at the same time makes the *en banc* panel more like a committee than a court. It is for this reason that the U.S. Court of Appeals for the Ninth Circuit has an *en banc* panel of far less than its entire membership.

When Wisconsin created its intermediate appellate court, it divided the court into four districts, but each is part of a single court. To prevent inter-district conflicts without an *en banc* procedure, it created a publications committee composed of one judge from each of the four districts and the chief judge. The committee's responsibility is to determine which of the opinions written by panels in each of the four districts are to be published thereby becoming binding precedent for the entire state.

Whatever procedure is used, there must be some means of resolving disagreements among panels so that the law is uniform throughout the entire jurisdiction, whether it be the United States or a particular state. If the supreme court of the jurisdiction can perform that function, no other procedure is necessary. If, however, the number of decisions of the intermediate appellate court is so large that it is impossible for the supreme court to perform this function effectively, then some procedure must be developed to permit the intermediate appellate court to resolve conflicts among its panels.[54]

4. Principles of Appellate Review

a. The Right to Appeal

An essential feature of appellate review in the federal system and in all but three of the states, is the opportunity of any person aggrieved by a final judgment to have that judgment reviewed by at least one higher court.[55] The right to appeal means the right to present the record in the court below and written argument to a panel of judges who give thoughtful consideration to the merits of the appeal.[56] In most jurisdictions this right is granted by statute but in a few states it is specifically provided for in their constitutions.

Notwithstanding the almost universal acceptance of the right to appeal, the United States Supreme Court has consistently refused to include this right as a fundamental right guaranteed by the due process clause of the federal constitution. Thus, if a state decided to eliminate appellate review altogether it could do so.

b. What Can Be Appealed

Before a person can exercise the right of appeal to an appellate court, the action of the lower court sought to be challenged must be of the type that is subject to appeal, that is, within the jurisdiction of the appellate court. In the federal system and in most states the final judgment rule is the principal limitation on what actions can be appealed. Under this rule only decisions of the trial court classified as final are subject to appeal. This limitation is always included in a constitutional or statutory provision and is considered a limitation on the subject matter jurisdiction of the appellate court, whether stated in jurisdictional terms in granting the right to appeal, or in defining what can be appealed.

A final judgment is defined as one that determines all of the issues as to all of the parties, leaving only execution of the judgment to be completed. Its historic roots lie in English practice by which the King's Bench reviewed the actions of lower courts. The notion of jurisdiction over a case was directly tied to possession of the record, that is the court that had the record in a case had exclusive jurisdiction of it. There being only one record, it was impossible for two courts to have jurisdiction over the same case.[57] The appellate court would not order the lower court to relinquish the record until it was finished with it, and this occurred only when a final judgment was entered. The inability of more than one court to have jurisdiction over a case at any given time is also attributed to treating the case as a single "judicial unit" that cannot be subdivided for purposes of jurisdiction.[58]

The modern justification for the final judgment rule is quite different. It is simply to avoid the delay and the expense of piecemeal appeals. If a party can appeal any non final decision of the trial court, one party can subject the opposing party to substantial expense by appealing every adverse action of the trial court. If proceedings in the trial court are stayed until the appeal is resolved, the final resolution of the dispute will be delayed. This type of appeal will also overload the docket of the appellate court, thereby delaying its resolution of other appeals.

Notwithstanding the strong policy considerations in favor of the final judgment rule, there are a substantial number of cases in which immediate appeal may be desirable. The party against whom the decision was rendered may suffer irreparable harm if the appeal is delayed until a final judgment is rendered; the decision may not be effectively reviewable at that time; the decision may finally dispose of a matter unrelated to the remainder of the case; or the decision is on a matter that will control the direction of the remainder of the proceedings and all concerned would prefer to have an immediate review. There have been three types of responses to these situations. In the federal system and most states some of these matters can be appealed as of right and others at the discretion of the trial court, the appellate court, or both. In a few jurisdictions such as New York almost every interlocutory order can be appealed as of right, while in a few others such as Wisconsin any interlocutory order can be appealed in the discretion of the appellate court.

Even when an interlocutory order is not appealable either as of right or in the discretion of the trial or appellate court, an appellate court may still attempt to review the order if it thinks that strict enforcement of the final judgment rule will create undue hardship for the appealing party. In such a case the appellate court is attempting to "do justice" notwithstanding the restrictions of the final judgment rule. A court can accomplish this by simply creating an exception to the final judgment rule, designating the issuance of the order as a special proceeding, or using an extraordinary writ such as mandamus or certiorari.

c. Who Can Appeal

A less technical but nonetheless highly important restriction on appellate review governs who can appeal. One of the few rules that is applicable in all 51 American jurisdictions is that only a person who is "aggrieved" by a final judgment can appeal from it. A person who is aggrieved by a judgment is the person with an interest recognized by law that is adversely affected by it. The effect of a judgment is adverse if the person has less under it than would have been the case under a different judgment.

In order for a person's interests to be adversely affected by the judgment, the person must in some way be bound by the judgment. In most cases that means the person will have been a party of record in the case. There are, however, many court proceedings such as domestic relations, bankruptcy, class actions, contempt proceedings, and estate proceedings, in which a person appears, participates or has the opportunity to do so, is legally bound by the judgment rendered, but does not become a formal party. So long as the person is bound by the judgment and the judgment is adverse to its interests, that person is aggrieved by the judgment and can appeal from it if no other party is likely to appeal the portion of the judgment that affects the person seeking to appeal or if the person's interests will not be protected by a party who does appeal. In most circumstances, however, the person must intervene formally in the proceeding in the trial court in order to exercise the right to appeal.

Even though a litigant has a judgment rendered in its favor, it can still be aggrieved if the litigant receives less than it sought or is required to pay or do more than it is willing to pay or do. This applies to a plaintiff who sought $10,000 but received a judgment for $9,999 and to a defendant who claimed no liability for the $10,000 claim but was ordered to pay $1.

A party who is aggrieved by a judgment can lose the right to appeal if it acts in such a way as to indicate acceptance of the judgment. Thus a plaintiff who accepts payment of a judgment that does not grant all of the relief sought cannot appeal the judgment. Similarly a defendant who voluntarily (that is other than pursuant to a writ of execution) pays a judgment cannot appeal from it.

d. Standard of Review

When an appellate court is confronted with an appeal the court must first decide the standard of review it will apply to the appeal. The standard will vary depending upon whether the nature of the issue raised by the appellant is factual, legal, or discretionary.

If the challenge is to a legal ruling by the trial court, the review by the appellate court is *de novo*, that is, with no special deference given to the legal interpretation of the trial court. If the appeal is from a factual determination, the standard of review will depend upon whether the finder of fact was a jury or a judge. A jury's finding will be upheld if there is sufficient evidence to support it; that is, if a reasonable jury viewing the same facts could come to the same conclusion. The factual finding of a judge is tested by a clearly erroneous standard. This means the judge's finding stands if it is plausible in light of the entire record, even if the reviewing court would have decided the matter differently had it been the trier of fact. When a matter is committed to the discretion of the trial court, the review of the action is in terms of an abuse of discretion. For an abuse to be found, the trial court must have ignored a relevant factor that should have been given significant weight; an irrelevant or improper factor was given significant weight; or if, when all and only relevant factors are weighed, there was a clear error of judgment. In non lawyer terms, this means that the appellate court must be convinced that the trial judge was not only wrong but really wrong.

e. Reversible Error

In most appeals the principal question confronted by the appellate court is whether the trial court committed reversible error. Reversible error means some error relating to procedure, the facts, or the law that may have affected the result in the case. Appellate courts are not concerned with harmless error, that is an error that the court concludes did not affect the result.[59] For an error to be harmless, it must be clear from the record that it could not have affected the result. If there is any doubt, the appellate court will assume the error was not harmless.

The requirement that an error must not be harmless to permit a reversal is included in a statute in many jurisdictions.

Typical is the federal statute that specifies that on appeal the court shall give judgment "without regard to errors or defects which do not affect the substantial rights of the parties."[60]

The principal types of error are procedural, factual, or legal. A procedural error may involve any failure to follow the procedural rules governing the type of proceeding. For example, not giving adequate notice of a hearing or denying the right to call or cross examine witnesses are procedural errors. A factual error includes deciding a case without sufficient facts to support the decision while a legal error involves misconstruing or failing to follow a binding legal authority.

f. Issues That Can be Raised

The general rule in the United States is that only those issues presented to and decided by the trial judge can be raised on appeal. This general rule, which had its origins in the writ of error, has been subjected to a multitude of exceptions. The principal exceptions are issues that go to subject matter jurisdiction,[61] involve only legal questions for which the record has been fully developed, or involve plain or fundamental error. In an earlier article, the author has criticized non adherence to the general rule because of the unfairness to the opposing party and the trial judge who might have avoided the alleged error had it been raised in the trial court. It is clear, however, that the general rule against raising new issues is honored as much in the breach as in the observance.[62]

C. Comparison

1. Historical Development

Given the fact that the American legal system is a direct descendant of the English legal system, it is surprising to find that there are more differences than similarities in the historical development of the civil appeals systems in each country. Part of the reason for this is that the English system was still developing while the American colonies were being settled and thus there was no well defined model for the colonists to copy. Another is that there was great variation among the colonies in their governmental and legal structures and there was no effort to impose on them any specific judicial system, much less any specific court structure or system of appellate review. Each colony developed independently of the others and subsequently each state and the federal government developed its own separate judicial system.

While the colonial, state, and federal law maintained the distinction between law and equity, they did not establish two completely different judicial structures to administer each, as was the situation in England until 1875, nor did they establish different judicial structures for civil and criminal cases. Essentially each judicial system in the United States had one court system that administered both law and equity and civil and criminal law. Most importantly, in almost every state appellate review was done by a single appellate court. Later when intermediate appellate courts were established, this basic consolidated approach did not change.

The English structure developed quite differently. Until 1875, law and equity each had a separate court structure and appellate review system. Thereafter law and equity were combined in a single appellate system, although as a matter of tradition separate law and equity panels did develop on the Court of Appeal. Criminal appeals, however, have never been integrated into the system at the Court of Appeal level, even though the criminal appellate court is technically a division of the Court of Appeal and the judges of the Civil Division also sit on the Criminal Division. A panel of the Criminal Division, however, is almost always composed of one Lord Justice and two High Court judges, thus appellate judges almost never constitute a majority when the Criminal Division sits. In addition, the criminal appeal procedures are completely different than those for civil appeals.

The major difference between supreme courts in the United States and the House of Lords as a judicial body is that each of the former is composed of a fixed panel of judges--every appeal is heard by the same judges. In the House of Lords, however, the membership of any given appellate committee of five members can be drawn not only from the ten law lords but may also include the Lord Chancellor or any member of the House of Lords who has had substantial judicial service. The person who determines the membership of any given Appellate Committee has the opportunity to influence the decision in a particular case because of which persons he chooses to sit on it. In addition, the eligibility of the Lord Chancellor, who as a practical matter holds office at the pleasure of the Prime Minister, to sit on the Appellate Committee has no counterpart in the United States.

Although the appellate review procedures in the two countries have common origins, they have deviated sharply since the latter part of the eighteenth century. In each country, two separate procedures developed, writ of error for common law proceedings and appeal for equity. Because the Americans had only one appellate court structure in each jurisdiction, there was a tendency to have only one appellate procedure applicable to both law and equity proceedings. The choice was made to adopt the writ of error procedure with its emphasis on procedural technicalities rather than the rehearing nature of the equity appeal. When England in 1875 combined appellate review in the Court of Appeal for both common law and equity, the equity rehearing approach was made applicable to appellate review of both common law and equity proceedings. In the twentieth century, however, the two systems have been moving toward each other. The American effort has been to simplify appellate procedure to enable appellate courts to get to the merits of the appeal. In England, on the other hand, the idea of the appeal as a true rehearing has not developed. As a result, today there is little difference between American and English appellate courts in their approach to performing their review function. This is discussed more fully in the next section.

2. Purpose and Function of Appellate Review

In theory, the purpose and function of appellate review in the United States differ widely from those of appellate review in England. In the former, the principal function of intermediate appellate courts is error correction and only incidentally law development. The ability of appellate judges to do justice between the parties is not an independent function of appellate review, but a by-product of the other two functions. Occasionally, the doing justice function can subsume the other two functions. The function of a supreme court in a jurisdiction with an intermediate appellate court is primarily law development and only incidentally error correction and doing justice. The primary importance of error correction in the intermediate appellate court is consistent with the writ of error approach to the purpose of appellate review.

In England, which adopted the *de novo* hearing approach of the equity appeal, it would be expected that the function of doing justice would be paramount. Law development should be only incidental to doing justice, and error correction should play no part whatsoever in appellate review. As the discussion in section 1 B indicates, however, the English appeal concentrates as much on a search for error as does its American counterpart. This crucial change in function results primarily from the limitations imposed by the Court of Appeal itself and not by virtue of any statute, rule, or decision of the House of Lords. The means for the imposition of these limitations have been the adoption of standards of review for various types of questions. It is significant that only recently has the function of the English appellate courts been discussed in terms of the functions of error correction and law development.[63]

A comparison of the standards of review for questions of law, fact, and discretion in the two countries shows that they are almost identical. As to questions of law, both follow the principle that in a hierarchical court system the standard of review by a higher court of a question of law decided by a lower court is, in the nature of things, *de novo*, that is the higher court is free to come to its own conclusion and is not bound by that of the lower court. Similarly, finding of a jury on basic facts can be set aside only if the appellate court concludes that no reasonable jury could have reached the same conclusion. The same type of findings by a trial judge can be reversed in either system only if the appellate court thinks the judge made a grievous error, not simply that the appellate judges would have come to a different conclusion. In the United States a judge's finding must be characterized as clearly erroneous before the appellate court will interfere. In both countries, however, when the review is of ultimate facts, the review is again *"de novo"* because it involves the application of law to the basic facts as found by the trial judge or jury. When reviewing the exercise of discretion by the trial judge, an appellate court in either country will reverse only if the judge made an error of law, took into account something he should not have, failed to take into account something he should have, or simply made a clear error of judgment.

It is commonly thought that English and American courts differ sharply on the extent to which they will engage in law development when there is existing binding precedent. To describe this in another way, it is generally believed that the doctrine of *stare decisis* has a much stronger influence in English appellate courts than in American. The difference between the two countries, however, is overstated. For intermediate appellate courts in both countries, the rule is the same-- a decision of a panel of a court applying a legal principle to a set of facts is binding in a later case before another panel of the same court involving substantially the same facts. For the United States Supreme Court and state supreme courts, they can and do overrule prior decisions and change the law when they consider that the legal rules set forth in prior decisions no longer meet the needs of modern society. They do not take the position that the law, once judicially declared, must remain the same until changed by the legislature, although this once was a commonly held view and is still held by some judges. This they regard as a "slavish" adherence to precedent. They consider that under the common law principles, it is the responsibility of judges to reexamine legal doctrines to ensure responsibility of judges to reexamine legal doctrines to ensure that the circumstances that gave rise to them no longer exist, making adherence to them unjustified. Essentially this has been the position of the House of Lords since 1966.

Two factors may give rise to the common perception that precedent means less in the United States than in England. One is the fact that the United States has a written constitution drafted over two hundred years ago. That document contains a number of words that can and have been interpreted differently in different contexts, particularly over several centuries. The number of occasions when the United States Supreme Court actually overrules its prior constitutional interpretations is relatively few, but they are usually cases of national import and they receive substantial attention.

The other factor is that American appellate courts decide so many more cases than English appellate courts--approximately 150 times as many--that the opportunities to make law and to modify existing law are far greater. It is not surprising, consequently that American courts appear to be less concerned with precedent than English courts. The fact is that in both systems the principal opportunities for law development are when a court is faced with applying a legal doctrine developed in one era in cases with common fact patterns to disputes arising in a new era with totally different fact patterns or resolving disputes with such novel fact patterns that existing legal doctrines and precedent are only marginally relevant.[64]

3. Principles of Appellate Review

a. The Right to Appeal

A major variance between American and English appellate justice concerns the right to appeal. Essentially the two countries have gone in opposite directions. In the United States, both state and federal statutes originally imposed major monetary limitations on the right to appeal and some types of decisions were not subject to appeal. Over the years there has been a steady trend not only to expand the legal right to appeal but also to make that right meaningful by reducing the cost of taking an appeal. Today there is a consensus that there should be the right to at least one appeal in every case. In this context, it is important to understand that the right to appeal means a right to have a decision on the merits of an appeal, not simply a right to ask the court to review an order of judgment. In jurisdictional terms, this is referred to as mandatory rather than discretionary jurisdiction. The explosion in the number of appeals in the last three decades has not jeopardized efforts to reduce the cost of taking an appeal and to reduce delay in deciding appeals. In fact, the approach has been one of the causes of the explosion. In England, on the other hand, the trend is in the opposite direction. One of the responses to the relatively minor growth in the number of appeals over the last 20 years is a provision in the County Courts Act of 1959 that allowed the Supreme Court Rules Committee to define the classes of orders for which leave would be required--in other words to restrict the right of appeal. Neither the 1981 Supreme Court Act nor Order 59 provides any criteria for granting or denying an application for leave to appeal. It can be granted by the trial judge or a single judge of the Court of Appeal. No notice of the application is initially given to the prospective respondent and there is no review of the decision of the single appellate judge.

The combination of these provisions is unfortunate. One of their premises is that the potential validity of an appeal can be predicted based on the amount involved, the court from which the appeal comes, the type of order involved, or some other objective criterion. There is no evidence offered to support this premise. Another premise is that the right to appeal only means the right to seek access to the appellate court, not the right to a review of the merits. Similarly, allowing a rules committee to restrict the right to appeal places in a committee a decision that is properly legislative in nature. Allowing the trial judge to grant an application for leave to appeal allows the judge whose decision is challenged to influence whether such a challenge will be permitted, a curious position in which to place a judge. For obvious reasons, judges are not allowed to sit on appeals of their own decisions. This procedure is inconsistent with that restriction. Giving the trial judge the authority to grant the application also permits a lower court judge to determine the caseload of a higher court, an unhealthy situation. (This same problem exists with regard to the provision that gives a panel of the Court of Appeal the power to grant an application for leave to appeal a decision of the panel to the House of Lords.) Allowing the application to be decided by a single judge of the Court of Appeal with no review of his decision merely allows one judge to substitute his judgment for that of another. Even worse, obtaining judicial review can turn on the chance of which judge hears the application. Sir Jack Jacob has noted that in this regard "the practice of the Judge in Chambers, in my experience at the Bar, varied enormously and I imagine it still does. Some Judges used to give such leave very readily, almost for the asking; others were affronted to be asked, as though their decision was being questioned, which it was."[65] It is likely that the same variation operates with the judges of the Court of Appeal.

Additionally, the lack of a requirement of notice of the application or its initial consideration to the winning party in the trial court means that the losing party is attempting to take away the benefits of the favorable order without the winning party knowing about it. The justification for this is that it will save the party the expense of responding to the application. The choice of whether or not to incur this expense should be left to the party; a court rule or procedure should not make the decision for it. At the very least, the winning party would want to know about the application to prevent taking any action that may create difficulties for it if the order is ultimately overturned.

Although Sir Jack Jacob has referred to the right of appeal as part of the fundamental right to a fair trial or hearing, yet at the same time he approves the restrictions and limitations that "greatly curtail or inhibit the exercise of this right." He further comments that "the cumulative effect of these restrictions and limitations is to trim down the number of appeals that are brought to a manageable total with which the appellate court can adequately cope and which they can dispose of after due deliberation."[66] Restricting the right to appeal should be the last option for responding to an increase in the number of appeals, not one of the first. For these reasons, no comparable procedure exists in the American appellate process for the initial appeal of a final judgement.

The problems with restricting the right of appeal from final orders will be exacerbated if a provision in the Government's bill concerning the courts and the legal profession (introduced in the House of Lords on December 6, 1989 as HL 13) is enacted. Under clause 7 of Part 1 of the bill, section 18 of the Supreme Court Act of 1981 would be amended to extend the provision authorizing the Supreme Court Rules Committee to determine which classes of final orders of the county courts can be appealed only with leave of court. If this provision is enacted the rules committee could extend the leave to appeal requirement to every final order of any court, including the High Court, or tribunal over which the Court of Appeal has jurisdiction. The provision was the subject of a heated debate in the House of Lords on the bill on January 25, 1990.[67] The basic argument in favor of the proposal was that because many appeals are without merit, it should be left to a committee to determine which, if any, classes of final orders should be appealable as of right. If the provision is enacted the right to appeal in England could be eliminated without further legislative action. Even without further action of the Rules Committee, the final orders subject to leave to appeal will be greatly expanded because the same bill includes another provision (clause 1 of Part I) that will permit the Lord Chancellor to reallocate the division of judicial business between the High Court and the county courts. The Lord Chancellor had previously stated in the July, 1989, White Paper his intent to give jurisdiction over most contract and tort litigation to the county courts (discussed in Chapter 2, section A 1, *infra*). Unless the provisions in Order 59 governing appeals are changed, many final orders now appealable of right would require leave to appeal.

It should be noted, however, that the Federal Courts Study

Committee in its April, 1990 final report suggested that study should be given in the future to whether to restrict the right of appeal in the federal system in the United States.[68]

b. What Can Be Appealed

The English and American views on what can be appealed are quite similar, but with some major distinctions. In making this comparison, it is important to keep in mind the difference between appeal as of right and appeal in the discretion of the appellate court.

In the United States any judgment that can be classified as "final" can be appealed as of right. Final judgment for this purpose is one that determines all issues as to all parties, leaving only execution of the judgment to be accomplished. In England, however, there are certain classes of orders that, even though final, can be appealed only if leave to appeal is granted. The most common of these is the order of a county court for an amount less than half of the maximum monetary jurisdiction of the court. Another twist is that in matrimonial causes, there is not only the right to appeal a decree *nisi* granting a divorce, if the decree *nisi* is not appealed immediately then the right to appeal the final decree is lost.

Another major difference concerns interlocutory orders. Both in England and the United States there are statutory exceptions to the final judgment rule that allow some interlocutory orders to be appealed as of right. In most jurisdictions in the United States, including federal, any interlocutory order that is not appealable by virtue of a statutory exception cannot be appealed even with leave of the appellate court. In England, however, an application for leave to appeal can be sought for any interlocutory order not appealable as of right. There are substantial advantages to the position taken by England and several American states that allows a party to seek review of any interlocutory order but gives discretion to the appellate court on whether or not to hear the appeal. The appellate process is thus flexible enough to prevent irreparable harm but the work load of the judges is not substantially increased. General guidelines on the exercise of discretion, while probably helpful, do not impose meaningful restrictions. Allowing this safety valve procedure is the best means to prevent statutory or judicial exceptions to the final judgment rule that unnecessarily create the right to appeal in certain types of cases.

Two other aspects of the English approach to the final-interlocutory order distinction deserve comment. The first is the curious rule that makes the distinction turn upon the order that might have been granted, not the order actually granted. This has the effect of converting some orders that are clearly final into interlocutory orders that require leave before they can be appealed. This is a peculiar way in which to cut down on the number of appeals coming to the court. Also peculiar is the authority given to the Rules Committee to classify orders as final or interlocutory. This power not only has an Alice in Wonderland aspect to it, by allowing the committee to make an order final or interlocutory by fiat without regard to the essential nature of the order, but more importantly it allows the committee to determine the right of appeal, a power normally reserved for a legislative body.

c. Who Can Appeal

The English and American approaches to who can appeal are textually different but in operation are substantially similar. The important factor in England is actual or potential status as a party. The American rule looks to whether a person can demonstrate that he is aggrieved by the judgment. A person who is not a party in the trial court but who is aggrieved must, however, intervene to become a party before he can appeal. Theoretically a party to an English proceeding can appeal even if it is not aggrieved by the order. In practical terms this is unlikely. There would be little or no reason to appeal unless the party were aggrieved by the order. The one circumstance when this might occur is when the party is aggrieved not by the order but by the reasoned judgement, but in such a case there is no right to appeal.

The major difference between the two systems concerns who grants party status so that a non party can appeal. In the

United States it is the trial judge while in England it is the Court of Appeal. It makes more sense to put the decision in the hands of the trial judge who is more familiar with the course of the proceedings and can more easily determine whether the person seeking party status is entitled to it. In the United States a person seeking to intervene for the purpose of taking an appeal must show that no other party is likely to appeal that portion of the judgment adverse to the intervenor. Once it makes the showing a petition to intervene will be granted. There does not appear to be any English decision on this point.

d. Standard of Review

The comparison of the standards of review in the two countries is made in section 2, *supra*. As the discussion there indicates, they are virtually identical.

e. Reversible Error

Both the United States and England expressly provide that a judgment or order should not be reversed for harmless error. In the United States a common provision in statutes provides that appellate courts should not take into account errors that do not affect substantial rights. In England, Order 14 specifies that a new trial should not be ordered unless there was a substantial wrong or a miscarriage of justice. These provisions appear to be substantially comparable.

f. Issues That Can Be Raised

Both English and American appellate courts have adopted the general rule that unless an issue is first raised in the trial court it cannot be raised on appeal. With an exception for issues of law that do not require the development of additional facts, the Court of Appeal adheres to the rule notwithstanding the status of the English appeal as a rehearing. The American courts, on the other hand, have made a virtual mockery of the general rule in their effort to "do justice" in individual cases. The unfairness to the winning party and the waste of judicial resources of permitting a party to remain silent in the trial court, and then, after all the proceedings are completed, raising a new issue should require strict enforcement of the general rule. The English adherence to the general rule is much to be favored.

ENDNOTES

1. As in most books about English legal institutions, the terms "England" and "English" as used in this book include "Wales" or "Welsh."

2. Origins of the English judicial system are covered briefly in R. Walker, *The English Legal System* 3-57 (6th ed. 1985) and R. Jackson, *The Machinery of Justice in England* 1-8 (6th ed. 1972). A more complete description can be found in 1 W. Holdsworth, *History of English Law* (3rd ed. 1923). Other standard works are F. Pollock and F. Maitland, *The History of English Law* (1968) and T. Plucknett, *A Concise History of the Common Law* (1956).

3. The development of equity as a separate legal system is the focus of Holdsworth, *supra* note 2 at 395-476.

4. The evolution of the systems of appellate review for law and equity is the subject of Holdsworth, *supra* note 2 at 222-26, 244-45, 370-74, and 642-45; and R. Pound, *Appellate Review in Civil Cases* 25-27, 38-71 (1941).

5. Pound, *supra* note 4 at 47-58.

6. Holdsworth, *supra* note 2 at 370-72; Pound, *supra* note 4 at 58-60.

7. Holdsworth, *supra* note 2 at 372-75; Pound, *supra* note 4 at 63-66. Walker, *supra*, note 2 at 46.

8. Walker, *supra* note 2 at 47.

9. Holdsworth, *supra* note 2 at 633-50; Walker, *supra* note 2 at 76-85.

10. Holdsworth, *supra* note 2 at 368-76; L. Blom-Cooper & G. Drewry, *Final Appeal* 18-29 (1972).

11. 5 Atkin's *Court Forms, Appeals* ¶¶ 61 & 64 (2d ed. 1984). Walker, *supra* note 2 at 186-87, however, states that the House has no power to issue an order but only makes recommendations that the lower court then incorporates into its own order. Blom-Cooper & Drewry, *supra* note 10 at 96 n.1 supports Walker.

12. Sunderland, *Improvement of Appellate Procedure*, 26 Iowa L. Rev. 3, 7-12 (1940).

13. 9 W. Holdsworth, *History of English Law* 368-69 (1923).

14. Blom-Cooper & Drewry, *supra* note 10 at 47.

15. See generally the Supreme Court Act of 1981, sections 15-18 and Order 59 of the Rules of the Supreme Court.

16. Until recently, the exception as to points of law did not apply to appeals from county courts. The Court of Appeal in 1989 held, however, that the rule treating appeals from county courts differently was no longer justified and decided not to follow it. This decision is particularly interesting because in so holding, the Court rejected a rule established by the House of Lords. *Pittalis v. Grant*, 139 New Law J. 578 (April 28, 1989).

17. M. Zander, *The English Legal System* 523-62 (5th ed. 1984), Walker, *supra* note 2 at 189-91 and 423-37, and D. Karlen, *Appellate Courts in the United States and England* 80-104 (1962) are good general discriptions of the Court of Appeal.

18. J. Jacob, *The Fabric of English Civil Justice* 231-33 (1987).

19. M. Zander, *The Law Making Process* 159-95 (2d ed. 1985); Walker, *supra* note 2 at 133-54; Blom-Cooper & Drewry, *supra* note 10 at 65-78.

20. Walker, *supra* note 2 at 134.

21. The statement of Lord Gardiner, the Lord Chancellor, is printed at [1966] 3 All E.R. 77, [1966] 1 W.L.R. 1234.

22. R. Stevens, *Law and Politics* 589-627 (1976) reviews the activity of the House of Lords until 1976 and concludes the changes in the law made by its decisions were incremental. A later list of cases in which the Appellate Committee considered a change in the law and the result is found in A. Paterson, *The Law Lords* 163-65 (1982). See also P. Atiyah and R. Summers, *Form and Substance in Anglo-American Law* 267-271 (1987)

23. Lord McCluskey, *Law, Justice and Democracy* 18 (1986).

24. *Pittalis v. Grant*, 139 New Law J. 578 (April 28, 1989).

25. Doing justice to the appellant was, however, the sole basis on which the Court of Appeal in *Pittalis v. Grant*, note 24, *supra*, decided to ignore the precedent of the House of Lords and consider an issue of law not raised in the county court. The court stated that not to do so would visit the sins of counsel on the client, thereby doing an injustice to the party seeking to raise the issue in the name of doing justice to the other party.

26. Although the statute refers to "judgment or order" the term "order" is the common terminology in the English system to the action of the lower court that is the subject of review in a higher court. For that reason the term "order" is used in this book rather than "judgment" or "judgment or order."

27. These statutes are listed in Atkin's *Court Forms, supra* note 11 at ¶ 61.

28. *Id* at ¶ 71.

29. *Id* at ¶ 67.

30. *Id* at notes 8-17.

31. Supreme Court Practice 1988 note 59/1/15. See also Atkin's *Court Forms, supra* note 11 at ¶ 71 note 8.

32. Supreme Court Act 1981 s. 18(1)(h)(vi).

33. Supreme Court Act 1981 s. 54(6).

34. Order 59 n. 14(4).

35. Atkin's Court Forms, *supra* note 11 at ¶ 68. The Court of Appeal can grant leave when it is just and convenient to do so. *Asphalt and Public Works Ltd. v. Indemnity Guarantee Trust Ltd.* [1969] 1 QB, 465, 471, [1968] 3 All E.R. 509, 511 CA.

36. *Lake v. Lake* [1955] 2 All E.R. 538 CA.

37. See, generally, Criminal Appeal Office, *A Guide to Proceedings in the Court of Appeal Criminal Division* (1983) and D. Meador, *Criminal Appeals: English Practice and American Reform* (1973).

38. Home Office, 4 Criminal Statistics 100 (1985).

39. These statistics were provided by the staff of the Court of Session, copies in the files of the author.

40. On the legal system in Scotland see generally A. Paterson & T. Bates, *The Legal System of Scotland: Cases and Materials* (2d ed. 1986) and *The Legal System of Scotland* (Her Majesty's Stationery Office, 3rd ed. 1981).

41. The history of appellate review in the United States up to the early twentieth century has been exhaustively detailed in Roscoe Pound's *Appellate Procedure in Civil Cases* (1941). The colonial period is covered at pp. 72-105, the nineteenth century at pp. 106-320 and improvements in the

twentieth century at pp. 321-374. A more recent effort covering the colonial period is J. Goebel, I *History of the Supreme Court of the United States* 25-35 (1971). A history of one colonial appellate court is recounted in C. Bond, *The Court of Appeals of Maryland* (1928).

42. R. Pound, *supra* note 4 at 385-88 (1941); Sunderland, *Improvement of Appellate Procedure*, 26 Iowa L. Rev. 3 (1940).

43. Pound, *supra* note 4, at 319-20.

44. This growth is detailed in Chapter 4, section B, *infra*.

45. The relationship between the state and federal court systems and between their systems of appellate review is explored more fully in C. Wright, *Law of Federal Courts* 268-346 (4th ed. 1983).

46. A typical procedure is found in Ohio Supreme Court, Rules of Practice XVI effective July 15, 1988. Under the rule the court may answer a question of state law certified by a federal court that may be determinative of a case pending in that court and on which question there is no controlling Ohio precedent. Once certified, the parties file briefs in the Ohio Supreme Court on the question. Oral argument is in the discretion of the court. If the court decides to answer the question it prepares a written opinion that is sent to the parties and to the federal court that requested it. The Ohio court may refuse to answer any question. This procedure was initiated by committees of federal and state judges designed to reduce friction between federal and state courts. For a list of the states that have adopted this type of procedure, see Le Bel, *Legal Positivism and Federalism, The Certification Experience*, 19 Ga. L. Rev. 999, n.1 (1985).

47. Review of decisions of state supreme courts by the United States Supreme Court is discussed in C. Wright, *Law of the Federal Courts* 736-54 (4th ed. 1983) and R. Stern, E. Gressman, and S. Shapiro, *Supreme Court Practice* 106-87 (6th ed. 1986). One of the most controversial issues in these cases is whether the Supreme Court will find that the case was decided on an adequate state ground, thereby precluding review of the federal issues in the case. The Supreme Court's most recent effort on this question, *Michigan v. Long*, 463 U.S. 1032 (1983) has generated substantial discussion. See the discussion in Hart and Wechsler, *The Federal Courts and the Federal System* 547-54 (3rd ed. 1988).

48. 28 U.S.C. § 1652. The term "laws" includes judicial decisions as well as statutes. *Erie R.R. v. Tompkins*, 304 U.S. 64 (1938).

49. Article IV Section 1 of the U.S. Constitution requires that "Full Faith and Credit shall be given in each state to the . . . judicial proceedings of every other state." By the same section Congress is given authority to pre-

scribe the manner in which the proceedings must be proved and their effect. The Congressional enactment is found in 28 U.S.C. § 1738. It provides in part that a judicial proceeding of a state court has the same effect in every state or federal court that it has in the courts of the state in which the proceeding was held.

50. Parker, *Improving Appellate Methods*, 25 New York Univ. L. Rev. 1 (1950).

51. R. Martineau, *Modern Appellate Practice - Federal and State Civil Appeals* 19-21 (1983); P. Carrington, D. Meador & M. Rosenberg, *Justice on Appeal* 2-4 (1976); American Bar Association Standards for Appellate Courts § 3.00 (1977).

52. For an interesting collection of articles on these topics, primarily by federal judges, see M. Cannon and D. O'Brien (Ed.), *Views from the Bench--The Judiciary and Constitutional Politics* (1985). The views of a thoughtful state supreme court justice on the law-making role of judges are found in Traynor, *Transatlantic Reflections on Leeways and Limits of Appellate Courts*, 1980 Utah L. Rev. 255. (Not coincidentally, this article was originally given at a colloquium on Methods of Law Reform, University of Warwick, England. Justice Traynor had also served as the Sir Arthur Goodhart Professor of Legal Science at Cambridge University, England in 1975-76.)

53. Tate, *The Art of Brief Writing: What a Judge Wants to Read*, 4 Litigation 11 (Winter, 1978).

54. The Institute of Judicial Administration (U.S.) recently announced a study of the ways in which state intermediate appellate courts in the United States deal with the problem. 22 IJA Report 8 (Nos. 1-2, 1990).

55. American Bar Association Standards for Appellate Courts § 3.10 (1977). Virginia and West Virginia have usually been listed as the only states that do not have a right of appeal. Lilly and Scalia, *Appellate Justice: A Crisis in Virginia* 3, 12-13 (1971); Dalton, *Taking the Right to Appeal (More or Less) Seriously*, 95 Yale L.J. 62 (1985). New Hampshire, which has traditionally been listed as having the right to appeal, has stated that the right of appeal "is limited to obtain a discretionary determination by this court as to whether it will accept the appeal." *State v. Cooper*, 498 A.2d 1209, 1213 (1985). There is thus no right to a review of the merits, meaning there is no right to appeal. A few matters in Virginia are appealable as of right. Barrow, *The Discretionary Appeal: A Cost Effective Tool of Appellate Justice*, 11 George Mason U. L. Rev. 31, 49 (1988).

56. American Bar Association Standards for Appellate Courts § 3.10 (Commentary) (1977).

57. Crick, *The Final Judgment as a Basis for Appeal*, 41 Yale L. J. 539, 542-44 (1932).

58. *Sears, Roebuck & Co v. Mackey,* 351 U.S. 427, 431-32 (1956) citing Metcalfe's Case, 11 Co. Rep. 38a, 77 Eng. Rep. 1193. In *Jason's Foods, Inc. v. Peter Eckrich & Sons, Inc.,* 768 F.2d 189 (7th Cir. 1985), however, the appellate court held it could order a limited remand to permit the trial court to take additional evidence on a jurisdictional issue while the appellate court still retained nominal jurisdiction over the appeal, a position in apparent conflict with the judicial unit theory. It is also generally held that during the pending of an interlocutory appeal the appellate court has jurisdiction over all matters not affected by the appeal.

59. R. Traynor, *The Riddle of Harmless Error* (1970).

60. 28 U.S.C. § 2106

61. For a challenge to the almost universally held position that even subject matter jurisdiction should be allowed to be raised for the first time on appeal see Martineau, *Subject Matter Jurisdiction as a New Issue on Appeal: Reining in an Unruly Horse,* 1988 Brigham Young U. L. Rev 1.

62. The extent to which courts find reasons not to follow the general rule is discussed in Martineau, *Considering New Issues on Appeal: The General Rule and the Gorilla Rule,* 42 Vanderbilt L. Rev. 1023 (1987).

63. J. Jacob, *supra* note 18 at 222; Jolowicz, *Comparative Law and the Reform of Civil Procedure,* 8 Legal Studies 1, 11-12 (1988). It is interesting to note, however, that when the Judicature Acts of 1873-75 were first adopted, this very distinction was made by an English barrister.

> A court of last resort should be exhaustively deliberative, eminently patient, nothing if not careful; it should therefore not be too easy of access, and should treat every case brought before it with the utmost minuteness and detail of which it is susceptible; and if the courts below be properly constituted, the appeals with which it will have to deal with be few enough to warrant, and important enough to demand, this treatment: and thus, and thus only, can such a court fulfil the great object of its existence by definitively 'settling the law' to which all other courts and judges are necessarily to conform, and which, when once settled, ought to be incapable of being disturbed, except by Act of Legislature. A court of first appeal, on the other hand, ought to be ready of access, rapid of decision, supplying an immediate correction to the tendency to divergence inherent in the multiplicity of the courts of first instance; and ought to aim rather at the termination of the specific contest than the determination of any abstract legal principle. If so constituted as to

command public confidence, appeals to it will be numerous, from it few; these few being confined to cases involving some point of especial novelty or difficulty, or where the value of the property at stake is so great as to induce the loser to risk the costs of appeal upon the doctrine of chances merely.

Miller, *Supreme Court of Judicature Act (1873) Amendment Bill No. 2 So Far as Relates to Appeal*, 19 Solicitors' Journal 536 (1875) quoted in Note, *The Reform of the New Zealand Courts*, 7 Civil Justice Q. 198, 201 (1988).

64. For a comparison of the functions of courts of last resort in England and the United States see P. Atiyah & R. Summers, *supra* note 22 at 267-71.

65. Jacob, *Leave to appeal - to give or not to give*, 5 Civil Justice Q. 3, 4 (1986). A similar criticism is made by Lord Justice Woolf in Woolf, *A Hotchpotch of Appeals - The Need for a Blender*, 7 Civil Justice Q. 44, 46-47 (1988).

66. J. Jacob, *supra* note 17 at 217-18; Woolf, *supra* note 65 at 47.

67. The debate is reported in 140 New Law Journal 136 (Feb. 2, 1990). A remarkable feature of the original language in HL 13 was that leave to appeal could be granted only by the court or tribunal whose final order was sought to be appealed. Because of the opposition to the entire provision, the Lord Chancellor argued to introduce an amendment to authorize the Court of Appeal to grant leave to appeal, a power it currently has over those orders that require leave to appeal. Without such an amendment, the ability of a litigant to challenge a final order could be solely dependent upon the discretion of the person or agency that issued the order.

68. Federal Courts Study Committee, Report 116 (1990).

Chapter 2   The Personnel of Appellate Review

A. England

When a party seeks review in the Court of Appeal of a decision of the High Court or a county court it will be represented by at least two lawyers, a solicitor and a barrister, or the party will represent itself. Also involved in the appeal are the trial judge or a single appellate judge if leave to appeal is required, and a panel of two or three appellate judges. Court staff and official shorthand reporters must also assist in processing the appeal both in the trial court and in the appellate court.

1. The Lawyers

The legal profession in England (as well as the rest of Great Britain and in some Commonwealth countries but not in the rest of the world) is divided into two branches--solicitors and barristers.[1] The historical reasons for the division and the justification for its continuation are beyond the scope of this book, but it is significant that there is continuing pressure to modify or eliminate it.[2] At the present time, however, both barristers and solicitors play significant roles in the appellate process.

a. Barristers

The traditional function of the barrister is to serve as an advocate for a client before a court or other legal tribunal. The position grew out of the activities of persons known by various designations including pleaders, narrators, or counteurs who were employed by litigants to speak on their behalf in court. Their sole task was persuasion but the litigant was not bound by what the advocate said and could disavow it when convenient. These courtroom advocates were employed on the basis of their oratorical skills rather than legal knowledge. It was not necessary to be admitted to practice before the court in order to appear before it in this capacity and there was no regulation of them by the judges.[3]

Eventually, as the English legal system became more formal and structured, persons performing these functions became known as barristers. In order to appear on behalf of a litigant in court, termed a right of audience, it became mandatory to obtain membership in one of the four Inns of Court in London-- Middle Temple, Inner Temple, Gray's Inn, and Lincoln's Inn. This requirement exists today. The origins of the Inns and how they gained control over admission to the bar are lost in history. The accepted view today is that the Inns derive their authority from the judges who have an inherent control over who is permitted to appear before them on behalf of another. It is said that the judges have delegated the responsibility for admission (and discipline) of the barristers, but this delegation is not express. It is based, rather, on tradition.[4]

To become a barrister a person must meet certain academic and vocational requirements. The candidate must be admitted as a student member of an Inn of Court, dine at the Inn at least three times during eight seperate terms (there are four terms a year), and pass the bar examination. After being called to the Bar, however, a barrister cannot practice on his own before serving a pupillage under an experienced barrister.

The first step, admission as a student member of an Inn, has no fixed educational requirements. Most students have a university degree which may but need not be in law. The law degree is not from a graduate professional school but is simply another undergraduate major, earned in the normal three year program of most English universities. If the degree is not in law, attendance at a diploma course is required. This is a one year program in substantive and procedural law run by the Council of Legal Education. A student member, whatever his educational background, must also attend the Inns of Court School of Law operated by the Council of Legal Education for a nine month period. This is usually done while a student is keeping terms at an Inn of Court. The program at the law school was until 1989 little more than a cram course in substantive law in preparation for the bar examination with little or no skills training in advocacy. After passing the bar examination the student is then called to the Bar as a member of an Inn. The new barrister must then serve for one year as a pupil in the chambers of a senior member of the bar (but not a Queen's Counsel). Pupillage involves observing the barrister in court, assisting in the preparation of briefs, and sitting in on interviews with clients for the first six months. During the second six months the new barrister may handle matters independently. When the pupillage is completed, the barrister is then free to appear on behalf of clients in any court, although obtaining clients is another matter.[5]

In 1987 the Council of Legal Education and the General Council of the Bar appointed a Committee on Continuing Education and Training for the Bar. In its first report dated October 7, 1987, it stated that because barristers are specialists in advocacy their education and training should foster and improve those skills. It concluded that the present program was heavily weighted toward substantive law and allowed little time for specialized practical skills, especially court advocacy, professional conduct, and communication skills. It observed that the practical exercises included in the present program gave only a limited opportunity to speak as an advocate. The Committee recommended that time should be made available during the student's tenure at the Inns of Court School of Law for the systematic teaching of advocacy, communication techniques, and skills and that students should engage in practical advocacy during the year. After the end of pupillage, the Committee recommended that a barrister just starting to practice should be required to attend a course in advocacy modeled upon those developed in the United States by the National Institute for Trial Advocacy.

Pursuant to these recommendations, the Council of Legal

Education adopted, effective October, 1989, a new curriculum for the vocational course in the Inns of Court School of Law. Under this curriculum students will devote two thirds of their time to receiving skills training in the following: legal research, information management and problem solving, opinion writing, interviewing, negotiating, drafting, and advocacy. The method of instruction will combine instruction and exercises in the various skills. In the final term students will manage the conduct of two cases, one for the plaintiff and one for the defendant. Although it is not expressly stated, it does not appear that the handling of the cases will go beyond the trial level; there will, thus, be no training in appellate advocacy. The recommendation that new barristers be required to participate in a course in advocacy based upon an American model was not implemented.

The next step for the hopeful barrister is to find a place in one of the established chambers. In the past, barristers could only practice out of a chambers, but in view of the lack of open places in chambers, the Bar has eliminated all restrictions on where a barrister may conduct a practice. Chambers, most of which have been located in the Inns of Court, are loose affiliations of barristers who share expenses and a clerk but who are not in partnership. Because of space limitations in the Inns of Court, barristers' chambers are overcrowded and it is very difficult for a new barrister to find a chambers. The number of barristers practicing in chambers has increased substantially in the past twenty years, from approximately 2000 in the late 1960's to almost 6000 today.[6]

Part of the changes made in the vocational program in 1989 extends into the pupillage period. Under Part V of the Consolidated Regulations of the Inns of Court, before a barrister can accept a pupil, the barrister must register and be approved as a pupil master. The duties of a pupil master are set out in an annex to the Code of Conduct for barristers. Under the new regulations an employed barrister is eligible to be a pupil master. In view of the difficulties of some new barristers in finding a barrister to serve as a pupil master, the Bar has pledged to make it easier to do so, as well as relieving the problem of overcrowded chambers.

Most barristers in private practice specialize in one of several areas--principally commercial, chancery, criminal, or family. There are no appellate specialists. Approximately 5000 barristers are not, however, in private practice but are employed by private businesses, local government, or departments of the government, often not in a legal capacity. These employed barristers have only recently been given rights of audience. Of the total number of barristers, less than 2000 are likely to handle a civil matter that might be appealed to the Court of Appeal.[7]

The Bar is divided into two classes, Queen's Counsel, of whom there are almost 600, and the remainder, who are referred to as junior counsel whatever their age. Queen's Counsel are the elite of the Bar and are designated by the Lord Chancellor from those barristers who seek the title. When a Queen's Counsel appears in court he is almost always assisted by one or more junior counsel (such assistance was required until very recently). Status as a "Q.C." or "silk" (from the silk gown they wear) is sought because of its prestige, the consequent ability to charge higher fees, and eligibility for judicial office. The number of Q.C.'s is kept at about 10% of the practicing Bar, and is divided among the specialties of practice.[8]

Under a structure adopted in 1987, the highest body of the Bar is the General Council of the Bar, composed entirely of barristers representing the circuits, bar associations, and the Inns, and 51 elected members. It regulates admission of students, call to the bar, legal education, and discipline of the bar, but actual disbarment is done by the Inn of which the individual barrister is a member. It is responsible for policy matters and the professional conduct of the members. Each Inn of Court is controlled by its Masters of the Bench, who are judges and senior members of the Bar. They direct the activities of the Inn, particularly the admission of students and calling students to the bar, but under regulations adopted by the Bar Council and a Treasurers' Council.[9]

The key privilege of a barrister is the right of audience.

They have the exclusive right of audience in the High Court, the Court of Appeal, and the Appellate Committee of the House of Lords (and to be eligible for appointment to those judicial bodies).[10] This exclusive right is the principal point of disagreement between barristers and solicitors. In addition to courtroom representation, barristers also draft documents conveying property, pleadings, and other legal documents. They also give advice on the law. When they are retained on a matter, they are said to have received a brief or been given instructions. The brief or instructions are received from a solicitor, not the client. In theory, the solicitor is the client of the barrister. The initial contact of the solicitor is with the barrister's clerk. The barrister never sees the client without the solicitor being present and until 1990 could not appear in court without being attended by a solicitor.[11] Barristers in chambers operate on the basis of the "cab rank rule." This means they are obligated to handle any matter brought to them if their schedules permit.

b. Solicitors

Solicitors have their origin in court officials who prepared pleadings and other legal documents for persons engaged in litigation or who required assistance in preparing documents intended to have a legal effect and to be enforceable in the courts. In the law courts these officials were called attorneys and in the chancery court solicitors. The unique privilege granted to them was that they were authorized to act on behalf of others and their clients were legally bound by what they did or did not do for them. Eventually persons who did not hold court offices began acting as attorneys and they sought and gained the status of officers of the court. When persons who held other court positions stopped acting for clients, the remaining attorneys retained the status of officers of the court.

The positions of attorney and solicitor were combined by the Judicature Act of 1873 with the title of solicitor chosen to apply to the persons who were members of this branch of the legal profession. Historically neither attorneys nor solicitors engaged in court room advocacy, this task being reserved for those who developed into the profession of barristers.[12] At one time a person could be both an attorney or solicitor and a barrister, but this has been prohibited by the Inns of Court since the sixteenth century. Today, if a solicitor wishes to become a barrister, or vice versa, the solicitor or barrister must resign from the one profession before qualifying for the other.

The solicitor does some of the things a barrister does, including courtroom advocacy in inferior courts and tribunals (referred to as "contentious" practice), but primarily engages in an office practice handling the legal and often business affairs of clients. Conveyancing has been the single most important activity of solicitors, in part because by statute only they were permitted to engage in the activity. When litigation is necessary, the solicitor will select the barrister and be present when the barrister interviews the client. The solicitor also handles most other aspects of any litigation including preparations and filing of pleadings and other documents, negotiating settlements, instructing the barrister on positions to be taken, interviewing witnesses, and all other matters connected with the conduct of litigation except advocacy in the superior courts. The solicitor is also present in court when the barrister is appearing on behalf of the client, sitting directly behind the barrister and often whispering suggestions or giving instructions on behalf of the client. One of the most important functions of the solicitor is to prepare the "brief" for the barrister. The brief includes copies of the important documents in a dispute including pleadings if the matter is already in litigation, summaries of facts, statements of witnesses, and other helpful material.[13]

The requirements for becoming a solicitor are set forth in rules adopted by the Law Society as well as by statute. No formal university training is required but most now have it, usually obtaining their degree in law. Those who do not must pass an examination. All candidates must attend a year long program in a "law school" designed to prepare students for the solicitor's final examination. The program at these "law schools" does not include skills training such as drafting, negotiating, or advocacy.[14]

After passing the final examination the candidate is admitted to practice by being included on the roll of solicitors maintained by the Law Society. The new solicitor must serve as an assistant solicitor with an established solicitor. This training period is termed being articled, and after two to five years (depending upon the academic training) the solicitor can practice independently. Solicitors are permitted to form partnerships or to incorporate and a number of very large firms with offices in various locations have developed.[15] The number of solicitors has increased almost as dramatically as barristers. In 1965 there were 20,000 solicitors in private practice. In 1988, that number was over 50,000, with over 20,000 in other types of employment. The demand for solicitors is growing even faster than new entrants into the profession.[16]

Solicitors are regulated by a substantial number of statutes. The governing body for solicitors is the Law Society, a voluntary association exercising statutory powers. The Society acts through a council consisting of 70 members, most of whom are elected by the members of the Society. The powers of the Society extend to education, training, and admission to practice. It can also adopt rules relating to the handling of clients' funds, indemnity of persons who suffer financial loss as a result of improper conduct by a solicitor, as well as generally regulating the professional conduct of solicitors. Discipline of solicitors is done by the Solicitors Disciplinary Tribunal, an independent body whose decisions can be appealed to the Court of Appeal, but the High Court and the Court of Appeal have inherent authority to discipline solicitors, even to the extent of striking them from the roll of persons admitted to practice. Many of the rules adopted by the Law Society are subject to approval by the Master of the Rolls or other major judicial officers.[17]

2. The Judges

The system for selection of judges in England is unique to that country. High Court judges are appointed by the Queen upon nomination by the Lord Chancellor. Court of Appeal judges (Lord Justices of Appeal), the presidents of the divisions of the High Court, law lords, the Master of the Rolls, the Lord Chief Justice, and the Lord Chancellor are nominated by the Prime Minister. Lower court judges are named by the Lord Chancellor.

By statute the eligibility requirements for judgeships in the High Court severely limit the pool of candidates. In practice the pool is even smaller. For appointment to the High Court, a statute requires that a person be a barrister of at least ten years experience. In practice, only those barristers who have become Queen's Counsel and who have had part time judicial experience are appointed and only those who have specialized in the practice before a particular division are appointed to that division. For a Court of Appeal judge, the statute requires that person be a High Court judge or a barrister of fifteen years standing. In practice, only High Court judges are appointed, usually from the same division as the previous judge. Law lords must be barristers of at least of fifteen years experience or have held high judicial office for at least two years, but again are almost always chosen from the Court of Appeal.[18] The effect of the formal requirements and custom is to establish a screening and refining process that allows only those with the highest professional qualifications on the Court of Appeal and as law lords.

Notwithstanding the fact that the selection system virtually guarantees judges of the highest professional and personal qualifications, the system is criticized by some because of the similarity of the backgrounds of persons who attain judicial office. Almost without exception they have been male and products of either Oxford or Cambridge (collectively referred to as Oxbridge) and are likely to share an establishment background or viewpoint.[19] Whether the substantial expansion of the number of barristers and the number of women joining the profession will have any substantial effect on this situation remains to be seen. The argument that opening higher judgeships to solicitors would have a leavening effect is also debatable. The traditions of the English bar and judiciary are such that even the fact that during much of the period since World War II the Lord Chancellor and the Prime Minister have been members of the Labor Party appears to have had little effect on the judicial selection system or on the type of persons selected for judicial office.

By protocol, the three highest ranking judges are the Lord Chancellor, the Lord Chief Justice, and the Master of the Rolls, in that order.

The Lord Chancellor is an office that has no counterpart in any other judicial system. The person who holds the position is simultaneously the highest ranking judicial officer, the spokesman for the Government in the House of Lords, and head of the Lord Chancellor's Department, which is part of the executive branch of government, and a member of the cabinet. The office is a political one with the holder selected by and holding office technically at the pleasure of the Queen but practically at that of the Prime Minister.

The powers of the Lord Chancellor are unparalleled. As a judge he is President of the Supreme Court and an *ex officio* member of the Court of Appeal, but sits only on as a member of the Appellate Committee of the House of Lords. He can increase the number of judges on the Court of Appeal and lower courts; he selects those who serve as Queen's Counsel and those on the lower courts and nominates all judges on the High Court. As head of the Lord Chancellor's Department he also is responsible for the administrative side of the court system. His direct influence on the law is relatively minor because he seldom sits as a judge. His indirect influence is extensive, especially through his control over who becomes Queen's Counsel or a High Court judge.[20]

The Lord Chief Justice's authority is not nearly as broad as the title may imply. He is both the president of the Criminal Division of the Court of Appeal and of the Queen's Bench Division of the High Court but seldom sits as a judge on either court because of his administrative responsibilities.

The Master of the Rolls, on the other hand, has a title that gives little clue as to the significance of the position. The "MR" is an *ex officio* member of the Court of Appeal and is the president, or chief judge, of the Civil Division of the Court of Appeal. Just as important, he regularly presides over one panel of the Civil Division and hears and decides as many or more cases than any other Court of Appeal judge. His opinions carry special significance, both because of the office and the caliber of the persons who have held the office.[21]

The number of superior court judges is remarkably small for a nation of over 40 million. In late 1987 the maximum number of Court of Appeal judges was increased from 23 to 28 judges and High Court judges from 80 to 85 but as of late 1989 only three additional judges had been appointed to the Court of Appeal. The maximum number of law lords is ten. There are thus only 39 full time appellate judges authorized in England, and not all of those positions are filled.

A judge of the High Court or Court of Appeal or a law lord must retire at age 75. A judge can be removed only by an address of both Houses of Parliament or, arguably, by the Crown if a judge acts improperly. In any event, no judge has been removed under either power since the Act of Settlement in 1700.[22]

3. Staff

There are two remarkable aspects of the staff of the English courts--there are very few personal staff of the judges, and neither they nor the court staff are legally trained nor appointed by the judges or persons under their control. A judge of the Court of Appeal or the High Court is assisted by only one person--a clerk who is a civil service employee within the Lord Chancellor's Department. The clerk has no legal training or university training and usually not even secretarial training. Most are male, often retired military or police personnel. Their duties are primarily of a personal nature, such as those performed by the batman of a British military officer. They may be transferred to other duties at the discretion of administrators in the Lord Chancellor's Department who themselves are civil service employees. The situation for the law lords is even worse. They do not even have clerks, and all share two secretaries.[23]

Prior to mid-1989 the only legally trained person on the Court of Appeal staff was the Registrar of Civil Appeals, a position created in the 1981 Supreme Court Act.[24] The Registrar performs quasi-judicial duties such as hearing and ruling on incidental applications. He, through the Civil Appeals Office, receives all documents submitted to the Court and can give directions as to whether and in what form documents are to be lodged. He assists the Master of the Rolls in his administrative duties and is very much involved with the scheduling of cases for hearing and the processing of cases through the system. He also gives advice to the personnel of the Civil Appeals Office in the proper interpretation of the statutes and court rules governing appeals. The Registrar is appointed by the Lord Chancellor with the approval of the Minister of Civil Service, but is directly supervised by the Master of the Rolls.

Beginning in mid 1989 additional legal staff were assigned to the Court of Appeals. The function of this staff was described briefly in the explanatory statement of the Master of the Rolls accompanying a Practice Direction issued on March 1, 1989 (reprinted in Appendix C). The explanatory statement recited that a working party of the Court of Appeal had proposed a number of changes in the procedures of the Civil Division, many of which were incorporated in the March 1 Practice Direction. In addition, the Master of the Rolls stated that the proposals "also included the establishment of a team of lawyers to assist the Civil Division, along the lines of the system of office lawyers" serving the Criminal Division (see Chapters 1, section A 4, *supra*). He further indicated that the need for the legal staff had been accepted by the Lord Chancellor and was in the process of being established. The statement did not define more precisely the duties of the staff. The only suggestion as to what they will do can be found in the 1988 annual review of the Master of the Rolls in which he contemplated that staff should review the documents in an appeal including the time estimates filed by counsel to establish the length of the hearing on the appeal. The significance of this role for staff is discussed in Chapter 4, section A 2 b, *infra*.

The day to day processing of cases is done by personnel of the Civil Appeals Office, headed by a chief clerk. All of the employees of this office are civil service employees in the Lord Chancellor's Department. Two other types of personnel perform duties in the courtroom. Persons termed "associates" sit in each courtroom to keep a formal record of what cases are heard and who appears. They also review the documents lodged with the Court, prepare the orders of the Court, and prepare summaries of applications heard by single judges. Associates are not legally trained and are civil service employees in the Lord Chancellor's Department. The only other personnel serving the Court are the ushers, who are responsible for seeing that the judges have copies of the various reports from which counsel read, and the Librarian of the Supreme Court. The senior civil service officer responsible for the administrative services of the Supreme Court including the Court of Appeal is the Administrator of the Royal Courts of Justice. The only judicial officers with private secretaries are the Lord Chief Justice, the Master of the Rolls, the President of the Family Division, and the Vice-Chancellor. Even they do not appoint their own secretaries, however; this is within the authority of the Lord Chancellor.[25]

Case processing in the House of Lords is done by employees of the Judicial Office of the House of Lords, headed by a principal clerk.[26] Two ushers assist the law lords during hearings in the same way that ushers assist the Court of Appeal. The ten law lords share two secretaries.

4. Reform of the Legal Profession

During the past decade the legal profession has been under almost constant scrutiny and evaluation, both from within and without.[27] The first was the Royal Commission on Legal Services (called the Benson Commission after its chair Sir Henry (later Lord) Benson). This commission was appointed in 1976 and filed its report in 1979 (Command Document 7648). Although the commission had a majority of non-lawyer members, it concluded that the public was being well served by the present system. In particular it recommended continued division of the legal profession between barristers and solicitors, limiting rights of audience to barristers and conveyancing to solicitors. Notwithstanding the fact that in 1983 the Government formally stated that it accepted the report, pressure for reform continued. In 1985, an act was passed to permit conveyancing to be done by persons who were not solicitors. The Government's support for this act led to the Law Society raising the question of giving to solicitors' rights of audience in the higher courts. In 1986, it published a discussion paper "Lawyers and the Courts: Time for Some Changes." The Bar rejected the proposal, but the heat generated by the dispute led the leadership of the Bar Council and the Law Society to appoint a 19 member committee on the future of the legal profession. It consisted of 6 barristers, 6 solicitors, and 7 "independent members" i.e. non lawyers. Lady Marre, one of the non lawyers, was named chairman thus giving the committee its informal name as the "Marre Committee." It filed its report, entitled "A Time for Change" in July, 1988.

The Committee began its report with several general statements that appeared to promise recommendations that lived up to the report's title. First was that "if the legal profession, and the professions generally, themselves do not initiate appropriate change then it will be forced upon them" (¶ 4.6); second, "in examining restrictive practices . . . a balance has to be struck between de-regulation on the one hand and the need to safeguard consumers on the other" (¶ 4.15); and third, "the legal profession should retain only those rules which are essential for the maintenance of professional standards in the public interest" (¶ 4.22). Notwithstanding these promises, however, the committee's recommendations made only modest suggestions for change in the structure and practices of the profession. The only change in rights of audience for solicitor was that some solicitors would be permitted to appear in the Crown Court (the principal criminal court) and this was opposed by four of the six barristers on the committee. Direct access of clients to barristers without the intervention of a solicitor would be permitted only for members of professions, not the public generally. Employed barristers would have rights of audience only in magistrates' courts and county courts and have direct access to barristers. Solicitors would, however, be eligible for appointment to the High Court. In all other respects, the *status quo* would remain although further study of some subjects was advocated.

All the while the committee was deliberating, various committees within the Bar, working alone or in cooperation with other groups, were developing proposals for reforms such as in discipline, vocational training, pupillage, and professional standards. The efforts of the Bar to achieve reform did not deter the Government from proposing more fundamental changes.

In January, 1989, the Lord Chancellor issued in the name of the Government a Green Paper (Command Document 570) entitled "The Work and Organization of the Legal Profession" setting forth a variety of proposals concerning the legal profession. The nature of the proposals as they would affect both the providing legal services generally and the representation of litigants before courts in particular were far reaching and could have almost revolutionary consequences.

The premises that underlay the report were stated as follows:

(1) free competition between the providers of legal services "will, through the discipline of the market, ensure that the public is provided with the most efficient and effective network of legal services at the most economical price" (par. 1.2);

(2) "the key element in ensuring an adequate quality of service to the public is the identification of the education, training, qualifications and standards of competence and conduct which are appropriate for those who practice in each area of legal services (par. 1.3);

(3) "[d]epending on the area of legal services in question, such providers may or may not need to be lawyers" (par. 1.3); and

(4) "practitioners must be able to show their clients that they possess the necessary competence to perform the particular service . . . it is not sufficient for practitioners to belong to a particular branch of the legal profession" (par. 3.2).

Under the proposals outlined in the Green Paper, any professional group whose members wished to provide legal services would have to have a code of professional conduct which would be subject to the approval of the Lord Chancellor after review by the Lord Chancellor's Advisory Committee on Legal Education and Conduct. Any professional code would have to comply with certain general principles adopted by statute. The Advisory Committee would also advise the Lord Chancellor on the education, qualifications, and training of those providing legal services. Enforcement of the codes of conduct would initially be the responsibility of each professional group, but a legal services ombudsman would be appointed by the Lord Chancellor to oversee the enforcement activities of the professional groups.

The Green Paper distinguished between two types of legal services, advisory and advocacy. Advocacy was not expressly defined but the phrase "the presentation of both the facts and the legal authorities on which the judge's decision will be based" was used to describe the responsibility of an advocate. The key element in advocacy is the right of audience, that is the right to represent another before a court. The basis for restriction rights of audience was stated in the Green Paper as arising from the dependence of the judges upon the adequacy of the presentations by the advocate because the judges work without legal staff support. Inadequate representation not only hurts the client but may delay the proceedings thereby adversely affecting other litigants. Further, the state of the law may be affected because the decision may not be based on the most relevant authorities. Such a decision may affect the outcome of other cases because of the doctrine of precedent. Just as important is the requirement that the court be able to rely on the representation of counsel not to mislead the court. The Green Paper stressed the paramount duty of counsel to the court over the interests of the client. It further stated that the "presentation of cogent legal argument is a highly skilled task requiring not only knowledge of the law but also constant practice in advocacy" (par. 5.5). For these reasons, the Green Paper concluded that rights of audience must be limited to those who will give quality service to clients as well as to enable the quality of justice and the standards of advocacy to be maintained.

To accomplish this goal the Green Paper proposed that rights of audience be limited to those who are:

(1) properly trained
(2) suitably experienced, and
(3) subject to codes of conduct that maintain standards.

A person who can demonstrate appropriate education, training and qualifications, and is bound by an appropriate code of conduct should have the right of audience. The Lord Chancellor would decide which professional bodies have members who satisfy these qualifications. The requirements may vary for different courts. The key point was made, however, that distinctions in treatment of the different branches of the legal profession will disappear. "The basic premise is that satisfaction of such requirements should, for the future, alone be the test for granting rights of audience; and not whether an advocate happened by initial qualification to be a lawyer, whether a barrister or solicitor, and whether in private practice or employed." (par. 5.8).

The Green Paper then proposed that rights of audience be dependent upon obtaining an advocacy certificate. These certificates would be of two types: full, entitling the holder to appear in any court, and limited, which would be restricted to lower courts. The Lord Chancellor, subject to advice by his Advisory Committee on Legal Education and Conduct (composed of a majority of non-lawyers), would establish the requirements for these certificates. These requirements would include an academic course in law, a vocational course that included advocacy training, and practical training in advocacy. To obtain a full certificate, practice for a period of time with a limited certificate would be required. The Paper went on to give details as to the various stages of training. For transitional purposes, all barristers would be given full advocacy certificates and all solicitors would be given limited certificates.

In addition to proposing changes in rights of audience, the Green Paper also attacked certain practices of barristers. It recommended that advocates be able to have direct relationships with clients without having a solicitor as an intermediary and whether a barrister must be attended by a solicitor in court be up to the client. Further barristers should be allowed to join in partnerships with other barristers or with solicitors, establish chambers wherever they wish, and practice without a clerk.

The changes in rights of audience would also affect eligibility to become Queen's Counsel and a member of the judiciary. Both would be open to persons with full advocacy certificates, whether or not barristers.

The most obvious effect of these proposals would be to take away the monopoly that barristers have in the right of audience in the higher courts and eligibility to become Queen's Counsel and judges on the higher courts. Even more significant, however, would be the transfer of authority over the legal profession and practice in the courts. At present, regulation of solicitors is divided among Parliament, the Law Society, the Lord Chancellor, the courts, and certain high judicial officers. Regulation of barristers is by the General Council of the Bar, Treasurers' Council, and the Inns of Court, with token supervision by the judges. If the Green Paper were implemented, virtually all authority over those who provide legal services would reside in the Lord Chancellor, advised by a committee of whom a majority would be nonlawyers. The Lord Chancellor in exercising this responsibility would be acting in his capacity as a member of the Government and not as the highest judicial officer. Regulation of those who represent others in court would thus be transferred from the professions and the judges to the Government.

The Law Society on behalf of solicitors decided to oppose only details of the recommendations in the Green Paper; the Bar, however, made an all out attack on them. Opposition also came from the judicial establishment.

The Bar's views on the Green Paper were contained in a 270 page document entitled "Quality of Justice: The Bar's Response." Essentially it was one of almost total opposition to the major proposals in the Green Paper, but with some minor changes proposed or already adopted. Essentially the Bar wanted to keep rights of audience in the higher courts limited to barristers practicing individually under the "cab rank" rule. If solicitors were to be given rights of audience, they would have to practice under the same conditions as barristers. In any event, control over rights of audience should be in the judges, not the Government. Direct access of clients to barristers should not be permitted. Whether a barrister could appear in court unattended by a solicitor should be up to the barrister. Barristers should not be allowed to form partnerships, either with other barristers or solicitors, or other professionals, or to incorporate. The Bar did support, as did the Marre Committee, the eligibility of solicitors who were circuit judges to be appointed to the High Court.

Many other organizations and individuals also commented on the Green Paper. Most important were the judges of the High Court, who were as outspoken as the Bar in opposition to many of the Government's proposals, particularly as to rights of audience.

In late July, 1989, the Government published its White Paper (Legal Services: A Framework for the Future, Command Document 740) containing the proposals that it would include in legislation to be introduced in Parliament later in the year. Substantial modifications were made in many of its proposals in the Green Paper. Most significant was the recognition of the decisive role the judiciary should play in determining who should be able to practice as an advocate in the courts. Rather than this power being brought within the control of the Government, it would by statute be placed in the hands of the senior judges (i.e., the Lord Chief Justice, the Master of the Rolls, the Vice-Chancellor, and the President of the Family Division, along with the Lord Chancellor).

Under the proposed statute, the rights of audience of the Bar will remain unchanged. Any change in the Bar's rules for education, training, and professional conduct will, however, be subject to approval by the senior judges and not simply, as at present, by the General Council of the Bar. Rights of audience of employed barristers will be covered by this provision.

For solicitors, they will retain their present rights of audience in the courts beneath the High Court. The Law Society will be given the authority to recognize a solicitor as qualified to be an advocate in a particular court or courts. Solicitors who wish to obtain right of audience in the High Court will have to undergo additional training under supervision, followed by testing to determine competence. Rules governing the required training and the conduct of persons granted right of audience will also have to be approved by the senior judges.

In addition, the statute will provide that other bodies may be authorized to grant rights of audience. Before this can occur, however, not only must the senior judges approve but an Order in Council on the recommendation of the Lord Chancellor must be made, subject to approval in draft by both Houses of Parliament.

All matters that are subject to approval by the senior judges will be reviewed in advance by the Lord Chancellor's Advisory Committee on Legal Education and Conduct which will be composed of a judge, two barristers, two solicitors, two academic lawyers, and eight non-lawyers. It will act, however, only in an advisory capacity.

The conduct of litigation, other than courtroom advocacy, is now exclusively in the hands of solicitors by virtue of the

Solicitors Act. This statutory monopoly will be repealed, and will be replaced with a scheme essentially the same as that concerning rights of audience with the possibility of groups other than the Law Society being authorized to grant the right to conduct litigation.

Eligibility to become Queen's Counsel or a High Court judge would be expanded to include any person with the right of audience in the High Court.

The Green Paper made a number of proposals relating to the practices of the bar. The White Paper, on the other hand, chose to leave most of those matters up to the Bar, including the question of direct access by lay clients, and the question of partnership either among barristers or between barristers and solicitors or members of other professions. In responding to the Green Paper's criticisms of certain practices, the Bar pointed out that a barrister was no longer required to employ a clerk and was investigating alternatives to practicing as a member of a chambers. It further proposed to drop the prohibition against a barrister meeting with a professional client in the latter's office. With the support of the Bar, legislation will be proposed to enable barristers to contract with clients for the payment of their fees. Many of the traditional restrictions on the manner in which barristers practice were eliminated in a new code of conduct for the bar adopted by the Bar Council and effective March 31, 1990. They can now adventure more freely, open chambers whenever they wish and can even practice from their homes, appear in court without a solicitor, visit soliciors' offices, and even have conferences with clients in solicitors'offices.[28]

It is difficult to estimate what impact the changes in the vocational training of barristers and the potential for solicitors (and others) to be qualified as advocates with rights of audience in the High Court and above may have upon the competence of those who will handle appeals in the Court of Appeal and the House of Lords. The new vocational curriculum makes no mention of appellate advocacy. The chances of a pupil participating in an appeal during the year of pupillage are slight, given the limited number of appeals. As to the possibility of solicitors being given rights of audience in the Court of Appeal, at least one commentator has suggested this is highly unlikely in view of the fact that all of the senior judges who must approve such a measure actively opposed the proposal in the Green Paper that persons other than barristers be qualified as advocates.[29] All of these judges were, of course, barristers before becoming judges. Given the circumstances under which the judges obtained this power and the fact that both the Lord Chancellor and his Advisory Committee on Legal Education and Conduct (whose 15 members will include only 2 practicing barristers) will play in the process, not to mention the high quality of the individuals who hold the positions, it seems unlikely that any proposal to expand rights of audience for solicitors will be automatically rejected.

The proposals contained in the White Paper were incorporated into House of Lords Bill 13, Courts and Legal Services, introduced by the Lord Chancellor on December 6, 1989. It was debated in the House of Lords in January, February and March, 1990. Once final action is taken there, it will go to the House of Commons. Final enactment is expected in late spring, 1990.

One change mentioned by the Lord Chancellor in his Introduction to the White Paper may, in fact, have a greater impact on the division of labor between barristers and solicitors and ultimately, upon rights of audience in the High Court and the Court of Appeal than any of the matters discussed in the White Paper. In the Introduction, the Lord Chancellor stated that legislation would soon be brought forward "to allow a major distribution of civil cases between the High Court and the county courts. The High Court will be reserved for judicial review and other specialist cases, and for general cases of unusual substance, importance or difficulty. Other cases will be heard in the county courts. This change will apply first to personal injury cases . . . and then will be extended to debt and housing cases." Such a provision was, in fact, included in clause 1 of Part I of the Courts and Legal Services Bill. The clause did not make the transfer; it only authorized the Lord

Chancellor to do so, but in light of his announced intention in the White Paper the implementation of the change seems more than likely.

The significance of this change on the future of rights of audience of solicitors may be substantial because solicitors already have rights of audience in the county courts. After the transfer of jurisdiction from the High Court to the county court, the opportunity for solicitors to engage in advocacy in a courtroom will sharply increase and it is entirely possible that some solicitors may appear in court as an advocate as often as many or even most barristers. When these cases are appealed to the Court of Appeal, it may be difficult to deny to the solicitor who tried the case the opportunity to argue it on appeal and instead require that the appeal be handled by a barrister who has no more training or experience in appellate advocacy than the solicitor.[30] Such a requirement may be justified if knowledge of appellate procedure and skill in appellate advocacy were part of the training of a barrister. Such is not the case, as noted above, even in the new curriculum of the Inns of Court School of Law. In fact, the syllabus for the final bar examinations for barristers identifies final appeals from the High Court to the Court of Appeals as a topic on which no questions will be focused and will be dealt with in outline only. Thus neither the knowledge nor the skills of appellate litigation will be any part of the training of a barrister in the forseeable future. It may well be that a solicitor in active practice in the county courts will be better qualified than a barrister to handle an appeal in the Court of Appeal.

B. United States

There are three types of personnel involved in every appeal in addition to the litigants: lawyers, judges, and staff. Each party to the appeal is usually represented by a lawyer; each appellate court consists of a panel of at least three judges. Each appellate judge is assisted by a personal staff. Finally, the appeal, both before and after it is considered by the judges, is processed by court staff.

1. The Lawyers

The legal profession in the United States is a direct descendant of the profession in England. It was not uncommon in colonial times for Americans to go to England to study, be admitted to the bar, and then return to the United States to practice. Given the financial and practical difficulties involved, however, only a small percentage of colonists could do this so an American bar developed with each colony and later each state establishing its own system for training, admission, and discipline.[31] In most of the colonies, and later in the states, the profession was not divided into solicitors and barristers because of the lack of a central legal center and the small number of legally trained persons.[32]

In the United States today there are over 600,000 lawyers who are admitted to practice in one or more states and the total is growing by over 30,000 each year.[33] Regulation of the bar in each state is under the exclusive control of the state's supreme court. To be admitted to practice in a state a person must first have a degree from a four year accredited college or university; have a degree from one of the 180 accredited law schools with a three year program; and pass a bar examination and a character check, both administered under the authority of the state's supreme court. When all of these conditions are met, the supreme court will grant a license to the applicant entitling the lawyer to practice in any court in the state.

Each state system is entirely separate from the other state systems. The only recognition given by an individual state to admission in other states is:

(1) admission "on motion" under which a lawyer with a specified number of years of practice in one state will be admitted on request in other states without the necessity

of taking the bar examination, and

(2) admission *"pro hac vice"* under which a lawyer from another state may be permitted by a court to appear in that court for a single case if accompanied by a lawyer admitted to practice in that state.

Some states, particularly those in the South and the West, do not permit admission on motion in order to make it difficult for retirees and other persons who seek to move to those states to enter practice.

Admission to practice in the federal courts is handled on a completely different basis. There is no general admission to practice in the federal courts. Admission to practice in the United States Supreme Court is good for that court only and does not automatically qualify a lawyer to practice in any of the 13 federal courts of appeal or 94 district courts. Each of the lower courts is responsible for admitting persons to practice before it. As a practical matter a lawyer who is admitted to practice in any one state can be admitted to practice in any federal court. Being admitted in a state is, however, a prerequisite to admission by a federal court. Most federal courts do not conduct their own bar examinations or character investigations, although a few district courts require the taking of an examination limited to federal procedure or observation of several federal trials.

Once admitted to practice in a state, a lawyer can appear in any court in the state, including the appellate courts. No special training or experience is required and there is no separate trial bar or appellate bar. Discipline of attorneys is also under the exclusive control of the court that admits the attorneys. In the states that court is each state's supreme court while in the federal system it is each individual court.

One of the major developments in legal education in the past two decades has been the acceptance of skills training as well as intellectual training in legal reasoning and analysis as essential to a sound legal education. For the better part of the 20th century law schools concentrated only on the latter, believing that the other "practical" skills of the lawyer should be obtained after graduation from law school. Beginning in the early 1970's, however, legal education was subjected to substantial criticism for ignoring trial practice skills as well as those of legal drafting, negotiating, interviewing, counseling and inter-personal skills in general. More recently, the lack of training in the skills of the appellate lawyer has been criticized.[34] After some initial resistance, skills training is now an accepted part of a sound legal education and is required to be offered to students by the American Bar Association's Standards for the Approval of Law Schools.[35]

2. The Judges

Each of the 51 jurisdictions in the United States has its own system for selecting judges. Almost every state requires that a judge be a lawyer, but that is the only requirement. In the federal system, even that minimal requirement does not exist. It is theoretically possible for a non-lawyer to be appointed to the United States Supreme Court, but it has never happened. Every federal judge is appointed in accordance with the procedures established in the federal constitution--nomination by the president with confirmation by the Senate.[36] Appointments are during good behavior which means for life unless a judge is impeached.[37]

Appellate judges in the states are selected under a variety of systems including appointment by the governor, election by the legislature, election by the voters, or a combination of appointment and retention elections. No prior experience as a lawyer or judge is a prerequisite to sitting on an appellate court. The terms for appellate judges vary. In only a few states, primarily those in New England, are judges' terms for good behavior. In most states, particularly those in which judges are elected, terms are less than ten years. A judge whose term is expiring and wants to serve another term must seek re-election in the same manner as any other candidate for the position.

During the past fifty years, in an effort to reduce the harmful effects of having judges run for office, a system that combines features of the appointive and elective systems has been developed. Under this system, called the Merit Plan, to fill a judicial vacancy the governor appoints from a list of three persons nominated by a judicial nominating commission composed of lawyers and non-lawyers. After the appointed judge serves an initial term, usually two years, the judge must stand for retention in office for a full term in a "non-competitive" election, that is, the judge's name appears on the ballot and the voters vote on the question of whether the judge should be retained in office. If over 50% of the voters say yes, the judge serves the full term. The judge can be elected to additional full terms under the same procedure.[38] Whatever the means of selection, the low number of women and minorities on the bench has caused criticism. There have been some efforts to seek out persons other than white males for judicial positions, but progress has been very slow.

The traditional means for removal of a judge who has engaged in misconduct is impeachment which in the federal system and most states involves charges voted by the lower house of the legislature and trial before the upper house. The process is so cumbersome that it is almost never used and it is appropriate only for the most egregious misconduct. To remedy this situation, since 1962 most states have amended their constitutions to give their supreme court authority to discipline judges for misconduct. Each of these states has a judicial conduct commission which investigates complaints against judges. If it finds probable cause for the complaint, the commission or another body conducts a hearing and makes a recommendation to the supreme court on whether the judge acted improperly and if so what sanction should be imposed. Final authority lies in the supreme court in all but a few states.[39] Impeachment is still the only procedure available to remove a federal judge.

One of the major effects of the enormous growth in appeals over the past several decades (discussed more fully in Chapter 4, *infra*) has been the increase in the number of appellate judgeships. Some of the additional positions have resulted from the creation of new intermediate appellate courts in states in which these courts did not previously exist. There have also been substantial additions to the number of judges, not only on previously existing courts but also on new courts. There are currently 177 federal appellate judgeships, consisting of the nine members of the Supreme Court and 168 judges of the United States courts of appeals. The United States Court of Appeals for the Ninth Circuit, which has jurisdiction over the far western part of the United States including Alaska and Hawaii, alone has 28 judges.

The number of justices on the state supreme courts ranges from 5 to 9 with a total number of 313 including the two supreme courts of criminal appeals. In 1986 there were 732 judgeships on state intermediate appellate courts, but that figure is constantly increasing. The state of California which has 9 supreme court justices recently increased the number of intermediate appellate court judgeships from 77 to 88. The total number of appellate judges, both federal and state in 1986, was 1213, but it is inevitable that this number will increase further as caseloads continue to mount.

3. Staff

The staff assisting the judges of an appellate court is divided between personal staff and court staff. Each appellate judge has at least one secretary and one law clerk who, while technically employees of the court, are appointed by and subject to the exclusive control of the judge. Depending upon the status of the court and the control it has over its funding, a judge may have several secretaries and up to four law clerks. The principal activity of the secretary is to type the opinions written by the judge as well as other correspondence. Law clerks are usually recent law school graduates who serve as legal assistants to the judges for one or two year terms.[40] They assist in reading briefs and records, and in preparing memoranda on the contentions of the parties and on legal issues raised in the briefs or that the judge thinks may be relevant to disposition of the case. They also assist in the drafting of opinions, review draft opinions prepared by other judges, and perform any other task the judge requests. The relationship between the judge and the judge's law clerks is a very personal one and will vary from judge to judge and from law clerk to law clerk. Many judges treat their law clerks as legal confidants and discuss the merits of the positions of the parties, how the case should be resolved, and what the opinion to be issued by the court should say.[41] Because it is such a valuable experience these positions are sought after by the highest ranking law graduates.

The staff serving the entire court includes the traditional positions: a clerk, deputy clerks, reporter of decisions, marshal, and librarian. A relatively recent addition to court staff is the staff attorneys. Some courts appoint an administrator to supervise the other staff while others have an administrative assistant to the chief judge of the court. Most of the staff perform essentially ministerial duties in processing the documents related to the appeal, scheduling oral arguments, and issuing the opinions and judgments of the court. If the court or the state government itself publishes the opinions the reporter of decisions also supervises their publication. The reporter may also prepare headnotes, that is summaries of the key legal points in the case, that are published with the opinion. The staff attorneys provide services of a legal nature such as screening cases to ensure that the court has jurisdiction and that the proper procedures have been followed in taking the appeal. They may recommend whether oral argument is necessary and prepare draft opinions on meritless cases. They may also review and recommend action on motions filed by the parties.[42] Some courts have also appointed a staff member to hold settlement conferences with attorneys or to develop individualized briefing schedules.

Most personnel serving the court are appointed by the court and serve at its pleasure. They are employees of the state or federal government and receive all the fringe benefits given to their civil service counterparts working for the executive branch of government. Their salaries and periodic raises are usually determined by the court or its administrator, but some may have limits on their salaries established by statute or by a salary classification system.

C. Comparison

1. The Lawyers

Although the American legal profession traces its roots directly to the profession in England, there are few similarities between them today. The most obvious distinction, of course, is the division of lawyers in England into barristers and solicitors and the combined profession in the United States. From this distinction and others flow variations in educational requirements, the extent of regulation, by whom it is imposed and administered, and the nature of the practice. The requirements for both the solicitor and the barrister involve fewer years of formal education and a substantially shorter period of professional education than in the United States, but each has an apprenticeship that Americans are no longer required to have. Perhaps the most significant difference has been that skills training is a major part of American law schools while skills training in the one year professional law school for barristers in England has just begun.[43]

The professional education received by American law students is substantially different from that received by their English counterparts. It is graduate level education and includes substantive and procedural law and professional skills training. Civil procedure is required in the first year in most law schools in the United States while in England it is at best a third year elective. Sir Jack Jacob in his 1986 Hamlyn lecture commented that "it remains a deplorable fact that England is perhaps the only country in the world where civil procedure is not generally taught as a required subject for the first degree in Laws, and where there is hardly any research taking place in the subject . . .." He went on to make a plea for English academics to focus on civil procedure and civil justice.[44] Legal research and writing, legal analysis, and advocacy, both written and oral, are likewise required for first year students in almost every law school in the United States but are not a formal part of English academic legal education. The English classes are primarily lecture while American classes rely much more on Socratic dialogue and problems.[45]

Apprenticeship or pupillage is one area where the English system may be more demanding than the American, although that system was widely used in the United States in the nineteenth and early twentieth centuries. The development of the American law school as graduate level training was a direct result of the perceived inadequacies of the apprenticeship system. The reasons for the weaknesses are readily apparent. The quality of an apprenticeship depends almost entirely on the mentor's willingness to spend the time necessary to teach and the ability to do so. There has been, however, little or no screening process to ensure that barristers who fulfill this role are qualified to do so, although under the new regulations on pupillage this should change. The assumption, for which there is no demonstrable basis, appears to have been that association with any barrister can be beneficial to the student. In fact, it is just as likely to do more harm than good because the mentor may as likely be passing on poor skills and professional habits as good ones. In any event, the reality in American legal education today is that most law students have opportunities during summer vacation and after school hours to obtain employment in law firms or in the legal departments of public agencies or large corporations or have had internships in various types of legal offices as part of a law school program. Very few law students, consequently, graduate from law school without having had three or more months of an experience that is equivalent to an apprenticeship or pupillage.

The division of the English legal profession into office lawyers and advocates at first blush would appear to be more likely to produce superior courtroom advocates than the American system of allowing every lawyer to appear in any court in any state in which admitted. This conclusion is based on the premise that a person can become skilled at something by doing it repeatedly. Some critics of the advocacy skills of American lawyers, notably former Chief Justice Warren Burger, have pointed to the English system as preferable. It is likely that most American lawyers share this perception. There is, in fact, no basis for a conclusion that English barristers are superior courtroom advocates to their American counterparts. There has been no effort to prove this empirically, assuming that it could be done. There certainly has been nothing in the training of English barristers that would provide them with any of the skills they will use in their profession, although with the new curriculum in the Inns of Court School of Law that deficiency will be remedied.[46] Further, much of the litigation in the United States is done by litigation specialists. Many individual lawyers and small law firms devote all or most of their practice to litigation. Almost every law firm with more than 20 lawyers has a litigation department as do most large governmental units. Prosecutions are the responsibility of prosecutors offices and public defender offices do much of criminal defense work.

In so far as appellate litigation skills are concerned, there is no appellate bar in England or the United States. For this reason, expertise based solely upon experience cannot be claimed. Based upon his almost thirty years experience as an appellate litigator, appellate court law clerk and administrator, participant in appellate court studies, and teaching and writing about appellate advocacy, including the observation of close to 1000 oral arguments in the United States as well as his experience in England, the author has concluded that only a small percentage of appellate advocates in either country can be classified as highly competent, with the remainder ranging from adequate to incompetent. (The specific inadequacies of the English barrister as an appellate advocate are discussed more fully in Chapter 3, section A, *infra*.)

There is in the United States a growing recognition that appellate litigation requires special knowledge and skills. The Appellate Judges Conference of the American Bar Association has recognized that the knowledge and skills necessary to be an effective appellate advocate differ sharply from those of the trial advocate. However competent trial lawyers may be in either country, the knowledge and skills they develop in the trial court are of little assistance to them in making a presentation in the appellate court. Efforts are being made to expand the teaching of appellate litigation in American law schools as well as to lawyers by continuing legal education programs.[47]

One of the reasons for the increased emphasis on appellate skills training in the United States is the remarkable fact that the lawyers are called upon to exercise appellate skills almost as often as trial skills. In the federal courts, for example, in 1988 there were as many appeals decided by the courts of appeals on the merits after the filing of briefs with or without oral argument as there were cases tried before a jury or judge in the federal district courts. The number of oral arguments in the courts of appeals equaled the number of jury trials in the district courts. The appellate judges in the United States have been in the forefront of the effort to improve the quality of the appellate advocates who appear before them. The ABA Appellate Judges Conference has recently drafted Standards for Appellate Litigators in an effort to detail the special skills and responsibilities of those lawyers who handle appeals. There is no similar effort in England either by the Bar or the judges. It is not surprising, consequently, that the new curriculum in the Inns of Court School of Law makes no mention of appellate advocacy training.

2. The Judges

In no area are there greater contrasts between England and the United States than in the methods of selecting appellate judges. In the United States any relationship between the qualities necessary or desirable to sit on an appellate court and the qualifications of those selected is remote and usually coincidental, particularly under elective systems. There are no formal qualifications and there is no tradition of informal qualifications. The most important criteria may be political party membership, political party activity, friendship with those who are instrumental in the selection process, politically attractive name, having held prior public office, gender, race, newspaper or union endorsements, and the like.

Name recognition is so important in elections in some states that it may be the difference between winning and losing. During one period in the early 1980's, the seven member Ohio Supreme Court was composed of two persons named Celebreeze and two persons named Brown, both well-known political names in that state. For one short period three persons named Brown were on the court at the same time. The attorney general's position, also elective, was held by a Brown who was succeeded by a Celebreeze.

Professional and personal qualifications are seldom significant except under a merit plan. Even when professional and personal qualifications are a factor, there is no consensus on which, if any, of the qualifications are significant. There is not even a consensus on the desirability of prior judicial experience because of the significant differences between what trial judges and appellate judges do. The sheer number of appellate judges exacerbates the problem. Notwithstanding these weaknesses in the selection process, in fact it does produce a surprisingly large number of very good appellate judges and remarkably few very poor ones. In part, this results from the collegial nature of the appellate process and the support provided by staff.

In England, on the other hand, appointment to the Court of Appeal is the result of a screening and selection process that will almost inevitably put on the appellate bench judges who are well qualified professionally for the position. In part this flows from the dominance of the oral tradition throughout the entire system. Skilled oral advocates are selected to be trial judges. They in turn function almost exclusively in oral proceedings and from their ranks are chosen appellate judges who again are engaged in an almost exclusively oral process. The original pool of barristers is small to begin with, and as the screening process moves from one step to the next the pool becomes smaller and smaller. Even more important, however, is the simple fact that in any group, there will be some who by virtue of their basic intelligence, drive, education, and experience are highly competent. The same people would be highly competent, however, no matter what profession they would follow. For both of these reasons, the strong likelihood is that any one who ultimately is appointed as a law lord or to the Court of Appeal is highly qualified to sit there.

That does not mean that the process is not subject to some criticism. The original screening process whereby certain barristers are chosen to be Queen's Counsel is done with no public involvement or accountability. The same is true in the selection of judges of the High Court and the Court of Appeal as well as selection of the law lords. This has brought about criticism that the selection system does not take into account the needs of a pluralistic and democratic society and thus almost all of the judges come from a very narrow background.[48] Whatever may be the validity of these criticisms, the fact of the matter is that it would be difficult to find a group of appellate judges who are better qualified personally and professionally to perform their duties than those who sit on the Court of Appeal or as law lords.

3. Staff

The advantages the English system has over the American system in the method of selecting appellate judges are almost canceled out by the difference in support staff provided the judges in each system. In England the law lords and judges of the Court of Appeal have virtually no personal support staff, such as secretaries or law clerks, to assist them in their judicial duties. The court staff until 1989 had only one legally trained person, the registrar of civil appeals. All of the other court staff, as well as the personal clerks of the judges are civil service employees who are not selected by the judges or persons under their control. In addition, the staff are subject only to civil service administrators for classification of positions, salary increases, promotions, discipline, and discharge. The judicial branch is thus entirely dependent upon the executive branch for the staff support to perform their judicial function. In 1987 two senior English judges, the Master of the Rolls and the Vice-Chancellor, spoke out on the potential threat to the independence of the English judiciary that too much control by the executive over the operations of the judicial branch.[49]

Judges in the United States have long recognized the close relationship between the staff and facilities available to the courts and the ability of the courts to fulfill their role as the judicial branch of government. For this reason, during the past century state courts have developed the doctrines of separation of powers and inherent power to justify their selection and supervision of the staff who assist the judges and the courts free from substantial control by either or both of the other branches of government. The doctrine has even been extended by some courts to permit them to determine the level of staffing as well as the salary levels of court employees. State (but not federal) courts have relied on the inherent power doctrine to employ additional staff or the setting of staff salaries only as a last resort when normal budget making procedures create staffing problems that threaten the proper administration of justice.[50]

The close relationship between funding and independence of the judiciary is so well recognized in the United States that a common provision in federal and state law is that the budget developed by the judiciary must be included without change by the executive in the budget submitted to the legislature.[51] Under such provisions the budget for the judiciary is subject to review and reduction by the legislature, but not by the executive. In any event, once funds are appropriated by the legislature, the expenditure of these funds is under the exclusive control of the judges and their staffs and the staffs themselves are employees of the judicial branch.

The result of these differences is that American appellate courts are well provided with both personal staff for the judges and court staff. At a minimum a judge will have a personal secretary and a personal law clerk. It is shocking to the American observer that in England only the highest ranking judicial officers with administrative duties have personal secretaries, the judges of the Court of Appeal have no secretaries, the 10 law lords who constitute the supreme court of Great Britain share two secretaries, and neither the law lords nor the Court of Appeal judges have any legal assistance. As long ago as 1972 the authors of the most comprehensive study of the House of Lords recommended that they be provided with law clerks, although the same authors thought that one full time and one part time secretary to serve all 10 law lords was adequate.[52] The ability of American appellate courts to dispose of almost three times as many appeals per judge as the English Court of Appeal can be traced at least in part directly to the staff assistance available to the former.

There are dangers, of course, that when judges have staff to assist them in their judicial duties the judges may delegate too much responsibility to the staff resulting in a reduction in the personal accountability of the judges for the decisions and the opinions or judgments. This is a concern whenever a bureaucracy is created to assist public officials in the performance of their duties. Although there have been expressions of concern by some observers, there is no hard evidence that this situation has developed in the United States, and given the quality of the English judges, it is even less likely to occur there.

The English have gone beyond the Americans in their willingness to give quasi-judicial authority to persons who are not judges. The use of masters and registrars is common in the High Court and has been adopted by the Court of Appeal in appointing a registrar of civil appeals. Similar officials called referees, magistrates, or commissioners are used in American trial courts but not American appellate courts. The English approach is to be favored because it relieves judges of the responsibility for deciding matters that do not go to a resolution of the merits of the appeal.

ENDNOTES

1. Lord Chancellor's Department, *The Work and Organization of the Legal Profession* (Command Document 570, 1989) (hereinafter referred to as the Green Paper). R. Megarry, *Lawyer and Litigant in England* 6-33 (1962); P. Atiyah & R. Summers, *Form and Substance in Anglo-American Law* 360-75 (1987).

2. Lord Chancellor's Department, *Legal Services: A Framework for the Future* (Command Document 740, 1989); Green Paper, *supra* note 1 at ¶ 5.8; M. Zander, *A Matter of Justice* 5-44 (1988); P. Reeves, *Are Two Legal Professions Really Necessary* (1986); Cohen, *The Divided Legal Profession in England and Wales -- Can Barristers and Solicitors Ever Be Fused*, 12 J. of the Legal Profession 7 (1987); *The Economist*, May 7, 1988 at 17-20.

3. For the historical development of the position of barrister see the authorities cited in Martineau, *The Attorney as an Officer of the Court*, 35 South Carolina L. Rev. 541, 543 at note 3 (1984).

4. R. Walker, *The English Legal System* 266-76 (6th ed. 1985). See also M. Zander, *Legal Services for the Community* 245-48 (1978). The most recent case and the one most directly on point is *Abse v. Smith*, (1986) 1 QB 536 (CA), which concerned the power of an individual High Court judge to permit a solicitor the right of audience in an uncontested matter. Sir John Donaldson, Master of the Rolls, in a judgment to which both of the other judges on the panel agreed, stated the general rule as follows:

> In my judgment the well established proposition that every court has inherent power to regulate its own practices, unless fettered by statute or, possibly, by ancient usage, applies to the judges of that court collectively as well as individually and it is for the judges collectively -- as a collegiate body -- to decide whether or not to modify established general practices and to promulgate such modifications by practice directions. (Id. at 555.)

5. The requirements for admission to the Bar are set forth in the Consolidated Regulations of the four Inns of Court. See also Green Paper, *supra* note 1 at Annex B; R. Abel, *The Legal Profession in England and Wales* 37-56 (1988); and G. Williams, *Learning the Law* 183-225 (11th ed. 1982). On the education and training of the Bar in England see M. Zander, *supra* note 4 at 142-63 and Megarry, *supra* note 1 at 94-116. Megarry criticizes the lack

at 142-63 and Megarry, *supra* note 1 at 94-116. Megarry criticizes the lack of advocacy training of the Bar at 100-05.

6. Green Paper, *supra* note 1 at 38-42, 58.

7. Green Paper, *supra* note 1 at 59 and Annex E, Par. 19-21; *The Economist*, May 7, 1988, at 17-18; Abel, *supra* note 5 at Table 1.16, p. 342.

8. Green Paper, *supra* note 1 at 32; M. Zander, *The English Legal System* 574-75 (5th ed 1988); *The Economist*, May 7, 1988, at 17-18; Abel, *supra* note 5 at Table 1.24, p. 354.

9. M. Zander, *supra* note 8 at 576-78; Abel, *supra* note 18 at 126-36.

10. Green Paper, *supra* note 1 at Annex E.

11. Green Paper, *supra* note 1 at 28-32, 38-42; Walker, *supra* note 4 at 268-69; Abel, *supra* note 5 at 86-93, 114-19.

12. The historical development of solicitors is detailed in M. Birks, *Gentlemen of the Law* (1960).

13. Walker, *supra* note 4 at 253-65; Abel, *supra* note 5 at 218-34.

14. Green Paper, *supra* note 13 at 59; Williams, *supra* note 17 at 207-08; Abel, *supra* note 5 at 139-47. A committee of the Law Society has recently proposed that the training of solicitors be revised to include a 24 week legal practice course to include drafting, interviewing, advocacy, negotiation and legal research. 140 New Law J. (March 2, 1990).

15. Green Paper, *supra* note 13 at 59; Zander, *supra* note 19 at 584-85; Abel, *supra* note 5 at 149-62.

16. Green Paper, *supra* note 1 at 59-60; *The Economist*, May 7, 1988, at 17; Abel, *supra* note 5 at Table 2.41, p. 444.

17. Green Paper, *supra* note 1 at 13-14, Annex D, part 2; Walker, *supra* note 4 at 251-52; Zander, *supra* note 8 at 583-84; Abel, *supra* note 5 at 242-60.

18. Green Paper, *supra* note 1 at 34-35; Walker, *supra* note 4 at 229-30; D. Pannick, *Judges* 47-74 (1987); Atiyah & Summers, *supra* note 1 at 336-353. The most complete description of the English system for the selection of judges is found in Meador, *English Appellate Judges from An American Perspective*, 66 Georgetown L. Rev. 1349 (1978).

19. Pannick, *supra* note 18 at 57-62; Atiyah & Summers *supra* note 1 at 353-58. For a defence of the existing system see Megarry, *supra* note 1 at 117-29.

20. For a complete listing of the duties of the Lord Chancellor see R. Jackson, *The Machinery of Justice in England*, 534-36 (6th ed. 1972).

21. For a history of the office of Master of the Rolls see Lord Haverworth, *Some Notes on the Office of Master of the Rolls*, 5 Cambridge L. J. 313 (1935). The name originated with the person who kept the parchment with copies of the correspondence of the Chancellor and the Chancery. Lord Donaldson, the current Master of the Rolls, described his duties in the 1985 Holdsworth Lecture entitled "The Problems of A Master of the Rolls."

The influence of the office is such that Lord Denning, who served as MR from 1962 to 1982, resigned as a law lord to become MR. A. Paterson, *The Law Lords* 132, n. 55 (1982).

22. Walker, *supra* note 4 at 229-30.

23. L. Blom-Cooper & G. Drewry, *Final Appeal* 114 (1972).

24. Supreme Court Act 1981, sec 89(1) and Schedule 2, Part II (9). The creation of this position was one of the principal recommendations of the committee chaired by Lord Scarman appointed in 1978 by the Master of the Rolls to study the work of the Court of Appeal.

25. Supreme Court Act 1981 s. 98(1) and (3).

26. Blom-Cooper & Drewry, *supra* note 23 at 113-14.

27. For a more complete description of the events of this period see Zander, *supra* note 2 at 5-44.

28. 134 Solicitors J. 177 (Feb. 16, 1990).

29. Young, *Views of the Law Society of England and Wales*, 14 International Legal Practitioner 37 (June, 1989). The concerns expressed in this article were given some weight by a speech by Lord Donaldson to the Bar Conference on September 30, 1989. In this speech he outlined some areas that should be restricted to barristers. This prompted concern by solicitors and caused the Lord Chancellor to respond, suggesting the actions of the senior judges on proposed rules to expand rights of audience to solicitors would be subject to judicial review. 139 New Law J. 1402 (October 20, 1989).

30. The Lord Chancellor himself has made such a suggestion. 139 New Law J. 1402 (October 20, 1989).

31. The history of the American legal profession is examined in detail in R. Pound, *The Lawyer from Antiquity to Modern Times* (1953); C. Warren, *A History of the American Bar* (1911); and A. Chroust, *The Rise of the Legal Profession in America* (1965).

32. A. Chroust, *supra* note 31, at 227-28; Q. Johnston and D. Hopson, *Lawyers and Their Work* 357-58 (1967).

33. Statistics on the number of lawyers in the United States as reported in the 1980 federal census can be found in *Statistical Abstract of the United States* 167 (1987) published by the Federal Bureau of the Census. In 1980 the total number of lawyers was 542,208. In 1987 the estimated figure was 676,584. *The Lawyer's Almanac* 1988 at 163-64 (1988).

34. ABA Section of Legal Education and Admissions to the Bar, Report and Recommendations of the Task Force on Lawyer Competency: The Role of the Law Schools (1979). This report is known as the Cramton Report after the Task Force's chairman, Professor Roger Cramton of Cornell Law School. Subsequently various groups within the American Bar Association have issued other reports on related topics including Appellate Litigation Skills Training: The Role of the Law Schools, adopted by the ABA Appellate Judges Conference in 1985. The author, who served as a member of and reporter for the committee that prepared the report, was its draftsman.

35. The American Bar Association's Standards for Approval of Law Schools § 302(a)(iii) require that each law school offer "instruction in professional skills" without specifying what skills are to be taught.

36. U.S. Const., Art. II, Sec. 2. The coverage by the news media rejection by the Senate in the fall of 1987 of the nomination by President Reagan of Robert Bork to be a justice of the United States Supreme Court gave the general public in both the United States and Great Britain an understanding of the political process that lies behind this simple provision.

37. U.S. Const., Art III, Sec. 1.

38. L. Berkson, S. Beller, and M. Grimaldi, *Judicial Selection in the United States: A Compendium of Provisions* (1981).

39. The remarkable speed with which states adopted this alternative to impeachment is discussed in I. Tesitor, *Judicial Conduct Organizations* (2d ed. 1980).

40. The development of the position of law clerk is recounted in Baier, *The Law Clerks: Profile of an Institution*, 26 Vanderbilt L. Rev. 1125 (1973).

41. U.S. Circuit Judge Frank Coffin tells of his interaction with his law clerks in F. Coffin, *The Ways of a Judge* 161-66 (1980). For the discussion of the use of law clerks by another federal circuit judge see Mahoney, *Law Clerks: For Better or For Worse*, 54 Brooklyn L. Rev. 321 (1988).

42. The role of staff attorneys is described in P. Carrington, D. Meador, and M. Rosenberg, *Justice on Appeal* 46-55 (1976) and D. Meador, *Appellate Courts: Staff and Process in the Crisis of Volume* (1974). Weisberger, *A Profile of Appellate Staff*, 24 Judge's J. 31 (Summer, 1985) gives details on the extent of the use of staff attorneys.

43. McBrien, *The White Paper: A Non Sequitur or Jacob's Ladder?* 133 Sol. J. 1046 (1989).

44. J. Jacob, *The Fabric of English Civil Justice* 252, 255 (1987).

45. English and American legal education are compared in greater detail in Atiyah & Summers, *supra* note 1 at 388-98. For a tribute to American legal education by a person trained as a barrister, see R. Stevens, *Law School* (1983).

46. The misunderstanding about the training of a barrister is as great in England as in the United States. The Bar's formal response to the Green Paper, *Quality of Justice: The Bar's Response* (1989), included as Chapter 27 an Epilogue that consisted solely of a letter from a retired Welsh solicitor to the London *Times* in March, 1989. In the letter the writer argued against any changes in the training or experience of barristers in the following terms:

> The delicate arrangements which produce the standards of excellence and spirit of independence should not be tampered with, lest we undermine or even destroy the very qualities which are crucial to us all in both judge and barrister.

> The Inns of Court may seem mysterious places to most of us. But they produce the goods: a fearless judiciary and formidable advocates.

What the retired solicitor obviously did not know, and the Bar did not mention, was that it was not until after the letter was written and published that the education of barristers was revised to include any skills training, including advocacy.

47. ABA Appellate Judges Conference, *Appellate Litigation Skills Training - The Role of the Law Schools* (1985); Martineau, *Appellate Litigation: Its Role in the Law School Curriculum*, 39 J. Legal Education 71 (1989). The A.B.A. Appellate Judges Conference in 1986 established a Committee on Appellate Practice to coordinate the Conference's efforts to improve the

teaching of appellate litigation skills in the law schools, the bar, and within law firms. It is currently developing plans to establish a National Appellate Practice Institute to teach appellate skills to practicing lawyers, modeled on the National Institute of Trial Advocacy -- established in the early 1970's.

48. D. Pannick, *supra* note 18 at 47-73 (1987); Atiyah & Summers, *supra* note 1 at 353-58.

49. The Master of the Rolls' remarks were contained in his 1987 annual review. The Vice-Chancellor made his comments in a speech entitled "The Independence of the Judiciary in the 1980's," a copy of which is in the files of the author. The speech was delivered in November, 1987. For a brief description of the development of the English approach to judicial administration, see Note, *Judicial Involvement in Court Administration*, 7 Civil Justice Q. 103, 105-6 (1988).

50. C. Baar, *Separate But Subservient: Court Budgeting in the American States* (1975); Note, *The Court's Inherent Power to Compel Legislative Funding of Judicial Functions*, 81 Michigan L. Rev. 1687 (1983). For a more general discussion see R. Wheeler, *Judicial Administration: Its Relation to Judicial Independence* (1988).

51. E.g., 31 U.S.C. § 1105(b).

52. L. Blom-Cooper & G. Drewry, *supra* note 23 at 114, 406 (1972).

Chapter 3 The Written Tradition and the Oral Tradition

A. The Oral Tradition in England

1. Arguments of Counsel

The heart of the English legal system and upon which all major aspects of it are based is the oral tradition.[1] This tradition dictates that each step of the litigation process going to the resolution of a dispute submitted to the courts--the presentation of evidence, the arguments of counsel, the deliberations of the judge, the making of the decision by the judge, the announcement of the decision, and the reasons given for it-- must take place in open court. The tradition permits the public to observe every aspect of the process. One authority has described the tradition as "comprehensive orality."[2] It applies both to proceedings in the appellate courts as well as the trial courts.[3] The tradition goes beyond the principle that justice must not only be done but be seen to be done and requires that it be seen being done. The faithful observance of the tradition is thought to be what guarantees the accountability of English justice and maintains public confidence in it.

The oral tradition has a direct influence on the organization of the legal profession, the selection of judges, the nature of the proceedings in the courtroom, the process by which decisions are made, and the reporting of decisions. It is the basis of the division of the legal profession into two groups, with only those who specialize in oral advocacy having the right of audience. It also explains limiting the selection of judges to those who belong to the small group of courtroom advocates. It justifies the *ex tempore* judgment, that is the giving of the reasons for a decision in an oral opinion delivered at the conclusion of the hearing. In addition, it further justifies the requirement that for a report to be accepted as an accurate statement of the judgment, the report must be prepared by a barrister who was present when the oral decision was rendered.

A key corollary of the oral tradition is that counsel must be allowed to present their evidence and arguments in whatever way they see fit for as long as they deem appropriate, with little or no direction or control by the judge. It also means that counsel cannot be forced to proceed with the hearing before they are ready. The timing and length of the proceedings in open court are thus subject solely to the wishes of counsel. Another corollary is that the judges should come to the hearing with an open mind, with no predisposition to one side or the other. This is best achieved if the judges do no advance reading connected with the case. What they learn about a case must be learned orally in open court. Once again it is thought that this ensures accountability so that any observer of the proceedings will have heard all of the elements that went into the judicial decision--facts, law, and the arguments of counsel on behalf of the parties.

In the Court of Appeal the oral tradition also dictates that the only authorities considered by the court are those cited to it by counsel. The judges do no additional research on their own. The assumption is that the competency of counsel and the imperatives of the adversary system will result in all of the relevant authorities, statutory and case precedent, being brought to the attention of the court. If a member of the court is familiar with a decision that may be relevant but is not cited by counsel in argument, the judge can ask counsel to consider its implications in the case being argued. All of this done in open court. Strict adherence to the oral tradition means that the judges should never decide an appeal on the basis of an uncited decision without giving counsel full opportunity to argue its import.

A significant part of the oral tradition is literally seeing the judges come to a decision. This occurs during the course of the hearing as points are made by counsel, facts referred to, and authorities cited and discussed. As the judges are exposed to these aspects of the case, they demonstrate by their questions and comments how their thinking is running, what is bothering them about counsel's arguments on the facts and the law, and how they are slowly coming to a conclusion by accepting this and rejecting that. For counsel it is highly important to witness this process so that they can attempt through their skill as an advocate, to shift the judges from viewpoints that are unfavorable to their clients to more favorable ones, to give additional support if the judges appear to be going in a direction favorable to their clients, or explain away the arguments of opposing counsel.[4]

A variation on this theme applies to the raising of issues for consideration by the court. Counsel will endeavor to present any issues they think the judges may find significant. They present one issue after the other until they find one in which the judges appear to see some merit. They will then focus on that issue because that is the one they think the judges find dispositive.[5]

The first break in oral tradition occurred in 1962 when the judges of the Court of Appeal announced that they would begin reading some documents, particularly the judgment of the trial judge, in advance of oral argument. The purpose was to save the time in oral argument devoted to the reading of the significant documents. This break with the oral tradition was criticized on the ground that counsel would not know if the judges properly understood the document.[6] This initial effort at weakening the oral tradition was soon abandoned[7] because the judges did not have time for advance reading and there was no systematic effort to get the documents to the judges far enough in advance of oral argument to give them an opportunity to read them. It was not until 1982 that a major effort was made to have the judges pre-read in every case. This change and the reaction to it are discussed in section C 4, *infra*.

2. Judgments

A system of law based on precedent requires two elements--a statement of reasons in support of the decision reached in the case and a means whereby judges on the same and other courts, the legal profession, government officials, and other interested persons can read and study the statements. In England, a statement of reasons is referred to as a judgement. When a judgment appears in print it is said to be reported and the publication in which it appears is a law report or simply a report. In the House of Lords the judgments of the law lords are referred to as speeches.

The rendering of judgments by judges has been a feature of the English system for centuries. Although technically a judgment need not be reported to be cited as precedent--it is sufficient that a member of the bar who was present when the judgment was rendered attests to the content of the judgment or that the judge be personally familiar with it--the reality is that unless a judgment is reported it is not likely to be used as precedent. Notwithstanding the obvious significance of the reporting of judgments, there has never been nor is there today an official system for the reporting of judgments.

The first reports of judicial decisions were summaries of judgments that appeared in the Year Books from the late thirteenth century to the mid sixteenth century. They included judgments of both trial courts and of higher courts. These summaries were not reports in the modern sense because they were handwritten and were not originally prepared to be cited to or used by judges. Eventually, however, they were used for this purpose. With the advent of printing in the fifteenth century, some of the summaries were printed. The printed versions were discontinued in the sixteenth century and were replaced by reports made by an individual barrister or judge and printed under his name. These reports were published at the convenience of the reporter and often did not appear until long after the judgments were rendered. The report of a judgment usually contained the arguments of counsel and the reporter's summary of the judgment, which could be close to a word for word repetition of it but most often was not.

This system lasted until 1865 when the Council of Law Reporting for England and Wales was established. The Council consists of representatives of the Inns of Court and the Law Society. Although it is not a creature of the government or of the courts, its reports have a preferred status. The Council publishes a separate volume of reports for each of the three divisions of the High Court and one for the House of Lords. Judgments of the Court of Appeal are published in the volume of the division from which the appeal was taken. Judgments in county court cases appear in the Queen's Bench Division volumes. The Law Reports include not only the judgments but also arguments of counsel. The report of an individual judgment is prepared by a barrister who is present in court when the judgment is rendered. The Council also publishes the Weekly Law Reports, which include all of the cases that will be published in the Law Reports as well as some that will not. Arguments of counsel are not included.

The Law Reports and the Weekly Law Reports are classified as general series because they are not limited to cases in any one subject area of the law. The only other general series is the All England Law Reports published by a private company. They are published weekly and subsequently in bound volumes. In addition there is a wide range of specialized reports of judgments in limited areas of the law or from specialized courts.

A third type is the report that appears in newspapers, the most well known of which is the London *Times*. These reports are not simply newspaper stories but summaries of judgments prepared by barristers. These can be cited to a court and are cited by courts when the judgment is not reported elsewhere.

Until 1951 there was no official copy of the judgments rendered by the Court of Appeal. In that year the Lord Chancellor ordered that a shorthand reporter be present in the Court of Appeal whenever a judgment was given and to record the judgment verbatim in shorthand. The shorthand reporter then makes a transcript of the judgment, a copy of which is placed in the file of the appeal and another in the Supreme Court library located in the Royal Courts of Justice. A copy is not provided to the parties. The judges are given the opportunity to review and edit the transcripts before they are filed. If judgment is reserved, as discussed in the next paragraph, the judgement is written and a copy filed with the other transcripts and given to each party. These transcripts are bound together by year and are available for inspection by those permitted to use the library (judges, barristers, and litigants representing themselves). The transcripts, however, may not be copied. If anyone including a party or its counsel desires a copy of a transcript, it must be purchased from the shorthand writers association. In the past decade a copy of each judgment of the Court of Appeal has been included in computer based systems and are available to those with the proper equipment and access to the system.[8]

There are several other significant features of the system for preparing, issuing, and publishing judgments of the English appellate courts. First, when a panel of the Court of Appeal decides an appeal, each of the judges is free to and usually does render an individual judgment. There is seldom a judgment of the Court in the sense of one judgment in which all of the judges concur. Individual speeches used to be the usual practice in the House of Lords but a single speech delivered by one law lord and concurred in by the others is now more common.

Second, in the Court of Appeal most judgments are delivered *ex tempore*, that is orally from the bench immediately following the conclusion of the arguments of counsel. The judges may confer briefly on the bench or in their chambers for a few minutes, but this is for the purpose of agreeing on the result, not the form or content of the judgment. In a small percentage of cases the panel will "reserve judgment," that is delay the making of a decision and giving the reasons for it. In such cases, the judges will usually write out their judgments but do not read them in court when they announce their decision. These decisions are indicated in reports by the notation "*cur.*

ad. vult" or "*c. a. v.*" for *curia advisari vult* ("the court will advise"). Because reserved judgments are prepared with more care, they usually carry more weight.[9]

Third, the number of judgments that are published in the general series reports is only a small percentage of the judgments of the Court of Appeal. According to one study, of the total number of judgments filed in the Supreme Court library in the years 1955, 1965, 1972, and 1973 the percentage of judgments that were published in the Law Reports were 18%, 14%, 13%, and 9%, respectively. When the All England Reports were included the percentages went to 34%, 28%, 21%, and 22%. The percentage not published in any general or specialized series was 51%, 47%, 62%, and 53%.[10] The comparable figures for 1986 were: Law Reports 5.2%, general series 13.8%, and unreported 61.1%.[11] Not even all speeches of the House of Lords are reported.[12]

Fourth, no judge or court official plays any part in the decision whether or not to publish a judgment. This decision is made by the publisher of the particular report series, but there is no public reason given for a decision to publish or not to publish nor are there any announced criteria for making the decision.

Although the system for reporting of decisions has been criticized as both too informal and duplicative, there is no current effort to change it. A study was made in 1940 by a committee appointed by the Lord Chancellor. That committee concluded that the system was satisfactory. As to the possibility that some decisions that should be reported were not, the Committee stated that "in the numerous Reports, general and special, almost every decision of any possible importance to the body of English law will be found. What remains is less likely to be a treasure house than a rubbish heap in which a jewel will rarely, if ever, be discovered."[13] There does not appear to be among the judges and the bar any current dissatisfaction with the system except that some believe too many, not too few, judgments are reported.

Research into English case law is done primarily through legal texts and treatises.[14] *Halsbury's Laws of England* is a general text encyclopedia in a form that attempts to cover all areas of the law. *Halsbury's Statutes of England* is an annotated collection of statutes. *Statutes in Force* is a complete collection of the statutes but is not annotated. The *Supreme Court Practice Book* includes the text of rules adopted by the Rules Committee along with annotations and comments but it is not an official publication. *The Digest* is a compilation of case digests that arranges case by subject matter to assist in finding the case law in any given area, but each case is usually summarized on only one point. There is no publication of citations of every reported case in every other reported case or legal journals, but *The Digest* and *Current Law Citator* index references to cases that have been judicially considered, the latter since 1947.

B. The Written Tradition in the United States

1. The Brief

Initially, the arguments made by counsel to American appellate courts were exclusively oral because of the English heritage of the American legal system and the relative difficulty of having materials printed. Oral arguments lasting several days in a single case were common. Because there were no written arguments, the oral arguments were the only means by which the judges acquired knowledge of the facts of the case and the contentions of the parties.[15]

As caseloads increased and access to printers became easier, courts required written statements of facts and contentions and put time limits on oral argument. Oral argument was then limited to true advocacy, that is, why the facts and the law justified a decision in favor of one side or the other. The Supreme Court of the United States adopted this practice in

1849.[16] The same pattern was soon followed in state courts. The initial time limit on oral argument in the Supreme Court was two and one half hours per side. Over the years courts limited further both oral argument and briefs, shortening the length of each.[17] This forced counsel to limit the number of issues they raised and to concentrate the focus of their arguments. It also required the judges to prepare in advance for oral argument so that they could use oral argument to clarify their understanding of the facts of the case and the contentions of the parties. Judges moved from using oral argument as their initial and principal means of learning about the case, with the briefs serving only the purpose of a reminder of the position of each party during the subsequent consideration of the case and the preparation of a written opinion, to relying primarily on the briefs, with oral argument as a supplement, albeit a significant and even decisive one, to the briefs.[18]

The brief follows a format specified in the appellate rules and is limited in length, usually 50 pages for the principal brief for each party.[19] The brief consists of five major sections: statement of issues, statement of the case, statement of facts, argument, and conclusion. The first section, the statement of issues, contains the principal questions raised by the appeal from the standpoint of the person filing the brief. Each issue is cast either in terms of an error made by the trial court or the correctness of one of its actions. The best advice on brief writing is to limit the number of issues to no more than three, but lawyers often raise more. The statement of the case, a procedural history of the case from the filing of the complaint to the filing of the notice of appeal, is next. The statement of facts follows, giving an accurate summary of the facts of the dispute as reflected in the record on appeal. Then comes the argument section, with a separate section for each of the issues raised. In this section the lawyer relates the facts of the case to the applicable law to show why both the law and justice require a result in favor of the lawyer's client. The last section of the brief is the conclusion, which is simply a short statement of the precise relief requested from the appellate court.

The appellant files the first brief, usually thirty days after the record on appeal is filed in the appellate court. The appellee then has thirty days to file a brief in response. The appellant is permitted to file a reply brief to respond to any points raised in the appellee's brief that the appellant did not address in its opening brief.

Oral argument, its role in the appellate process, and its relation to the brief is discussed in Chapter 5, section A 8 c ii, *infra*.

2. Opinions

Almost from the very beginning of appellate review in the United States the written opinion has been one of its most significant features. For a short period of time in its earliest years the Supreme Court of the United States rendered its opinions orally at the conclusion of the oral argument, but it soon abandoned this practice in favor of writing out the opinion first and then reading it in open court. Another practice adopted initially but soon abandoned was to have each judge render an individual opinion in each case. It is a universal practice of long standing that one judge is assigned to write a single opinion speaking for the entire court. If a judge disagrees with the result the judge can, but is not required, to write a dissenting opinion. A judge who agrees with the result but not with the reasoning expressed in the majority opinion may, but again is not required to, write a concurring opinion expressing the judge's reasons for voting with the majority.

The opinion is designed to serve the purposes of its author, the other judges on the panel, the appellate court, the litigants and their lawyers, the legal profession, and the general public. For its author, writing out the opinion is one means to test that the correct result in the case has been reached. This practice reflects the generally recognized principle that the best way to organize one's thoughts is to write them out. For the other members of the court, the opinion tests their own reasons for joining in the decision. They are also free to propose modifications in the language of the opinion before it is issued so that it better reflects their views of the rationale of the decision. This means, of course, that often the opinion that is ultimately issued under the name of one judge is actually a compromise document that precisely reflects the views of no one single judge on the court, not even the principal author. In this drafting process a judge who initially disagreed with the tentative decision of the court may be persuaded to join the majority. Similarly a judge, after writing the opinion or reading the opinion of another member of the panel, may conclude that the tentative decision was incorrect and change the judge's vote. If a majority of the court is affected in this way, the decision will be changed and a new majority opinion is written. If the author of the original opinion is also persuaded that the tentative decision was incorrect, that judge will write another opinion explaining the new decision. If the judge still believes the tentative decision was correct, the original opinion may be issued as a dissenting opinion.

For the appellate court of which the panel issuing the opinion is a part, the opinion is the official means whereby the court develops the law and speaks to the various groups that rely on it for declarations of the law. It is also the means whereby the court speaks directly and authoritatively to the lower court telling it whether its actions were correct or in error and what further actions to take in the present case and future ones.

For the litigants in the particular case and their lawyers, particularly the loser, the opinion shows that their side of the case and the points they raised have been considered and rejected and the reasons for the rejection. The expectation is that they will be more willing to accept an unfavorable result if they know that the decision was not arbitrary but was obtained through principled reasoning. The legal profession and the general public look to the opinions for other reasons. Most importantly, the opinion is the sole means by which they learn what the law is and can guide their activities accordingly. The lawyer will use the opinion to advise clients and to argue the client's position with private individuals, governmental bodies, and before the courts. Both lawyers and the public will also use the opinions as the principal measure of whether the judicial system is functioning properly and serving the purposes for which it was created.

In comparing the functions of appellate review with the functions of written opinions, it can be seen that when an appellate court is performing the error correction function the written opinion primarily serves the interests of those immediately involved in the case -- the appellate judges, the trial judge, the litigants, and the litigant's lawyers. In law development cases, the principal audiences of the opinions are the legal profession, including judges of lower courts, and the public. If no opinion is written, none of the purposes of an opinion is met.

For an opinion to perform its law development function, its intended audience must have access to it. To a very limited degree, the audience beyond those directly involved in the case is first made aware of a decision of an appellate court through reports in the news media. These reports are necessarily brief and give only the highlights of the most newsworthy decisions. In addition, they are prepared by persons who are almost never legally trained. Newspapers seldom report an opinion verbatim beyond a sentence or two. Serious analysis of an opinion by lawyers, scholars, public officials, and interested members of the general public requires the full text of the opinion. This is provided by reports of the opinions of a particular appellate court. A report is nothing more than a bound volume of the opinions of an appellate court published in the order the opinions were issued by the court.

After some initial variation, opinions of the United States Supreme Court and most state supreme courts were printed and published by the court itself or the government of which it was part under the supervision of a court official called the reporter of decisions for that court. The reporter, who was always legally trained and was sometimes a judge of the court, made sure the opinions were published in the exact form issued by the court. The reporter also summarized the key points of the opinion. These are termed "headnotes." At one time the reporter also summarized the arguments of counsel but this practice has been almost completely abandoned. Today each volume issued is numbered separately with each volume having its own pagination. When a particular opinion is referred to in a subsequent opinion or other writing, the name of the case is usually accompanied by a citation to the volume of the reporter series in which it is published, the page of the volume where it can be found, the year of decision, and the name of the court unless it is clear from the title of the report. Reports published under the authority of the court have the status of official reports.

In addition to the court published reports, some private firms also publish their own reports of the opinions of various courts. They are free to do so because the opinions are considered public documents. One of these private publishers, West Publishing Company, established a national reporter system in the late nineteenth century that included in a series of reports organized by region or specific court all of the opinions of all of the appellate courts, both state and federal, in the United States. It also established a uniform headnote system that was common to all of its reports and a system of digests that included all of the headnotes for the entire county, a regional reporter, or an individual state. In recent years many states have abandoned their own separate official reports and designated the reports by West as the official report. When the U.S. courts of appeals were established in 1891, neither these courts nor the federal government established an official series of reports for their opinions. West then established a new reporter series for the opinions of these courts known as the Federal Reporter. While these reports have never been designated as official reports, they effectively have the same status because they are the only series including all of the published opinions of these courts.

Copies of the official reports and the national reporter system are purchased by law libraries throughout the United States. These law libraries are operated by law schools, states, local governments, bar associations, government agencies, and private law firms. The law school and state law libraries have complete collections for all federal and state courts, while the smaller law libraries will usually have the federal reports plus those of their own state and perhaps adjoining states. Most series of reports also publish "advance sheets" that include portions of the opinions that will appear subsequently in a bound volume. They are usually issued on a regular basis, either weekly, biweekly, or monthly depending upon the volume of opinions. Their purpose is to give quick access to the opinions without the necessity of waiting for the publication of a hard bound volume.

In recent years several computer based opinion reporting systems have been established. These give almost instant access to opinions but, of course, require computer equipment and access to the computer in which the opinions are stored.

There are various research aids to assist lawyers in finding relevant opinions. West's national reporter system has developed a "key number" system which breaks down all judicially created law into a whole range of classifications and subclassifications. When an opinion is published in the national reporter system it is preceded by a group of headnotes prepared by the staff of West. The key number and the paragraphs are then published in a digest that includes all of the key number summaries of all of the opinions within a particular classification of reporters; federal courts, region, or by state. There is also a general digest that includes all the regional reporters. These summaries are now also included in a computer data base.

Another publication includes, for each published opinion of an appellate court, all of the citations to other cases or selected legal journals where the main case has been cited.

When the number of opinions of an individual appellate court was relatively small, it was the practice for most appellate courts to have every one of their opinions published. During the late 1960's and early 1970's a concern arose that the sheer number of opinions being published was making legal research not only more expensive and more difficult. Appellate courts were encouraged to adopt publication plans that would establish standards for the publication of opinions.

Many courts adopted these plans and made a determination upon the issuance of an opinion whether it was to be published or not. The basic criteria for publication was whether the opinion made any significant contribution to the law. There was, however, a substantial amount of flexibility included in the plans so that if any member of the panel issuing the opinion wanted it published it was. To enforce the non publication rule, many courts also adopted a rule that an opinion not published cannot be cited to it.

Criticisms of the limited publication plans have been made on two grounds. One is the argument that in a common law system what a court does in any one case is precedent in subsequent cases and a no publication-no citation rule is inconsistent with the basic notion of precedent. The other is that courts, by designating an opinion for non publication, could hide what they did or save the judge from criticism, valid or otherwise. A third criticism made more recently is that inequalities of access to opinions is created by the limited publication rules because unpublished as well as published opinions are included in computer databases and are thus available to anyone who has access to the system. In addition, certain litigants, primarily government agencies and large corporations, can afford to collect unpublished opinions and use them either directly by citing them to the court or indirectly by simply following what the appellate court says and does in those cases in which the opinions are not published.

C. Comparison

1. Reasons for the development of different traditions

Nothing distinguishes the English and American appellate systems more than the reliance of the English system on the oral tradition and the American on the written tradition. The oral tradition in the context of the appellate process can be described as one in which:

(1) all matters factual, legal, and persuasive are presented by counsel to the judges in an oral hearing,

(2) the judges rely only on those matters in making a decision, and

(3) the judgments rendered by each judge are delivered extemporaneously in court immediately following the conclusion of the arguments of counsel.

The written tradition, on the other hand, is one in which:

(1) all of the matters factual, legal, and persuasive are presented to counsel in written briefs and an appendix or record

(2) the written material may be supplemented by an oral argument of 15-30 minutes in length per side, the principal purpose of which is to permit the judges to ask questions of the attorneys based on their prior reading of the written materials,

(3) the decision and the reasons in support of it are set forth in a single opinion written by one of the judges some time after the oral hearing or submission on briefs,

(4) relying on such authorities as may have been cited by counsel or found in additional research by the judges or their staffs.

The English oral tradition was developed to meet the needs of trial courts in which verdicts or findings of fact were based on the presentation of the testimony of witnesses and written documents and on counsel's arguments in favor of their client's interests based on both the law and the facts. Review of the decisions of trial courts was made by a group of trial judges, including the judge who originally heard the case, with the review being limited to errors of law reflected on the face of the pleadings in the trial court, supplemented by a document prepared by the judge recording the rulings made by the judge and the exceptions to them taken by counsel. There was no transcript of testimony and the legal authorities available to be cited to the judge were almost non existent and in any event did not include reports of judgments of courts in prior cases. The same process continued, however, even after appellate courts with full time appellate judges were established, full records including transcripts of testimony became available, and reports of the judgments in prior cases were published. The reasons for this adherence to procedures developed to accommodate different conditions can probably best be explained by three factors. First, the conditions under which the system operated changed only slowly with no single change demanding a reexamination of the traditional procedures. Second, the barristers and judges, who had all spent most of their time in the trial courts, were not only comfortable with the oral procedures used there, they delighted in them and saw no reason to deviate from them in the appellate court. The appellate judges were former advocates and trial judges used to doing everything in open court including rendering oral judgments at the conclusion of the case. Finally, and perhaps most important, by the time the Court of Appeal was established the oral tradition was so firmly fixed in the English legal process that to deviate from it would have created substantial, if not almost universal, opposition. The oral tradition was not looked upon solely as a convenient means to enable judges to decide cases, but as the primary means for public accountability of the judicial system, both for trial courts and appellate courts. The oral tradition has thus survived because it was a tradition, the players in the system liked it, and there was a strong policy reason to keep it.

Until the mid-nineteenth century, American appellate courts adhered to the oral tradition for the presentation of the arguments of counsel. In 1849, however, the United States Supreme Court simultaneously imposed a requirement for written briefs and put a limit of 2-1/2 hours per side on oral argument. The justification for the change was that the justices felt that most of the time devoted to extended oral arguments was spent in acquiring information about the case that could be acquired more efficiently through briefs prepared by counsel for each side, with the oral hearing restricted to counsel arguing their respective positions--in other words to engage in advocacy. Even before then, however, the justices did not deliver opinions extemporaneously at the end of oral argument; they wrote out their opinions and then read them in open court. The reasons for this are not hard to imagine--the justices were not selected for the Court because they were particularly skilled oral advocates. Additionally, they had little or no experience as trial judges rendering oral opinions. Also significant is the fact that in the new federal system the judges had no binding precedent to rely on to decide cases. Everything was new--the constitution, statutes, and the common law to be applied. It is little wonder that the justices decided to write out their opinions.

As case load pressures mounted, the judges had to find means to increase their productivity. Three steps were taken to reduce the amount of material they had to read and the amount of time they spent in court: page limits on briefs, further reductions in the time allowed for oral argument, and elimination of oral argument in many cases. What the judges found was that the greater the restrictions imposed, the more effective the document or the argument. Briefs are better when they do not exceed 50 pages, and often can be shorter, and oral argument per side need not be more than 15 or 20 minutes. In this framework oral argument is reduced to the judges asking the lawyers questions about the weak spots in their factual and legal arguments, identified by a careful pre-reading of the briefs by the judges and their staffs. Oral argument in this setting is advocacy in its purest form.

2. Accountability

The ultimate justification for the oral tradition is that it is the best means to ensure accountability of the judicial system to the public it serves. This rationale, however, confuses the ability to see a process in action with accountability for the result of that process. The major difficulties with relying on the opportunity to observe the oral hearing in the Court of Appeal or the House of Lords is that a person must be physically present to see and hear it and there is no permanent record of what is seen and heard.[20] What a person sees and hears exists only for an instant and then is gone forever, except as a recollection in the mind of the observer. Few people attend the oral hearings in the Court of Appeal and even fewer in the House of Lords. Those few who do witness some portion of the hearing are seldom there from beginning to end. Even if they do manage to last for the entire hearing, they seldom make notes and have no access during the hearing to the reports of the cases cited to the court. Even more importantly, they have no access to the bundles before, during, or after the hearing unless they obtain a copy from the appellant. Nothing is kept on file in the Court of Appeal or any other public place. Unless the observers take shorthand, they have no record of the judgments rendered. If they want a copy of the judgment, they must buy one from the shorthand writers association or have access to a computer based reporting system. They do not know when or if the judgment will ever be published in a report. If a person finds out about a case only by reading the judgments in one of the reports, it is too late to attend the oral argument or to inspect a copy of the bundles. If judgments are not published in one of the reports, the only way to find out what judgments have been rendered is to read the copies placed in the Supreme Court library (to which the general public does not have access) or from a computer based reporting system.

In the United States, on the other hand, accountability is far easier because copies of the briefs and records in every case decided by a court are on file, not only in the appellate court but usually in major law libraries in the jurisdiction of the court. Most opinions are published in the reports. Those not published are so designated by the court in accordance with published criteria and a list of those cases is published in the reports. If no opinion is written, however, there is no accountability.

In comparing the public accountability of the two systems, it can thus be seen that the accountability that flows from the oral tradition is substantially less than under the written tradition. Accountability for an appellate court depends upon the ability of interested persons, particularly legal scholars and members of the bar, to have easy access to the judgments or opinions of the appellate courts and access to the factual record and the arguments of counsel upon which those judgments or opinions are based. These are available in the American system if an opinion is written, but not in the English system.

Notwithstanding its deficiencies as a guarantor of accountability, the oral tradition could still be justified if it were either effective or efficient as a means of conveying to the appellate court the relevant facts and law and the parties' positions on how the appeal should be determined. The premise of the English system of appellate justice is that the oral tradition is both efficient and effective in accomplishing this objective. Once again this premise is not supported by a careful examination of the facts. Such an examination demonstrates that the English appellate system is neither efficient nor effective. This situation is a direct result of its reliance on the oral tradition.

3. Efficiency

Under the oral tradition most of the hearing is devoted to informing the judges of the text of relevant portions of the bundles and of the relevant cases as to each of the points raised by counsel. Only a very small portion of the oral hearing has been devoted to *why* the material cited is relevant, *why* it supports the position for which it is cited, and *why* it should require a decision in favor of the counsel's client. Even a shorter time -- usually only 15 to 30 minutes -- is devoted to the heart of the oral hearing -- the vigorous exchange between the judges and counsel on the points that the judges believe are crucial to their understanding and resolution of the appeal.

This process is inefficient because the information provided during the oral hearing in almost every instance can be provided more efficiently on paper. As the Master of the Rolls acknowledged in his 1986 annual review, "judges, like anyone else, can absorb written material more quickly if they read it to themselves than if it is read aloud to them." It was in recognition of this fact that the United States Supreme Court over a century ago required written briefs and imposed time limits on oral argument.

The essential fact when considering the ability of a court to dispose of appeals is that if every appeal is heard orally, the number of appeals a court can dispose of is fixed by the amount of time it takes to hear each appeal. The total amount of time available for oral hearings is finite. Under the current schedule of the Court of Appeal, the number of hours each judge spends on the bench is fixed at 37 weeks x 4 days per week x 4.75 hours per day, a total of 707 hours. To the extent that a judge spends any of that time listening to what could otherwise be read, that time is spent inefficiently. It is the author's judgment that, based on his observations in the Court of Appeal and the House of Lords over a period of three months, English appellate judges spend most of the oral hearing time passively listening not to advocacy but to the transmittal of information. Sir Jack Jacob made the same point in the following words:

> [T]he English court takes no active part in the initiation, conduct, preparation or presentation of a civil case before or at the trial or on appeal.[21]

That time is, consequently, spent inefficiently.

The key factor in this inefficiency is that part of the oral tradition that dictates that the manner and length of counsel's presentation is solely under the control of counsel - the court must listen to whatever counsel wants to say or read as long as counsel wants to speak. A system of appellate justice that operates on this principle cannot hope to use efficiently its most valuable resource--the time of its judges.

The relationship between the dictates of the oral tradition and the efficiency or productivity of the Court of Appeal was first recognized in 1982 when the Court began prereading some documents and requested but did not require skeleton arguments that would identify the points raised and the principal authorities but not argue them. Both were intended to reduce the time spent in court devoted to the judges learning basic information about the case.[22] The March, 1989, Practice Direction and the Master of the Rolls introduction to it make it even more clear that the Court of Appeal has accepted the necessity of reducing the length of oral argument to permit the court to hear and dispose of more cases. Lord Donaldson commented in the introduction that the purpose of the changes introduced by the Practice Direction was "reducing the amount of time spent in court and increasing the Court's productivity without detracting from the quality of our appellate system." The key features of the changes introduced by the Practice Direction were the mandatory filing of skeleton arguments at least four weeks prior to the scheduled hearing date, the appointment of a legal staff to review the estimates of counsel on the length of the oral hearing and to recommend shortening them when appropriate, a greater commitment to prereading by the judges, and an effort to give greater certainty to the scheduling of oral hearings.

The significance of these modifications of the oral tradition, particularly those made in 1989, cannot be overemphasized. What they represent are major limitations upon key elements of the oral tradition--allowing counsel to determine the length of the oral hearing and requiring that any matter considered by the judges be presented in open court--so that any observer would know everything the judges knew and on what they based their decisions. If the Practice Direction is fully implemented, it will eliminate the principal barriers to making the Court of Appeal more efficient. Particularly significant are the portions of the Practice Direction that counsel will not open their arguments with a recital of facts but "proceed immediately to the ground of appeal which is in the forefront of the appellant's case." This not only directs counsel to skip a statement of the facts but to concentrate on the principal issue raised by the appeal. Further, the Direction directs that the counsel should not read a case at length "but go immediately to the passage in the judgment where the principle relied on" can be found. Finally, when reading from the record "counsel should so far as possible avoid reading from them *in extenso*." As can be seen, the entire thrust of the Practice Direction is to restrict the oral hearing to argument, and not the providing of information.

The Court of Appeal's concern over these modifications of the oral tradition were such that the final paragraph of the Practice Direction instructed solicitors and counsel to explain the prereading procedures "so that the parties do not infer that, because the appeal hearing has been shorter than has hitherto been customary, their case has not been just as fully considered."

4. Effectiveness

Even if the oral tradition were inefficient it could still be justified if it were effective. The oral tradition depends upon the competence of the Bar as oral advocates and its ability to present to the court all relevant facts and legal authority. Based upon the author's observations in the Court of Appeal and the House of Lords over almost three months in a wide variety of appeals and in light of his experience in observing oral argument in American appellate courts for almost thirty years, it is his conclusion that most English barristers are not effective appellate advocates.

This conclusion is based on the following:

1. It took an inordinate amount of time for counsel to identify what their appeals were about, what the issues were, and what were their contentions. In most of the appeals observed by the author, the arguments began at 10:30 a.m. It was often 2:30 or 3:00 p.m. before he could ascertain what the key issues were. He contrasted this with his experience in American appellate courts in which it takes him no more than 15 minutes to ascertain the key issues and approximately 30 minutes to come to a conclusion on how the appeal should be decided. Getting to the point of the appeal for an English barrister seems to be some-

thing to be avoided, not achieved. On a number of occasions the presiding judge was forced to ask in an exasperated tone "But what is the point of your argument?" or "What point are you trying to make?"[23] This occurred as often with senior counsel as with junior.

2. Lack of preparation was demonstrated in a number of ways. Perhaps the most telling was that in most of the appeals the author heard argued by Queen's Counsel, the Q.C. was unable to answer even the simplest question about the appeal and had to turn to his junior counsel for advice on how to respond. This was true as to both factual questions and those on the authorities cited. The appeals had obviously been prepared by the junior with the Q.C. only bothering to achieve the most superficial understanding of the case before making his argument.[24]

By contrast, the judges were very familiar with the issues of the appeal before the hearing began and were prepared to get to the heart of the case whenever counsel would let them. In the Court of Appeal, the House of Lords, and the Inner House of the Court of Session the author had the opportunity to discuss with the judges the cases they were hearing either before the hearing or during recesses. In each instance it was clear that the judges were fully prepared on both the law and the facts but felt restrained by the oral tradition from forcing counsel by their questions to get quickly to the heart of the appeal before counsel was prepared to do so. In almost every other hearing the author attended, the same situation existed. It often appeared that the judges were indulging counsel out of deference to the oral tradition.

In other cases lack of preparation was evidenced by arguments that were repetitive or skipped back and forth from one point to the next and back again without any apparent plan. Precedents were cited and quoted from at length and when questioned as to their relevance, no explanation satisfactory to the judges was given. Confusion often reigned when copies of documents or judgments intended to be given to the judges could not be found. Questions as to specific documents or testimony in the bundles were often met by the hurried paging through of papers, followed by an apology for not being able to find the appropriate paper or quotation.

3. The basic approach of the barrister was to raise as many issues as possible, and as to each issue cites as many cases as possible, in the hope that some point would find favor with the court without any selectivity as to either. This is exactly contrary to the best advice given to American appellate advocates to limit sharply both the issues raised and the authorities cited.[25]

The raising of an excessive number of issues has been defended on the grounds that either the solicitor or the client may insist upon one or more particular issues being raised. This seems a peculiar defence in light of the asserted expertise of the barrister as a courtroom advocate, the claimed importance of having an independent bar, and the higher duty of the barrister to the court than to the client. In the United States, the responsibility of the lawyer to choose the arguments to be made has been recognized by the United States Supreme Court.[26]

4. Few of the barristers observed appeared to have much knowledge or understanding of the basic principles of public speaking. The rules governing eye contact, body movement, voice pitch, and reading extended passages were disregarded as often as those governing the limitation of points. Some barristers appeared to think that it was essential to say "My Lord" at least once in every sentence.

Similar, but more restrained, criticism of the performance of barristers in the Court of Appeal was made recently in an English legal journal.

A visitor to the Court of Appeal is not always impressed by the effectiveness of the oral argument he hears. It cannot be denied that in many cases there is a good deal of time wasted in getting the attention of the judges and the counsel appearing focused on the real points at issue. Sometimes judges, though clearly deeply committed to the oral tradition, find it very difficult to get counsel to state their best points succinctly and clearly and to engage counsel in a fruitful dialogue for the purpose of clarifying and testing these points. It has to be said that some counsel either have not mastered their briefs thoroughly or are not particularly adept at arguing points of law.[27]

This is not to say that all of the barristers observed were inadequate. Some of them were, in fact, outstanding. It was apparent, however, that these were the exception rather than the rule. The same is true in the United States.[28]

An examination of the educational requirements for barristers and the circumstances under which they practice explains why it should not be surprising that most are not effective appellate advocates. They have received no advocacy training in university or in their professional legal education, and are not likely to be exposed to competent appellate advocacy in their pupillage. Most do not have enough appeals for self training.[29] In these respects, they are not different from the American lawyer, whose training and practice have most of the same deficiencies. The principal difference between the two, insofar as the oral argument of a particular appeal is concerned, is that the American requirement of the preparation of a brief mandates that the attorney think through carefully what the issues are and the position to be taken on them. Just as importantly, the preparation of the American appellate judge for oral argument, the time limitations on it, and its principal purpose being to permit the judges to ask questions result in the oral hearing in American appellate courts being highly concentrated, narrowly focused exercises in advocacy, notwithstanding the inadequacies of the typical American appellate advocate.

The oral tradition, on the other hand, rather than forcing counsel to focus on the key facts and legal arguments, has allowed them to argue *ad infinitum* and often *ad nauseam* without the discipline of the written word or a time limit. The unlimited oral hearing is a perfect illustration of the point attributed to many great speakers including Winston Churchill on the amount of time necessary to prepare a speech--an hour's speech can be given on five minutes notice, but a five minute speech requires at least a week to prepare.

Perhaps the most extreme example of the effect of the lack of discipline of the oral tradition was an oral hearing attended by the author on how many days should be set aside for the appeal of a case that had yet to be tried. The estimates given by counsel for the length of the trial was eight days. The estimated length of the hearing of the appeal was eight to ten days, that is as long or longer than the original trial.

Even the simplest advance preparation of giving to the ushers the day before the hearing a list of cases to be quoted in argument seemed to be too much for many barristers. As a result the hearings were often interrupted each time counsel moved from one case to the next while the ushers try to find copies of the reports from which the judges could read along with counsel. When a recent decision yet unreported was cited, counsel often neglected to bring copies of the judgment for the judges or opposing counsel. At best the performance of many counsel, including some Queen's Counsel, would be termed sloppy. In a few cases unprofessional may be the more accurate term.

The strength of the oral tradition in England is such that every time a study is made of the current system or some alteration made in it, a rejection of the American brief and limited oral argument becomes *pro forma*. The first occasion the American system was formally discussed was in 1953 in the report of the Committee to Study Supreme Court Practice and Procedure headed by then Sir Raymond Evershed, the Master of the Rolls.[30] The committee stated that it had considered but rejected the American approach and gave the following reasons:

(1) the advantage of the judges discussing fully with counsel each point raised by each party, with each judge hearing the questions of the other judges and the responses of counsel;

(2) fewer dissents as a result of the judges working as a team during the hearing;

(3) the delay in bringing the case on for a hearing in the American system because of the time spent by the judges in reading the briefs and the record and the delay in the preparation of reserved judgments in every case, the judges being unable to deliver extemporaneous judgments;

(4) most important were the differences in the organization of the legal profession in each country; in England cost to litigants would increase because counsel who were specialists in oral advocacy would have to prepare twice, once to write the brief and once for the oral hearing.

It is significant that the committee noted that it had consulted with two Americans, Justice Felix Frankfurter of the United States Supreme Court and John W. Davis, a prominent New York lawyer, and that neither was enthusiastic about the American system. This is not surprising. Justice Frankfurter was known for his preference for oral argument over briefs,[31] and John W. Davis is generally recognized as the best American appellate oral advocate of the 20th century.

The experiment in reading the bundles in advance of the oral hearing by judges of the Court of Appeal that resulted from the Anglo-American exchange of judges in the early 1960's was quickly dropped.[32] Apparently no one thought it was a good idea to experiment with briefs. Confirming the worst suspicions of the English judges was the allowance of the filing of a written brief in one case in 1966. A brief of 116 pages was filed, followed by a reply brief of 9 pages. One of the judges commented in his judgment: "Both of these matters were wholly irregular and contrary to the practice of the court and in my opinion should not be allowed as precedent for future proceedings."[33]

The Scarman Committee in 1978 considered the American brief anew and again rejected it, primarily on the grounds of expense to the litigants and because "it is obviously impossible in [one half hour per side] to explore points in the depth that is customary in our courts."[34]

In 1982 Lord Diplock referred to the long standing practice of the members of the Appellate Committee reading in advance of the oral hearing the judgment of the lower court and the printed case filed by the parties. Lord Diplock stated that the purpose of the prereading was to reduce the length and cost of appeals. He immediately added, however, that it was not the purpose of the practice to lead to the introduction of American style briefs or to reduce the importance of oral argument.[35]

The two most recent statements on the subject by a high judicial officer have been by Lord Donaldson, the current Master of the Rolls. In his 1986 annual review, he attempted to quiet fears that the changes in procedure, particularly prereading and skeleton arguments, would be followed by a more dramatic shift to the American system. He stated that the court had gone as far as it should. He gave two reasons--the specialized corp of advocates upon whom the court relies to do much of the work done by judicial law clerks in the United States and the long tradition of oral argument in England.

In his introduction to the March, 1989, Practice Direction in which the Court of Appeal mandated the filing of skeleton arguments rather than having them discretionary, this issue was again referred to. Lord Donaldson commented that when skeleton arguments were first introduced, some lawyers took the view that this was the first step toward going to the American system of full arguments in writing and short oral arguments. He commented: "This is not the case. I cannot emphasize too strongly that the English Court of Appeal remains firmly wedded to its long established tradition of oral argument in open court. For that reason, as the Practice Direction makes clear, skeleton arguments should be confined to identifying the points, not arguing them."

There have been two public comments on the pre-reading and skeleton arguments by lawyers in England, one by a solicitor and one by a barrister. The former made an attack on virtually every change made in the last decade by the House of Lords and the Court of Appeal in their procedures.[36] He particularly viewed the practices of prereading and skeleton arguments as dangerous. The former he saw as "the thin end of the wedge which will eventually lead to the American-style 'brief' and the practical elimination of oral argument."[37] Prereading of the skeleton arguments and portions of the bundles would change the oral hearing because judges would no longer come to it with an open mind. "The suggestion that, having read all the papers, including the skeleton argument, a judge is still capable of keeping a truly open mind is no more than an illusion."[38]

In a program on judicial techniques in arbitration and litigation held in November, 1987, a prominent Queen's Counsel sounded a similar alarm.[39] His position was that by reading skeleton arguments in advance of the oral hearing "the basic premise of the oral system (i.e. a completely open and fresh mind of the Judge at the commencement of the hearing) may well be undermined."[40]

The question must be asked what prompts these virtual automatic rejections of a system with which few English have any direct experience. Lord Wilberforce, one of the most highly regarded senior law lords, in the same November, 1987, program made some telling responses to the uncritical defense of the oral tradition. He commented that "belief in the virtues of the oral process is largely instinctive and unscientific."[41] By the same token, so is the rejection of the written tradition.

Some key points about the written brief and the relation of oral argument to it need to be recognized. First, the American brief is not an unstructured document of unlimited length. The rules of appellate procedure in every jurisdiction tightly govern both form and length. The result is that any brief that meets minimum standards of competence is one that can be read and understood in a very short time--usually no more that half an hour--by an experienced appellate judge. The structure of the brief forces the lawyer to identify the key issues, the procedural history of the case, the principal facts, and to make the argument in the context of the facts and the issues. Oral argument based on a written brief becomes an intense exercise in advocacy in which the lawyers and the judges immediately confront the key areas of dispute that require resolution by the judges. Viewed in this light, oral argument loses none of its importance; if anything it becomes more important. This point was recognized in a report of the debate between the Queen's Counsel and Lord Wilberforce at the program on arbitration and litigation. In reporting on the opposition of the Q.C. to written briefs based on their supposed adverse effect on dialogue, the commentator "wondered whether dialogue might not be actively engendered by the use of written briefs or more or less skeletal arguments helping the tribunal to focus on the really crucial aspects of the case."[42]

One of the most significant similarities between the extended English oral hearing and the short American oral argument is the fact that in both types the amount of time actually devoted to the heart of the case--when the judges press counsel on their principal argument and the counsel either persuade or fail to do so--lasts for only a relatively brief period, usually no more than 15 to 30 minutes on each side. The principal difference between the two systems is the length of time it takes to reach that point.

In analyzing the objections to the American style brief and oral argument, it seems clear that the English view of the exact nature of the written brief and the oral argument based on it stems from a lack of understanding of how the American system works. Ignored is the fact that the American system has five separate checks on the ultimate decision to ensure its correctness--(1) the briefs, (2) prereading and checking of the briefs, (3) the oral argument, (4) the preparation of an opinion by one judge assisted by staff, and (5) a review and checking of the opinion by two other judges and their staffs. The preference for the oral tradition, on the other hand, is based on an unjustified belief in the competence of the English barrister as an appellate oral advocate. Overlooked are the dangers in relying solely on counsel for the wherewithal of the decision by the appellate court--the issues, facts, and law. Also overlooked is the fact that the American system is faster and the judges more productive than the English system, as detailed in Chapter 4.

It may be that an unstated reason for opposition to the American system is a fear that to adopt it for the English appellate system would remove one of the justifications for the continuation of the division of the legal profession into two branches, barristers and solicitors. There is, however, no necessary correlation between the two. The American system requires specialized skills of advocacy and communication just as much as the English oral tradition. It simply requires them to be of two kinds, written and oral, rather than just oral. If the right of audience in the English appellate courts is properly limited to barristers in the oral tradition, that same limitation can properly be applied to the written briefs and shorter oral arguments of the written tradition.

The most recent developments in England offer some prospect for improving the effectiveness of the oral tradition in the appellate process. One is the revision of the curriculum of the Inns of Court School of Law that, effective in 1989, devotes two thirds of the time of students to skills training, particularly advocacy. The emphasis in the Green and White Papers on advocacy and the need for skills training of those who have rights of audience was significant, no matter what the eventual disposition of the specific recommendations of the Government. The other is the changes introduced by the March 1, 1989, Practice Direction issued by the Court of Appeal. The implementation of this direction will mean that counsel will have to think through their arguments well in advance of the oral hearing, prepare a written outline of them in a skeleton argument, review the key facts in a chronology of events, cite key factual references in the skeleton argument, and devote their oral presentations to the substance of their argument, concentrating on their principal points and reading only the most relevant portions of cases and the transcript of testimony. Even more significant, the Court of Appeal has taken control over the length of the oral hearing and the renewed emphasis on prereading will permit the judges to take a far more active role in the oral hearing by questioning counsel. This should not only reduce the length of the oral hearing, but just as important, force counsel to be more effective advocates.

It should be noted, however, that none of the discussion of the need for improved advocacy training for barristers makes any mention of the difference between the skills necessary for effective advocacy in a trial court and in an appellate court. If the advocacy training concentrates on the examination and cross-examination of witnesses, as it does in the United States, this will be of little assistance in the appellate courts. It took almost 15 years in the United States for appellate judges to realize that improving trial advocacy skills had little or nothing to do with improving appellate advocacy skills and that separate appellate programs had to be developed for both law students and practicing lawyers. The same process should also occur in England.

5. Judgments and Opinions

There are four major differences between England and the United States with respect to the statement of reasons given in support of a decision of an appellate court--the number rendered in each case, the manner in which they are prepared, who makes the decision to publish them, and the method of their publication.

In the Court of Appeal each judge renders an individual judgement in almost every case (this is now less true in the House of Lords), while in the United States there is almost always one opinion in which the judges who agree on the result join and which thereby becomes the opinion of the court. The American system seems far preferable. If a decision is to serve as precedent, the greater the certainty in what constitutes the precedent the greater the certainty in the law. To the extent that an opinion speaks only for one judge, the law is less certain and more open to disagreement as to the precise principle of law for which the case stands. The reason for individual judgments in the Court of Appeal is understandable--with judgments given extemporaneously there is no opportunity for the judges to agree on any single judgment. These extenuating circumstances do not exist in the House of Lords, however, where the statement of reasons (speech) given by each member of the Appellate Committee is written rather than extemporaneous. Thus it is not surprising that Blom-Cooper and Drewry recommended the change to the American system in their study of the House of Lords judicial function and why the single speech in the House of Lords is today more the rule than the exception.[43]

The justifications given for continuing with separate judgments in the Court of Appeal are not convincing and seem more directed at simply preserving the status quo than anything else. The only rationale that appears substantial is that it is helpful to have the views of each member of the panel. This is achieved in the United States by the occasional use of concurring opinions by individual judges, but they become counter-productive when the concurring judge does not also join in the opinion of the court. If there is no opinion of the court, then there are only separate opinions of individual judges, but these are not and cannot be authoritative pronouncements of the law. Opinions and judgments should be something more than statements on the law by individual judges that derive their authority from their internal logic or the reputation of the author. They should, rather, be authoritative and binding statements of the law issued in the name of and with the authority of the court.

One of the major efforts in American appellate courts over the past fifty years has been to replace the "one judge opinion" with an opinion that truly reflects the views of a majority of the court. One judge opinions were common when there was only one record and one judge was assigned responsibility for the opinion prior to oral argument. As a result only one judge was prepared for oral argument and was concerned with anything but the outcome of the appeal. Copies of the opinion were not circulated to the other judges in advance of the opinion conference; the opinion was merely read at the conference by the author to the other judges. Unless they heard something highly objectionable, they simply accepted the opinion without careful study. They were primarily interested in the result, not the opinion. Recent efforts have been designed to make the opinion and not just the result the product of collegial deliberation.[44] A single opinion of the court has another advantage--it helps the efficiency of the court by requiring each judge to write an opinion on only one third of the appeals which the judge decides on the merits. It also cuts down on the number of opinions published.

It is hard to imagine a greater variance in method of operation than there is between the English and American processes for preparing the statement of reasons in support of a decision. Under both systems the statement of reasons serves the parties--by telling them why they won or lost[45]--and the legal and general public by informing them of the law. The American written opinion serves another major purpose, however, and that is to permit the judge writing the opinion and those who will concur in it to test their conclusion by the ultimate test of justifying it in writing. It also allows them to exercise extreme care in choosing the exact words to use in the opinion so that to the extent humanly possible the opinion says what the judges mean. The written opinion also allows checking of the record, further study of the authorities cited by the parties, and an opportunity to do additional research. Draft opinions can then be reviewed by the other judges on the panel and their staffs, and revisions made when appropriate. There is, thus, an internal quality control of the content of the opinion before it becomes the statement of the court.

Even more important than the issue of quality is that of the extent to which the judges rely on arguments and authorities not cited by counsel. The oral tradition dictates both are limited to those made or cited by counsel while under the written tradition the judges are free to rely on any legal argument supported by the record and any authority that is published. The former emphasizes the effect of the decision on the parties while the latter places more importance on the precedential effects of the decision. It has recently been argued that English judges should not be as passive as has been traditional.[46] This cannot occur, however, until the judges write their judgments rather than render them extemporaneously, take the time to do additional research before writing, and have the staff to permit them to do so expeditiously.

It is a tribute to the quality of the English judges that their extemporaneous judgments are as well done as they are, given the fact that preparation and public announcement are simultaneous. The weaknesses in this process have long been recognized. Almost four decades ago Lord Evershed, then Master of the Rolls, expressed concern that the judges of the Court of Appeal were not able to render more reserved judgments, acknowledging the benefits of time to think through a decision and carefully select the words to justify it.[47] Even more significant is the general view that reserved judgments are entitled to more weight than those delivered extemporaneously for the very reason that more care is given in their preparation.

Allowing the publishers of reports to determine which judgments are included in the reports rather than the appellate court making the decision is another major difference between the English and American systems. The difference is difficult to explain except in historical terms. In light of the fact that, practically, law is made and precedent established only when judgments or opinions are published, it should be the court issuing the judgment or opinion and not some private party deciding what to publish. If all judgments or opinions were published in any event, the question of who makes the decision would not be significant. But when, as is the case under both systems, substantial percentages of judgments or opinions are not published, then determining who makes the publication decision becomes crucial.

The principal justification for the English system is that not only all significant judgments are published but that an excessive number wind up in the reports. The proponents of this position offer no proof in support of their conclusion, nor can they because no study has been made of the precedential value of judgments not published in the general reports. The conclusion is, consequently sheer speculation. There is, however, substantial evidence that significant judgments are not published in the general reports. In a 1977 study of law reporting of Court of Appeal judgments, a total of 31 judgments cited in later judgments over a three year period were not published in a general series.[48] In 884 transcripts of appeals decided in 1986, the author found citations to 27 judgments that were published only in newspapers and not in either a general or special series. Of the five appeals detailed in the appendix, two of them were argued on the basis of judgments reported only in newspapers and one was decided on that basis. Only two of the five judgments have been reported in general reports and one was not reported at all. Delmar Karlen was correct in 1962 when he referred to the unpublished judgments in the Supreme Court library as "unexploded land mines, ready to do damage."[49] The problem of unpublished judgments has become so great that both a law lord and the Master of the Rolls have seen fit to criticize the citation to the appellate courts of judgments available only on the computer based systems and not published elsewhere.[50] To the author, this signifies the existence of an underpublication problem, not one of over citation. It is both ironic and telling that the judgment of the Master of the Rolls in which he discussed this problem was published only in a newspaper.[51]

In the United States, on the other hand, what is published is solely within the control of the court even though computer based systems include every opinion, both published and unpublished. Criticism of selective publication has been growing although the first two systematic studies of the unpublished opinions of two separate courts showed not only that no significant opinions were unpublished but that many that were non-precedential were still being published.[52] Some later studies indicate both underpublication and unequal access.[53]

In addition some courts have established a procedure that permits anyone to petition the court at any time to publish an opinion. Such a procedure should eliminate the need for citing an unpublished opinion as well as alleviate the problem of unequal access.[54]

To the extent that the American system of publication has been effective it has been because it is court controlled. The courts have adopted formal publication guidelines to aid the making of a decision on the publication of a particular opinion.[55] Essentially the standards provide for non publication if the opinion is simply repetitive of earlier published opinions and adds nothing because it neither involves a new legal principle nor applies an established principle to an unusual fact situation. Interestingly, and perhaps not coincidentally, these standards are very similar to those adopted by the Committee on Law Reporting in 1940.[56]

Difficulties have arisen with the American system for two principal reasons. One is that judges are not following the publication guidelines and are publishing opinions that do not meet the criteria for publication, or are failing to publish some that meet the criteria. The best way to deal with this problem is to establish an advisory panel of judges and court staff to review opinions and make recommendations as to publication.

An even greater problem, however, is the inclusion of unpublished opinions in non official publications such as computer based systems, specialists reports, or even legal newsletters. Such non official publications do create a problem of unequal access.[57] There are two solutions to the problem. One is to enforce strictly the rules against non citation of unpublished opinions. To permit these citations is to destroy the effectiveness of non publication rules. A non publication rule without non citation simply creates more problems than official publication of all opinions because it creates a two level publication system--official an unofficial. This makes research both more difficult and more expensive. A more drastic device would be to provide copies of the unpublished opinions only to the parties to the appeal and to prohibit them from providing them to any one who might publish it.

Arguably, in an earlier era in England when there were only two permanent panels of the Court of Appeal, one hearing all common law appeals and one all equity, the membership on the panels was permanent, and the bar was quite small, the judges and the bar would know about a decision even if it was not published. Under such circumstances, under publication probably did not create major difficulties. Today, however, the situation is much different. With 27 judges sitting in revolving panels and spending part of their time sitting in the Criminal Division, and an ever-growing bar, that assumption can no longer be the basis for a continuation of the traditional system of publication of judgments.

The problems created in the American system by the failure to write an opinion in every appeal, even if not published, are discussed in Chapter 4, section C, *infra*.

ENDNOTES

1. J. Jacob, *The Fabric of English Civil Justice* 19-21 (1987); R. Magarry, *Lawyer and Litigant in England* 167-73 (1962).

2. Megarry, *supra* note 1 at 167-73.

3. Id. at 167.

4. Jacob, *supra* note 1 at 21-23, A. Paterson, *The Law Lords* 59-61 (1982); R. Megarry, note 1 at 168-69; Meador, *English Appellate Judges from an American Perspective* 66 Georgetown L. Rev., 1349, 1366-67 (1978).

5. Id.

6. Megarry, *supra* note 1 at 170-71.

7. M. Zander, *The English Legal System* 535 (5th ed. 1988).

8. R. Walker, *The English Legal System* 154-61 (6th ed. 1985); M. Zander, *The Law Making Process* 203-221 (2d ed. 1985).

9. Walker, *supra* note 8 at 158, n. 18.

10. K. Eddey, *The Law Reporting of the Court of Appeal (Civil Division)*, 374 pp. undated. This thesis, a copy of which is on file in the Supreme Court Library, indicates it was completed in 1977.

11. These statistics were developed by the author based on data in LEXIS, ENGGEN Library, Cases file, Court (appeal) and date 1986, search.

12. In L. Blom-Cooper & G. Drewry, Final Appeal 249 (1972), it is reported that in their study of decisions of the House of Lords over a 16 year span, 25 were not reported in any series of reports. Only 71% of the English appeals to the House of Lords were reported in Appeals Cases.

13. Eddey, *supra* note 10 at 12.

14. Walker, *supra* note 8 at 162-67, G. Williams, *Learning the Law*, Chs. 3 & 12 (11th ed. 1982).

15. The exclusive reliance on oral argument in the United States Supreme Court in its earliest years is described in Shapiro, *Oral Argument in the Supreme Court: The Felt Necessities of the Time*, Historical Society of the United States Yearbook 22 (1985).

16. Id. at 25-26.

17. Id. at 26-27.

18. Martineau, *The Value of Appellate Oral Argument: A Challenge to the Conventional Wisdom*, 72 Iowa L. Rev. 1 (1986).

19. Federal Rule of Appellate Procedure 28 is typical.

Rule 28. Briefs

(a) Brief of the Appellant. The brief of the appellant shall contain under appropriate headings and in the order here indicated:

(1) A table of contents, with page references, and a table of cases (alphabetically arranged), statutes and other authorities cited, with references to the pages of the brief where they are cited.

(2) A statement of the issues presented for review.

(3) A statement of the case. The statement shall first indicate briefly the nature of the case, the course of proceedings, and its disposition in the court below. There shall follow a statement of the facts relevant to the issues presented for review, with appropriate references to the record [see subdivision (e)].

(4) An argument. The argument may be preceded by a summary. The argument shall contain the contentions of the appellant with respect to the issues presented, and the reasons therefor, with citations to the authorities, statutes and parts of the record relied on.

(5) A short conclusion stating the precise relief sought.

(b) Brief of the Appellee. The brief of the appellee shall conform to the requirements of subdivision (a)(1)-(4), except that a statement of the issues or of the case need not be made unless the appellee is dissatisfied with the statement of the appellant.

(c) Reply Brief. The appellant may file a brief in reply to the brief of the appellee, and if the appellee has cross-appealed, the appellee may file a brief in reply to the response of the appellant to the issues presented by the cross appeal. No further briefs may be filed except with leave of court. All reply briefs shall contain a table of contents, with page references, and a table of cases (alphabetically arranged), statutes and other authorities cited, with references to the pages of the brief where they are cited.

(d) References in Briefs to Parties. Counsel will be expected in their briefs and oral arguments to keep to a minimu references to parties by such designations as "appellant" and "appellee". It promotes clarity to use the designations used in the lower court or in the agency proceedings, or the actual names of parties, or descriptive terms such as "the employee," "the injured person," "the taxpayer," "the ship," "the stevedore," etc.

(e) References in Briefs to the Record. References in the briefs to parts of the record reproduced in the appendix filed with the brief of the appellant (see Rule 30(a)) shall be to the pages of the appendix at which those parts appear. If the appendix is prepared after the briefs are filed, references in the briefs to the record shall be made by one of the methods allowed by Rule 30(c). If the record is reproduced in accordance with the provisions of Rule 30(f), or if references are made in the briefs to parts of the record not reproduced, the references shall be to the pages of the parts of the record involved; e.g., Answer p. 7, Motion for Judgment p. 2, Transcript p. 231. Intelligible abbreviations may be used. If reference is made to evidence the admissibility of which is in controversy, reference shall be made to the pages of the appendix or of the transcript at which the evidence was identified, offered, and received or rejected.

(f) Reproduction of Statutes, Rules, Regulations, etc. If determination of the issues presented requires the study of statutes, rules, regulations, etc. or relevant parts thereof, they shall be reproduced in the brief or in an addendum at the end, or they may be supplied to the court in pamphlet form.

(g) Length of Briefs. Except by permission of the court, or as specified by local rule of the court of appeals, principal briefs shall not exceed 50 pages, and reply briefs shall not exceed 25 pages, exclusive of pages containing the table of contents, tables of citations and any addendum containing statutes, rules, regulations, etc.

(h) Briefs in Cases Involving Cross Appeals. If a cross appeal is filed, the plaintiff in the court below shall be deemed the appellant for the purposes of this rule and Rules 30 and 31, unless the parties otherwise agree or the court otherwise orders. The brief of the appellee shall contain the issues and argument involved in his appeal as well as the answer to the brief of the appellant.

(i) Briefs in Cases Involving Multiple Appellants or Appellees. In cases involving more than one appellant or appellee, including cases consolidated for purposes of the appeal, any number of either may join in a single brief, and any appellant or appellee may adopt by reference any part of the brief of another. Parties may similarly join in reply briefs.

(j) Citation of Supplemental Authorities. When pertinent and significant authorities come to the attention of a party after the party's brief has been filed, or after oral argument but before decision, a party may promptly advise the clerk of the court, by letter, with a copy to all counsel, setting forth the citations. There shall be a reference either to the page of the brief or to a point argued orally to which the citations pertain, but the letter shall without argument state the reasons for the supplemental citations. Any response shall be made promptly and shall be similarly limited.

20. This problem was noted in Paterson, *supra* note 4 at 82-83 (1982).

21. Jacob, *supra* note 1 at 12.

22. The Court of Appeal is not the only court to recognize the inefficiency of the oral tradition. In 1987 the Commercial Court, a part of the Queen's Bench Division of the High Court, imposed limits on the length of certain types of hearings and required counsel to submit estimates of the length of the hearings, but not to exceed the maximum set by the court order. Practice and Procedure Note, *Time - Limits in the Commercial Court*, 7 Civil Justice

Q. 1 (1988). It also required written submission by counsel in advance of a hearing.

23. The description of an opening statement by counsel in C. Hare, *Tragedy at Law* 69 (1942) (reprinted in C. Hare, *Murder in the Court* (1988), seems appropriate here. "Flack, an earnest middle-aged man with a particularly ugly voice, occupied the whole morning with his opening. This consisted ... in repeating in various tones of emphasis the words of a section of an Act of Parliament which appeared to have been composed by an illiterate with a talent for obscurity, and reading passages from judgments in other cases on other acts which seemed to have no bearing on the matter whatever." Hare is the pseudonym of Alfred Alexander Gordon Clark, a barrister who later served as a county court judge.

24. Similar observations were made by a former legal correspondent of the London *Times* who, during a 1979 labor dispute that prevented publication of his newspaper, sat in court proceedings to observe the competency of barristers. His findings were that "many young barristers seemed incapable of forming a grammatically correct English sentence . . . . Much more distressing was the poor, sometimes inexcusable standard of presentation of the lay client's case." Berlins, New Law J. 1117 (November 15, 1979) quoted in M. Zander, *A Matter of Justice* 75-76 (1988).

25. As the late Justice Robert Jackson of the United States Supreme Court, commented "One of the first tests of a discriminating advocate is to select the question, or questions that he will present orally. Legal contentions, like the currency, depreciate through over-issue . . . . receptiveness declines as the number of assigned errors increases . . . . multiplying assignments of error will dilute and weaken a good case and will not save a bad one." Jackson, *Advocacy Before the U.S. Supreme Court*, 37 Cornell L. Rev. 1, 5 (1951). The same advice is given to English advocates by a Queen's Counsel in Janner, *A Matter of Presentation*, Counsel 22 (June/July, 1989).

26. *Jones v. Barnes*, 463 U.S. 745 (1983).

27. Note, *Court of Appeal of Procedure*, 8 Civil Justice Q. 201 (1989). A Queen's Counsel recently recited his experiences at observing other barristers during his earlier days at the bar. "While some counsel were charming, articulate and at ease ... well-structured in their approach and maintaining eye contact with judges ... others 'ummed' and 'erred', mumbled and bumbled. Some projected their voices and enunciated their words. Too many others spoke with their eyes and their voices down, their sentences long and boring." Janner, *supra* note 25 at 22.

28. The author's assessment of the quality of the American lawyer as an appellate advocate is that approximately 10 to 15% are highly competent, 30 to 40% competent, and 50 to 60% incompetent. Martineau, *Appellate*

Litigation: Its Place in the Law School Curriculum, 39 J. of Legal Education 71, 78 (1989). In a survey conducted in 1987 by Senior U.S. Circuit Judge Myron Bright of chief judges of state intermediate appellate courts on the quality of oral argument in their court gave the following results:

Excellent	14.64%
Good	40.63%
Fair	30.09%
Poor	14.14%

In some major states, such as New York and Michigan, the total of the fair-poor advocates was 65% or higher. (Copy on file with author).

29. It is surprising, in view of the total lack of training in advocacy in the education of barristers, to find that training in advocacy is cited as one of the reasons for limiting rights of audiences to barristers. In *Abse v. Smith* [1985] 1 Q.B. 536, 555 (C.A.), for example, Lord Justice May stated that rights of audience should be limited to those "who have been thoroughly trained and practiced in the skills of advocacy, in the proper and expeditious conduct of litigation and in the law." Barristers have, in fact, been trained in neither of the first two.

30. Command Document 8878 ¶ 574 (1953) quoted in Zander, *supra* note 8 at 325-28.

31. Paterson, *supra* note 4 at 225-26 n.9 quotes a law lord as stating that Justice Frankfurter never read the briefs in advance of oral argument and wasted everyone's time by asking questions that were answered in the briefs.

32. Zander, *supra* note 7 at 535.

33. Zander, *supra* note 8 at 328-29.

34. Report of the Working Party on the Work of the Court of Appeal ¶ 6 (December, 1978) (unpublished, copy on file with the author).

35. [1982] 1 All E.R. 1024, 1026.

36. Mann, *Reflections on English Civil Justice and the Rule of Law*, 2 Civil Justice Q. 320 (1983).

37. Id. at 324.

38. Id. at 335. Chief Justice Rehnquist of the United States Supreme Court has noted the difference between the open mindedness of ignorance and that of impartiality. W. Rehnquist, *The Supreme Court* 277 (1987).

39. Littman, in *Written Briefs and Oral Advocacy*, in Papers delivered at the Program on Judicial Techniques In Litigation and Arbitration, London, November 30, 1987 at 107 (copy on file with the author).

40. Id. at 117.

41. Lord Wilberforce, id. at 120, 129.

42. Note, *Judicial Techniques in Arbitration and Litigation*, 7 Civil Justice Q. 204, 205 (1988).

43. Blom-Cooper & Drewry, *supra* note 1 at 401-02. Also see the discussion in Paterson, *supra* note 8 at 183-89. Criticizing the development is Mann, *supra* note 36 at 328-30.

44. R. Leflar, *Internal Operating Procedures of Appellate Courts* 36-40 (1976).

45. Although in English Court of Appeal the parties must still purchase copies of judgments delivered extemporaneously from the Shorthand Writers' Association.

46. Andrews, *The Passive Court and Legal Argument*, 7 Civil Justice Q. 125 (1988).

47. R. Evershed, *The Court of Appeal in England* 14-16 (1950).

48. Eddey, *supra* note 10 at 249.

49. D. Karlen, *Appellate Courts in the United States and England* 100 (1962).

50. R. Walker, *supra* note 8 at 132-33.

51. *Stanley v. International Harvester Co. of Great Britain, Ltd.,* (1983) *The Times,* 7 February, as noted in R. Walker, *supra* note 8 at 133.

52. Mueller, Unpublished Opinion Study, 1 State Court J. 23 (Summer, 1977); Wisconsin State Bar Committee on Administration of Justice and the Judiciary, Final Report, 57 Wis. Bar. Bull. 40 (August, 1984).

53. Robel, *The Myth of the Disposable Opinion: Unpublished Opinions and Government Litigants in the United States Courts of Appeals*, 87 Michi-

gan L. Rev. 940 (1989); Songer, Smith, and Sheehan, *Nonpublication in the Eleventh Circuit: An Empirical Analysis,* 16 Florida State L. Rev. 963 (1989); Honeysberg and Dikel, *Unfairness in Access to and Citation of Unpublished Federal Court Decisions,* 18 Golden Gate U. L. Rev. 277 (1988); Steinstra, *Unpublished Dispositions: Problems of Access and Use in the Courts of Appeals* (1985).

54. 42. E.g. U.S. Court of Appeals for the Seventh Circuit, Circuit Rule 53(d)(3); Wisconsin Supreme Court, Rule of Appellate Procedure 809.23(4).

55. Recommended standards are found in Advisory Council on Appellate Justice, Standards for Publication of Opinions 5-8 (1973). The U.S. Judicial Conference has required each U.S. Court of Appeals to adopt a plan for publication of opinions.

56. Eddey, *supra* note 10 at 259.

57. See the authorities cited in note 52, *supra.*

Chapter 4 Coping with Increased Caseloads

A. Caseload Growth and Responses

1. England

a. Caseload Growth

The number of appeals taken to the Court of Appeal has not changed dramatically over the years. Prior to 1982 the Court of Appeal did not keep any statistics of its own and the only available statistics are those prepared and published by the Lord Chancellor's Department. These statistics, along with those of other courts, are included in an annual report entitled "Judicial Statistics." According to these reports, the number of appeals set down in 1952 was 848, 749 in 1960, and 690 in 1961. The report also includes a statistic on the number of appeals terminated after hearing. This figure is misleading, however, because the number includes separate appeals by individual parties in the same case even though for all practical purposes all of the appeals are treated as a single appeal and have only one bundle, are heard together, and are covered by the same judgment. It is for this reason that the figures for appeals filed and terminated in the U.S. courts of appeals are adjusted to eliminate the effect of multiple appeals in the same case. The most accurate statistic of the productivity of the court, comes from the number of transcripts of Court of Appeal judgments filed each year in the Supreme Court library. According to L. Blom-Cooper and G. Drewry, the number of transcripts for 1961 was 475. The average for the years 1951-68 was 432 with no trend upward.[1] K. Eddey counted the transcripts in the 1970's and found the number of transcripts did increase; 1972--508, 1973--586, 1974--620, 1975--

772.[2] In 1986, by actual count by the author, the number of transcripts was 884.

Beginning in 1983, the Master of the Rolls has issued an annual review of the work of the Court of Appeal including statistical data, the efforts of the court to reduce its backlog, and prospects for the future. These annual reviews are an invaluable source of data and information about the appellate process in the Court of Appeal. Availability of the reviews is limited but the author has been provided with a copy of each of the six that have been issued prior to 1989.

The gross figures for filings, terminations, terminations after hearings and pending appeals, for the period October 1-September 30, for the years 1983-1988 in the annual reviews of the Master of Rolls show the following:

	SetDown	Terminated	Terminated on Merits	Pending
1982-83	1437	1633	1055	924
1983-84	1449	1406	1001	974
1984-85	1570	1547	1123	943
1985-86	1604	1581	1207	953
1986-87	1573	1500	1162	954
1987-88	1568	1532	1104	977

As can be seen from the above statistics the caseload of the Court of Appeal has been steady except for one substantial increase in 1984-85. Comparing 1961 to 1987 the total filings increased from 690 to 1573, an increase of 883 or 128%. The number of transcripts went from 475 in 1961 to 884 in 1986, an increase of 410 or 86%.

b. Responses

The idea that an appellate court and its judges had any responsibility, beyond deciding the merits of appeals and developing the law, played no part in the appellate process in England until late 1982. The philosophy that had prevailed since the origins of the adversary system--the responsibility for moving cases through the system up to the point they were heard by a panel of judges was solely that of the parties and in particular their legal representatives--was accepted without question. There were no statistics on how long it took cases to move through the system because only the lawyers and not the courts were concerned with the pace of litigation, and they were concerned only with their own cases, not other cases. If the system did not move fast enough to suit the demands of justice in a particular appeal, the lawyers could ask that the appeal be expedited. So long as the system could accommodate the individual requests, there was no reason to suspect that it was not performing adequately in meeting the needs of litigants and the public. Statistics were kept only on the number of appeals set down, terminated, and pending at the end of each year. When the first and the last figures increased substantially, then it was time to add new judges.

The length of delay finally became so long that an institutional response was necessary. In 1978 Lord Denning, the Master of the Rolls appointed a committee with Lord Scarman as chairman. It studied the problem of delay in the Court of Appeal. The committee in its report found three major defects in the current system:

(1) uninformative notices of appeal;

(2) bundles not filed in a usable form or in a timely manner; and

(3) absence of a central control over the progress of appeals from setting down to hearing.

It made four principal recommendations designed to reduce the amount of wasted time for all participants in the appellate process -- litigants, lawyers, and judges. The recommendations were to appoint a senior lawyer with the status of a master to be responsible for the processing of appeals; allow the new officer or a single judge to rule on procedural applications; impose greater restrictions on the right to appeal to the Court of Appeal; and tighten up the entire appeal process. The committee expressly refused to recommend any change in the oral hearing procedure.[3]

Until 1982, the principal response to the increase in workload was to provide for additional judgeships. The number of judgeships during this period went from 12 (including the Master of the Rolls) to 24 in 1987. The effective number sitting on the Civil Division in 1987 was 20 because there are always 4 assigned to the Criminal Division. As a result of the recommendations of the Scarman Committee, the Supreme Court Act of 1981 was enacted, and amendments made to Order 59, the court rule that governs appeals. Another major event was the appointment of Sir John Donaldson as Master of the Rolls, succeeding Lord Denning who had held the position since 1962. Subsequently, practice statements and directions have been issued by the Court of Appeal, and revisions made in the Court's internal procedures for processing appeals. The principal changes that flowed from the statutory enactment and rule amendments, practice statements and directions, and internal procedure changes prior to 1989 included: requiring leave to appeal for appeals from county courts in which the judgment was for less than half of its maximum jurisdiction; shortening the time for taking an appeal; giving authority to a single Lord Justice or the Registrar of Civil Appeals to hear and decide most applications; moving up the date for the filing of the trial court record with the Court of Appeal from just before the hearing on the appeal to shortly after the filing of the notice of appeal; establishment of a Civil Appeal office; establishment of the position of Registrar of Civil Appeals; centralizing the scheduling of hearings in a single office; adding to the types of cases that could be heard by two judge panels; reading of the appeal papers by the judges in advance of the hearing; suggesting the filing of "skeleton arguments" which are short statements of the points to be argued on appeal by each party; eliminating the reading of reserved judgments in open court; requiring the filing of a chronology of events setting out the basic facts of the case; and establishing a system of "floater" appeals that could be assigned for hearing on short notice.

In his 1987 annual review, the Master of the Rolls concluded that the Court of Appeal had done all that it could on its own to expedite the appellate process. The only additional changes that he could foresee would have to involve additional judges or enlarging the types of appeals that require leave to appeal.

One of the first steps taken in 1982 was to centralize the processing of appeals in a single office. Prior to 1982, notices of appeal were filed with an appeal clerk who was actually part of the Chancery Division of the High Court. His responsibility was to receive the notices of appeal and then to distribute them to the clerk of the presiding judge of the appropriate panel of the Court of Appeal. All applications concerning an appeal were filed with the latter clerk who scheduled them for hearing before the panel. Appeals were scheduled for hearing on the merits only when the solicitors or counsel for the parties notified the presiding judge's clerk that they were ready for the appeal to be heard. The bundles in the appeal were also lodged with the presiding judge's clerk but had to be lodged only seven days before the scheduled date of hearing. Each panel of the court effectively acted as a separate court insofar as the processing and scheduling of hearing of appeals was concerned.

The establishment in 1982 of a Civil Appeals Office and the appointment of a Registrar of Civil Appeals with overall responsibility for the processing and scheduling of appeals, the keeping of records, and the development of statistical data were radical changes from prior practice. It now became the responsibility of a single official of the Court of Appeal to ensure that litigants and their legal representatives complied with the requirements of the rules both as to what was done and when it was done. Each appeal was monitored and if the appellant did not respond to notices of default, the appeal was dismissed, but only after a hearing was held to give the appellant one last chance to explain his default. The scheduling of the hearings of appeals was also centralized in the Listing Office. This is part of the Civil Appeals Office and operates under the direct supervision of the Registrar. The Registrar was also given jurisdiction over most applications concerned with the processing of appeals prior to hearing on the merits. The only aspects of processing appeals, up to the point they are ready to be heard on the merits, that were still left almost entirely to counsel were when the hearing on the merits would be held and how long the hearing would last.

Notwithstanding the statement in his 1987 annual review that the Court of Appeal had done all that it could do on its own to increase its productivity, the Master of the Rolls established in 1988 a working party within the Court to study the matter further. Based on the recommendations of the working party, the Court, in March, 1989, issued a Practice Direction making further changes in the appellate process in the court.

The Practice Direction, which became effective in June, 1989, and is set out in full in Appendix C, represents another major step in court control of the pace of the appellate process. The filing of a skeleton argument and a chronology of events was made mandatory, and it must be filed at least four weeks prior to the scheduled hearing date. The court will employ legal staff, part of whose duties will include advising the court on how long the hearing of an appeal should take and scheduling cases accordingly. Most appeals will be given a fixed hearing date rather than simply a range of dates on which it could be heard. The length of the hearing will be set by the court, and not dependant solely upon the estimates submitted by counsel.

The nature of the oral hearing itself will be changed. The judges will read in advance, at a minimum, the judgment of the trial court, the notice of appeal, the chronology of events, and the skeleton argument, plus any other papers the judges think useful. The appellant is directed not to recite the facts but "to proceed immediately to the ground of appeal which is in the forefront of the appellant's case." Further, in citing an authority that is included in the skeleton argument, counsel are not to read the case at length, but only the most relevant passages. Similarly, when referring to facts in a transcript, the testimony should not be read at length because having been referred to in the skeleton argument, the judges will have read it in advance.

The whole thrust of the changes introduced by the Practice Direction is to reduce the length of each oral hearing to permit the court to hear and dispose of more cases. In the introduction by the Master of the Rolls to the Practice Direction, the relationship between the length of the oral hearing, the number of appeals the court can dispose of, and the effect of both of these on other litigants whose appeals are waiting to be heard is recognized. Most significant, the court has accepted the responsibility for taking measures to control the length of the oral hearing and not leave it solely to counsel, to increase the court's "productivity", and thereby reduce the delay in disposing of cases.

2. United States

a. Caseload Growth

It has been accurately observed that the controlling influence in the appellate process in the United States today is volume.[4] The growth in the caseloads of appellate courts, both federal and state, since 1960 almost defies comprehension.

Particularly overwhelming are the statistics for the United States courts of appeals. In fiscal 1961 (July 1, 1960-June 30, 1961) a total of 4204 appeals were filed, 4049 were terminated, and 2806 were terminated by court decision. In fiscal 1987 the comparable figures were 35,176, 34,444, and 18,502. These represent percentage increases in 27 years of 737, 751, and 559. During the same period the number of judgeships in regional federal courts of appeals was raised from 68 to 156, an increase of only 129%.[5]

Individual courts of appeals had even more dramatic increases. The Fifth Circuit, which includes much of the southern part of the United States, went from 630 appeals filed in 1961 to 8176 in 1987, an increase of 1198%. For the Ninth Circuit, which covers the western United States, the same period showed an increase from 443 to 5652, a 1176% growth.

The overall statistics for the states are not as easy to ascertain because there was no uniform system of record keeping for the states over the entire period.[6] One study has concluded that the number of appeals began to increase substantially in the 1960's and the rapid growth has continued unabated since that time. Statistics available from 43 states showed an increase from 1973 to 1983 of 112%.[7] Some states had substantially greater increases. In Connecticut it was 265%, Florida and Kentucky 186%, and Oregon 212%. Three states for which statistics over a longer period are available are Maryland, Michigan, and Wisconsin. All of them established intermediate appellate courts during this period--Michigan in 1965, Maryland in 1966, and Wisconsin in 1978. Between 1961 and 1987 the number of appeals in Maryland went from 356 to 1754, or 392%, Michigan from 1235 to 8186, or 563%, and Wisconsin from 331 to 2406, or 627%.[8] The total number of appeals filed in state appellate courts in 1985 was approximately 225,000. The total figure for federal and state courts was over 255,000.

b. Responses

Efforts to cope with these staggering increases in caseload included structural, personnel, and procedural changes. The most significant structural changes were the establishment of intermediate courts of appeals in states that previously had only trial courts and a state supreme court. In 1960, 14 states had intermediate appellate courts while by 1988 this number had risen to 37. The change usually occurred when it was clear that the state supreme court's caseload had reached the point where it was spending so much time on error correction issues that it did not have adequate time to devote to its law development function and the length of time it took to hear and decide cases was excessive.

The personnel changes were of two principal types; additional judges and additional staff. An initial response to increased volume in some states was to enlarge the state supreme court. This was found to be unsuccessful even in the short term because of the fact that these courts almost always sat *en banc,* that is with their entire membership. Additional judges meant the opinion writing workload could be divided among a larger number of judges, but the involvement of additional judges in the decision making and opinion writing process made the net improvement in the decision making capacity of the court marginal at best. Additional judges at the intermediate court level did, however, greatly expand the ability of a particular court to dispose of cases because these courts sat in three judge panels rather than *en banc*. Each additional judge on one of these courts is, consequently, an absolute increase in the court's ability to handle more cases. Increased judges, even on a court that sits in three judge panels, creates problems of its own.[9]

The increased use of staff to assist the judges in their judicial functions has been dramatic and, in the case of central staff, controversial. The tradition of a personal law clerk for a judge was well established and thus when courts that did not have law clerks added them, or when one law clerk per judge was increased to two, there were few complaints. When the number of personal law clerks went to three or four per judge, as they did in a few courts, some concerns were raised. There was concern that the judges became more like office managers with diminished personal responsibility for their decisions and opinions.

Even more substantial questions were raised when courts began employing central staff attorneys who served the entire court and not a particular judge. These staff attorneys were given a variety of duties including screening cases for oral argument or for summary disposition, recommending action to be taken on motions, preparing draft opinions for appeals decided without oral argument, and screening prisoner petitions. Some observers feared that these central staff could become a court unto itself with no public accountability and little supervision by the judges. While these concerns have not been totally eliminated, the worst fear--that the judges would lose control over the decision making process and be manipulated by their staffs--have certainly not been realized. Personal law clerks and central staff attorneys are now accepted features of the appellate process.

In addition to structural and personnel changes, which required legislative approval or funding, the appellate courts themselves adopted a wide variety of procedural changes designed to enable the courts to dispose of more cases in a shorter period of time as well as to make the cost of taking or defending an appeal less expensive. These changes included: shortening the time in which an appeal could be taken; expediting the preparation of the record on appeal, including the transcript of testimony; expressly placing in the appellate court control over the appeal as soon as the notice of appeal was filed; shortening the length of briefs and simplifying their form; eliminating printing requirements for the briefs and appendix; establishing a procedure for the parties to discuss settlement of the appeal under the auspices of the appellate court; considering summary disposition of appeals either at the initiative of a party or the court itself; shortening or eliminating oral argument; disposing of appeals with no opinion or a short unpublished opinion; imposing sanctions for taking an appeal found to be frivolous or for taking or not taking any other step without a reasonable basis or with an improper motive; and using staff to assist with both administrative and judicial activities.

What has occurred in the appellate process in the United States as a result of the crisis of volume can fairly be described as revolutionary.[10] Underlying this revolution was a recognition by appellate judges that restructuring the appellate courts or adding new judges were not ultimate solutions. If the capacity of appellate courts to dispose of large numbers of additional appeals were to be increased, the judges themselves would have to develop the solutions. This they did, with the result that the per judge disposition rate increased dramatically while the median time for the disposition of appeals was shortened or at least not substantially lengthened.

Of all of the changes that have occurred in the appellate process in the United States as a result of the crisis of volume, the one that is central and from which all of the others flow concerns the responsibility for moving appeals through the system. Until the 1960's, the consensus among both appellate judges and lawyers was that under the adversary system this responsibility was solely that of the parties and their lawyers and that the appellate court played little or no role in it. In practice, this meant that the responsibility for getting the appeal ready to be heard was exercised by the lawyers. The role of the appellate court was simply to perform its review functions when called upon to do so by the lawyers. The presumption was that the lawyers would act in the best interests of their clients and that the very nature of the adversary system would move an appeal expeditiously from one step in the appellate process to the next and ultimately to its disposition.

When courts began to develop statistical data and to analyze their processes in order to identify the principal causes of delay in the disposition of appeals, they found that the adversary system did not ensure that appeals would move through the system expeditiously. They discovered, rather, that virtually everyone in the system--lawyers, trial court clerks, court reporters, appellate court staff, and appellate judges themselves acted without regard to the effect of their actions on the total length of time it took for the disposition of an appeal. Each individual acted in response to pressures, but the pressures were seldom directed at prompt disposition of the appeal. Trial court personnel were more concerned with proceedings in the trial court; lawyers had other cases and clients to worry about; the appellate judges were primarily concerned with the substantive issues involved in the appeals presented to them; and appellate court staff dealt only with isolated steps in the process and no one person was given overall responsibility for monitoring the progress of individual appeals through the system. In addition there was usually one party whose interests were favored by delay. The combination of these factors and a greatly increasing caseload created enormous delays. It was not unusual to take two to three years to move from judgment in the trial court to disposition in the appellate court.

Another factor that made matters worse was psychological-- it was found that delay begets delay. When it became known that there were lengthy delays in the process, each person in the system who had the responsibility for taking an action could always justify postponing doing so because a little more delay added to a lot of other delay would not make much difference. The cumulative effect of this attitude simply made a bad situation much worse. There was also a suspicion that delay itself generated additional appeals when it was advantageous to the appellant to postpone enforcement of the judgement as long as possible.

At the heart of all of the changes made to combat delay was the decision by judges on one appellate court after another that the appellate courts themselves would have to take responsibility for the processing of appeals through the system. They found that unless the appellate court actively supervised the preparation of the record, the transcript of testimony, and the briefs, the result would be substantial delay. The commentary to Section 3.50 of the ABA Standards Relating to Appellate Delay Reduction (now part of the ABA Standards Relating to Appellate Courts) states that "Delay in appellate litigation is rarely the result of a single cause. . . . The first and most important is that appellate courts generally have exercised inadequate supervision of the movement of cases coming before them." At the same time, the courts became aware of the necessity for monitoring their own performance to ensure that the judges and the court staff were not themselves the cause of delay. These supervisory and monitoring activities became known as active case management. The changes made affected not only what lawyers, clerks of court, and court reporters did in preparing an appeal for submission to the court and when they did them, but also the entire process the court used to decide the appeal and announce its decision. The goals were to have the appeals ready for consideration by the court as soon as possible and to eliminate from the review process in individual cases those steps not necessary for an adequate consideration of the issues raised by the parties.

Just as important as the changes that were made were those not made. Only a few suggested that the taking of an appeal should become contingent upon the approval of either the trial judge or the appellate court and these suggestions gained little support.[11] No one suggested making an appeal so expensive as to discourage all but the richest and most persistent litigants. Even more remarkable were the efforts to reduce the expense of taking an appeal, particularly by eliminating printing requirements for the record, the appendix, and the briefs in the full knowledge that this would likely add to the growth in the number of appeals. The right to at least one appeal from a final judgment remained an important feature of the judicial process in every jurisdiction but three.

B. Efficiency

The efficiency of an appellate court in performing its functions can best be measured in two ways:

(1) by the number of appeals per judge terminated after hearing or submission on briefs and

(2) the time it takes for appeals to move through the appellate process from the filing of the notice of appeal to the final decision of the appellate court and between intermediate steps in the process.

The effect of the increase in caseload upon efficiency can be ascertained by comparing the data for 1961 with that for 1987. The specific points at which delay occurs can also be identified.

1. England

In the Court of Appeal in 1961 the number of dispositions on the merits (i.e. the number of transcripts) was 475. With 9 judges this was a per judge disposition rate of 52.7. In 1986, the comparable figures were 743 dispositions on the merits, 19.5 judges (one judge was appointed in the middle of the year), and a disposition rate of 38.1 per judge.[12] There are no published statistics on median time span from filing of the notice of appeal to disposition for all cases decided by the Court of Appeal. The only statistics that have been published have been in the 1984 and 1986 annual reviews of the Master of the Rolls. These show that while the cases that are given priority can be heard very quickly, the appeals in cases that make up the heart of any appellate court's caseload--appeals from final judgments and orders--the delay ranged from 12 to 18 months depending upon the court from which the appeal was taken. In attempting to determine how much of this time is attributed to the court and not to the parties, the most significant period is the period between when the appeal is ready to be heard and the time of hearing or submission, not the overall time from filing of notice of appeal to appellate court judgment. During this period no one is doing anything and the case is merely waiting to be scheduled. In the Court of Appeal only 1.4 months of the 12 to 18 month delay is attributable to filing of the bundles, and thus the balance of the 10.6 to 16.6 months is spent waiting for the appeal to be heard.[13]

2. United States

In 1961 with 68 judgeships on the United States courts of appeals and a total of 2,691 dispositions after hearing or submission, the per judge disposition rate was 39.6. During fiscal 1987, these courts terminated 18,502 cases after hearing or submission on briefs, that is on the merits and after full consideration. With 156 active judges, this gives a per judge disposition rate of 118.5. In some circuits it was almost 200 per judge. In some states it is even higher. In the Michigan Court of Appeals, for example, the figure was 232 per judge in 1987-88.

In measuring time, the statistics for the United States courts of appeals as developed by the Administrative Office of the U.S. Courts are used.[14] These are the only courts for which these types of statistics have been published for the entire period. The statistics measure the median time interval between each recorded step. The median rather than the mean is recognized as a more accurate measure of the average because it is only minimally affected by major aberrations.

For all circuits for all cases in 1987, the median time interval from the filing of the notice of appeal to final disposition in the court of appeals was 10.3 months. In civil cases only, the interval was 11.0 months.

The median time intervals between each major step in the appellate process for all circuits and for each circuit for all cases and for civil appeals only are as follows:

U.S. COURTS OF APPEALS
MEDIAN TIME INTERVALS IN CASES TERMINATED AFTER HEARING OR SUBMISSION, BY CIRCUIT DURING THE TWELVE MONTH PERIOD ENDED JUNE 30, 1987

CIRCUIT	FROM FILING NOTICE OF APPEAL TO FILING LAST BRIEF INTERVAL (MONTHS)	FROM FILING LAST BRIEF TO HEARING OR SUBMISSION INTERVAL (MONTHS)	FROM HEARING TO FINAL DISPOSITION INTERVAL (MONTHS)	FROM SUBMISSION TO FINAL DISPOSITION INTERVAL (MONTHS)	FROM FILING NOTICE OF APPEAL TO FINAL DISPOSITION
		ALL CASES			
TOTAL	4.7	2.9	2.8	1.1	10.3
DISTRICT OF COLUMBIA	5.3	3.6	3.3	.4	12.7
FIRST	3.9	1.6	2.8	1.6	8.7
SECOND	3.4	.7	1.2		
THIRD	3.7	3.2	1.5	.3	8.2
FOURTH	4.5	2.4	3.0	1.7	8.2
FIFTH	4.8	2.4	3.0	1.2	8.8
SIXTH	4.8	5.6	1.6	1.1	12.0
SEVENTH	4.2	2.8	4.7	.9	11.7
EIGHTH	3.2	3.4	2.8	1.1	8.3
NINTH	6.5	3.6	2.5	1.1	14.1
TENTH	6.0	4.6	4.6	1.0	16.1
ELEVENTH	5.3	2.1	3.8	1.5	10.3

U.S. COURTS OF APPEALS
MEDIAN TIME INTERVALS IN CASES TERMINATED AFTER HEARING OR SUBMISSION, BY CIRCUIT DURING THE TWELVE MONTH PERIOD ENDED JUNE 30, 1987

CIRCUIT	FROM FILING NOTICE OF APPEAL TO FILING LAST BRIEF INTERVAL (MONTHS)	FROM FILING LAST BRIEF TO HEARING OR SUBMISSION INTERVAL (MONTHS)	FROM HEARING TO FINAL DISPOSITION INTERVAL (MONTHS)	FROM SUBMISSION TO FINAL DISPOSITION INTERVAL (MONTHS)	FROM FILING NOTICE OF APPEAL TO FINAL DISPOSITION INTERVAL (MONTHS)
			CIVIL		
TOTAL	4.5	3.2	2.9	1.2	11.0
DISTRICT OF COLUMBIA	5.3	5.1	3.7	.3	13.5
FIRST	3.7	1.7	2.8	1.8	8.4
SECOND	3.2	.8	1.7	.4	6.2
THIRD	3.6	3.3	1.5	.3	8.2
FOURTH	4.3	2.4	3.0	1.8	10.3
FIFTH	4.6	2.7	3.3	1.4	9.2
SIXTH	4.6	6.1	1.7	1.5	13.0
SEVENTH	3.9	3.0	4.7	.9	11.6
EIGHTH	3.2	3.7	3.0	1.2	9.6
NINTH	6.7	3.7	2.7	1.2	14.9
TENTH	6.2	7.8	5.9	1.1	19.5
ELEVENTH	4.4	2.3	3.5	1.6	9.8

U.S. COURTS OF APPEALS
MEDIAN TIME INTERVALS IN CASES TERMINATED AFTER HEARING OR SUBMISSION DURING THE FISCAL YEAR ENDING JUNE 30, 1961

CIRCUIT	FROM FILING OF COMPLETE RECORD TO FILING LAST BRIEF INTERVAL (MONTHS)	FROM FILING LAST BRIEF TO HEARINGS OR SUBMISSION INTERVAL (MONTHS)	FROM HEARING OR SUBMISSION TO FINAL DISPOSITION INTERVAL (MONTHS)	FROM FILING OF COMPLETE RECORD TO FINAL DISPOSITION INTERVAL (MONTHS)
TOTAL	3.7	0.8	1.5	6.8
DISTRICT OF COLUMBIA	3.3	.7	1.6	6.6
FIRST	3.1	.4	1.6	5.0
SECOND	3.7	.1	1.4	5.9
THIRD	2.7	1.0	1.7	5.9
FOURTH	2.7	.4	1.7	5.2
FIFTH	3.3	.9	1.6	6.9
SIXTH	4.5	2.5	.8	8.8
SEVENTH	4.1	.7	1.1	6.5
EIGHTH	3.9	.5	2.6	7.6
NINTH	5.4	1.8	1.6	9.5
TENTH	3.2	.5	1.5	5.7

An exact comparison between all of the steps between 1961 and 1987 is not possible because the identical statistics were not computed and published at that time. For the median time interval for all cases the measuring period in 1961 began with the filing of the complete record in the court of appeals rather than the filing of the notice of appeal in the trial court. Nonetheless the time intervals for the steps after the filing of the record can be compared.

For civil cases only, the median time interval from the filing of the notice of appeal to the filing of the complete record was computed in 1961. These show the following:

	INTERVAL (MONTHS)
TOTAL	1.3
DISTRICT OF COLUMBIA	1.3
FIRST	1.2
SECOND	1.2
THIRD	1.2
FOURTH	1.3
FIFTH	2.4
SIXTH	1.3
SEVENTH	1.3
EIGHTH	1.3
NINTH	1.9
TENTH	1.7

If the 1.3 months for the period from the filing of the notice of appeal of the filing of the record in civil cases is added to the 6.8 months from the filing of the complete record to final disposition in all cases, a median time period in civil cases from filing of the notice of appeal to final disposition of 8.1 months can be approximated.

A step by step comparison between 1961 and 1987 shows the following:

	Filing Notice of Appeal to filing last brief	Filing of last brief to hearing or submission	From hearing or submission to disposition	From filing of notice of appeal to disposition
1961	5.0	0.8	1.5	8.1
1987	4.7	2.9	1.9	11.0

As can be seen, the only significant difference is the increase from 1961 to 1987 in the period from the filing of the last brief to hearing or submission, an increase of 2.1 months.

The median time interval from hearing or submission in 1987, 1.9 months, is misleading because it combines both cases in which oral argument is heard and those submitted only on briefs. Cases in which oral argument is heard took a median time of 2.8 months, while those submitted on briefs take only 1.1 months. This reflects the fact that the appeals scheduled for oral argument are usually more difficult and writing these opinions takes more time.

As noted in the previous section, the only time that can properly be classified as delay in the appellate process for which the appellate court is responsible is the period between when the case is ready for submission and when the case is actually heard or submitted on briefs. This is dead time in which nothing is being done by either the lawyers or the court or its staff. There is a great variation among the circuits, from 5.6 months in the Sixth Circuit to .7 months in the Second Circuit, with the median for all circuits 2.9 months.

C. Comparison

The responses of the English and American appellate systems to increased caseloads have both major similarities and differences. Both have used additional judges as a primary and initial response. The Americans discovered early on, however, that additional judges would never be more than a partial solution and that it was necessary at the same time to increase the productivity of judges. They also realized that they would have to monitor closely the processing of cases through the system to identify points at which delay occurred and its causes. This was accomplished by employing additional staff, both legal and clerical, to assist the judges, revising internal procedures, providing for settlement conferences, exercising active control over the processing of cases, reducing the time allowed for oral argument or eliminating it, limiting publication of opinions or eliminating opinions in selected cases, among others. The effect of all of these changes has been to increase dramatically the number of appeals per judge that an American appellate court can decide on the merits while at the same time speeding up the processing of cases or at least preventing substantial delays from developing.

The English system has relied on two major changes not utilized in the United States--sitting in two judge panels and requiring leave to appeal in certain types of cases--in addition to adding new judges. It has also tightened up the time limits for taking an appeal and lodging bundles. It originally requested but did not mandate the filing of skeleton arguments and chronologies of events. Judges of the Court of Appeal now spend one day per week prereading certain portions of the bundles, skeleton arguments, and chronologies of events to become familiar with the facts of an appeal before the oral hearing. The purpose of the prereading is to permit counsel to dispense with the reading of items from the bundles to establish the factual background of the appeal. The position of Registrar of Civil Appeals was created to supervise the processing of appeals and to rule on most applications. A central clerk's office for the Court of Appeal was also established. Some case management measures have also been adopted. The key elements of the oral tradition, however, remained until 1989--unlimited oral argument held when counsel agree to it, extemporaneous judgments rendered by the judges relying solely on the submissions of counsel without additional research or staff assistance, and with the judges playing no part in deciding which of the judgments will be published.

Of all of the changes made in the American system, the one most subject to challenge is the elimination of the written opinion in some appeals, particularly as a device to preserve oral argument in all or most appeals. This change eliminates from the appellate process the principal guarantor of the accountability of the judges for their decisions as well as the principal guarantor of the correctness of the decisions themselves. Without being forced to the discipline of justifying a decision in writing, the likelihood of sloppy thinking or the overlooking of a key fact or precedent is much more likely. Just as important, the principal check on whether one of these evils occurred is for the attorneys for the parties and other members of the legal public to review the written opinion and to call attention to errors in it. Without the written opinion, this essential review is precluded.

The English responses to increased volume are suspect both from the standpoint of some of the changes made and some not made. Eliminating the right to appeal from final orders in certain classes of cases is unwise because the importance of an appeal to the litigant or to the law does not depend upon the amount of money involved or the court from which the appeal is taken. Further, allowing the right to appeal to be denied upon the unreviewable decision of a single judge without a hearing not only destroys the appearance of justice, it undercuts the basic principle that appellate review should be by a panel of judges and not just a different judge.

Having certain classes of appeals heard by a two judge rather than a three judge panel is again suspect for the same reason as taking away the right to appeal in certain classes of cases--there is no relationship between the type of appeal and the importance of the appeal. Even more important is the different nature of a group of two as a deliberative body compared to a group composed of three.[15] The range of views, the extent of discussion, the nature of discussion, and the possibility of disagreement are all substantially less with two judges than with three. It is for this reason that the Standards for Appellate Courts adopted by the American Bar Association[16] provide for appellate panels to be composed of three judges and why only one American court has ever adopted two judge panels as a means of coping with increased caseloads. That there is a difference between the two types of panels is indicated by the fact that there are almost no reported instances of a disagreement between the initial two judges that resulted in the appeal having to be reheard by a three judge panel.[17]

The Master of the Rolls indicated in his 1987 annual review that the judges of the Court of Appeal had concluded that they had exhausted the internal changes that could be made to increase the productivity of the judges and that the only remedies open were more judges and putting further restrictions on the right to appeal. This reaction stemmed in large part from the fact that all of the changes made since 1982, including two judge panels, had virtually no impact upon the backlog -- it was the same in October, 1987 as in October, 1983, with only a 10% increase in filings and terminations. The increase in the number of appeals that could be heard as a result of the changes made during the period was offset by the reduction in sitting for each judge from five days to four days per week, a cut back of 20%.

The relative success of the two systems in responding to the crisis of volume best can be measured by comparing

(1) each system's per judge disposition rate in 1961 and 1986;

(2) each system's per judge disposition rate in 1961 and 1986;

(3) each system's median time span for the disposition of appeals in 1961 and 1986; and

(4) each system's median time span for the disposition of appeals.

Using the data for the U.S. courts of appeals, the per judge disposition rate in 1961 was 39.6 while in 1986 was 118.5, an increase of 199%. In the English Court of Appeal the rate was 52.7 in 1961 but dropped to 38.1 per judge in 1986, a decrease of 27.7%. In 1961 the English judges decided 33% more appeals per judge than the American judges but in 1986-87, the Americans were disposing of appeals at a rate over three times that of the English.

Between 1961 and 1987, the median time interval from filing the notice of appeal to final disposition in the federal courts of appeals went from 8.1 months to 11 months for civil cases. There are no comparable statistics for the English Court of Appeal in 1961, but in 1986 it ranged from 12 to 18 months. Approximating 15 months as an average, this is almost 5 months longer than in the United States.

These statistics made it clear that the productivity of English appellate judges will not increase substantially until measures are adopted that will permit the judges to use their time more efficiently. The American experience indicates that this would require providing the judges with additional legal and secretarial staff and, just as important, reducing the amount of time spent in court on each appeal, in other words reducing the length of oral argument in each case. The March, 1989, Practice Direction was the first step to this end and offers the opportunity for an increase in the productivity of English judges.

ENDNOTES

1. L. Blom-Cooper & G. Drewry, *Final Appeal* 139-40 (1972).

2. K. Eddey, *The Law Reporting of the Court of Appeal (Civil Division)* 87 (undated thesis, copy on file in the Supreme Court Library, Royal Courts of Justice, London).

3. Report of the Master of the Rolls Working Party on the Work of the Court of Appeal (Civil Division) filed December, 1978. This report was not published. A copy of the report is on file with the author.

4. Tate, *Federal Appellate Advocacy in the 1980's*, 5 Am. J. Trial Adv. 63, 66 (1981).

5. All statistics except percentages relating to the federal courts in this section are taken from the annual reports of the Director of the Administrative Office of the U.S. Courts, published by the federal government.

6. The National Center for State Courts has attempted to solve this problem partially by establishing a system for record keeping and the development of statistics based on those records. It has published eleven reports, the most recent for 1987. These reports are useful, but do not give the far more comprehensive data of the reports on the federal courts. The Center's statistics also suffer because there is no way for the National Center to force states to file reports, comply with reporting guidelines, or to ensure the accuracy of the reports submitted to it or to force compliance with the guidelines it has established for the reports submitted to it by the state courts.

7. Marvell, *Is There an Appeal From the Caseload Deluge?*, 24 Judges' J. 34 (Summer, 1985).

8. These statistics are taken from reports of the clerks of the intermediate appellate court clerks in Maryland, Michigan, and Wisconsin, copies of which are in the possession of the author.

9. These problems are described in Kaufman, *New Remedies for the Next Century of Judicial Reform: Time as the Great Innovator*, 57 Fordham L. Rev. 253, 256-61 (1988). The principal ones are loss of collegiality, decline of coherence and uniformity in the law, and a decline in prestige.

10. For descriptions and discussions of the various changes see P. Carrington, D. Meador, and M. Rosenberg, *Justice on Appeal* (1976); J. Martin & E. Hudson, *Appellate Court Delay* (1981); R. Leflar, *Internal Operating Procedures of Appellate Courts* (1976); Meador, *Appellate Case Management and Design Process*, 61 Virginia L. Rev. 256 (1975); Mills, *Caseload Explosion: The Appellate Response*, 16 John Marshall L. Rev. 1 (1982); Weisberger, *Appellate Courts: The Challenge of Inundation*, 31 American U. L. Rev. 237 (1982), and Martineau, *The Appellate Process in Civil Cases: A Proposed Model*, 63 Marquette L. Rev. 163 (1979). An evaluation of the effectiveness of the various techniques in increasing productivity is made in Marvell and Moody, *The Effectiveness of Measures to Increase Appellate Court Efficiency and Decision Output*, 21 J. of Law Reform 415 (1988).

11. Advocating this approach is Barrow, *The Discretionary Appeal: A Cost Effective Tool of Appellate Justice*, 11 George Mason L. Rev. 31 (1988). For a discussion of proposals to limit the right to appeal, see Carrington, *The Function of the Civil Appeal: A Late-Century View*, 38 South Carolina L. Rev. 411, 429-31 (1987).

12. In order to make a comparison to the United States per judge disposition rate two adjustments have to be made. First, the English figures have to be reduced to eliminate the effect of counting multiple appellants in the same case by multiple appellants and cross appeals. Both of these are included in the English statistics but not the American. Second, the English figures have to be reduced to reflect the fact that approximately one half of the English appeals are decided by two judge panels because all American appeals are decided by three judge panels. According to the 1987 review of the Master of the Rolls the total number of appeals disposed of after hearing in 1986-87 was 1162. Of these 792 or 68% were disposed of by 2 judge panels and 418 or 32% by three judge panels. In his inspection of the 884 transcripts filed in 1986, however, the author found that 427 (48.3%) were decided by two judge panels and 457 (51.7%) were decided by three judge panels. The statistics based on the transcripts will be used because they more accurately reflect actual workload. The first correction is thus made by counting the number of transcripts filed in the Supreme Court Library. For calendar year 1986 the total was 884. The second correction is made by taking the number heard by two judges (48.3% of 884 or 427) and reducing it by 1/3 (427 x 66% or 285). The result of 285 is then added to the number heard by 3 judge panels (285 + 457 or 743) to give the total number of dispositions calculated on the same bases as in the federal courts of appeals and in most state courts in the United States.

13. The Court of Appeal does not publish any statistics on the delay between each step in the appellate process as do the federal courts in the United States. The information necessary to make such calculations is available in the computer in which all of the records of the Court of Appeal are maintained. At the request of the author, data for all of the cases terminated

during calendar 1987 was prepared by the Civil Appeals Office. This data gave for each case the dates on which certain events occurred. This data showed that 1186 appeals were terminated on the merits by court action. Complete data was available only for 769 appeals, but the data was not broken down between interlocutory and final order appeals. For all 769 appeals, the median time from the setting down of the appeal to the lodging of the bundles was 1.4 months and this figure is used in the calculation in the text. It may be that the figure for appeals from final orders may be different but on the data available there is no way to make this determination.

14. The statistics prepared by the Administrative Office are published annually in the Report of the Director of the Administrative Office of the U.S. Courts. The Administrative Office also publishes Management Statistics for United States Courts each year. The statistics in this chapter all come from the annual reports of the director.

15. J. Jacob, *The Fabric of English Civil Justice* 220-21 (1987). The reservations of the Bar to two judge courts have been expressed in an undated memorandum prepared by Peter Scott, Q.C., Chairman of the Bar Council in 1987 (unpublished, copy in the files of the author).

16. American Bar Association Standards relating to Appellate Courts § 3.01(a) (1977).

17. In his 1983 annual review, the Master of the Rolls stated that of the 580 appeals heard by two judge panels, there had been no disagreements between the two judges. In his 1986 annual report, he stated that in the four years the two judge panels had been utilized, there had been disagreements between the two judges only 12 times, a rate of less than one half of one per cent. These figures were used to argue that two judge appeals were not a waste of time because there were so few rehearings. The greater significance of the figures is, however, that the rate of disagreement is so low as to suggest that the two judge panel is little different than one judge panel and thus the reasons for having review by a panel of judges rather than a single judge is lost.

Chapter 5   The Civil Appeals Process

A. England

1. The Appealable Order[1]

The types of orders that can be appealed are described in Chapter 1, section A 3 a. What makes a ruling an order that then becomes appealable is governed by Order 42. Rule 3(1) of Order 42 provides that an order is effective from the day of its date. Part (2) of the same rule provides that the order is dated the day it is "pronounced, given or made" unless otherwise expressly provided. Under Rule 5 of Order 42, an order (referred to in the rule as a judgment) of the Queen's Bench Division is drawn up by the appropriate party, presented to the appropriate officer, who after approving it files it and enters it in the judgment book. The order is sealed with the seal of the court and returned to the party. Rule 6 governs orders of the Chancery Division. Its orders are drawn up by the staff of the court and then filed in the court office.

2. Parties

In Chapter 1, section A 3 c it was noted that actual or potential status as a party in the trial court along with being aggrieved by the order sought to be appealed are the principal requirements to invoke the jurisdiction of the Court of Appeal. The party who first files a notice of appeal is termed the appellant. The person who was benefited by the order and who defends it on appeal is the respondent. A respondent who also wishes to challenge the correctness of the order may do so by seeking to have it varied or to have an order granted in its favor, but the designation of the respondent as such remains the same without the addition of words such as cross-appellant. If there are multiple parties with the same interests each of whom seeks to appeal, each party is designated as an appellant. Although there is nothing expressly stated in the rules or decisions, presumably each party appealing could file a separate notice of appeal or file a joint notice of appeal.

An unusual aspect of appellate practice that flows from the concept of the English appeal as a rehearing is the rule that a notice of appeal may be served on a person who was not a party in the trial court. Permission of the Court of Appeal must first be obtained for this. When a new party is served, the Court of Appeal may grant any relief for or against the party as if it had been a party in the trial court. Permission may also be obtained to serve the notice of appeal on a person who has no legal interest in the proceedings. The person may then be permitted to participate in the appeal hearing subject to whatever limitations the court wishes to impose.

3. Initiating and Perfecting the Appeal

a. The Notice of Appeal

The taking of an appeal is begun by the service of a notice of appeal by the appellant. As to the notion of appeal and all subsequent steps, they are the responsibility of each party's solicitor unless the party is unrepresented. The barrister becomes involved only in connection with the skeleton argument and the hearing. Technically Rule 3 of Order 59 provides that the appeal is brought by motion and the notice of the motion is referred to as a notice of appeal. There is no required form of the notice but it must give the following specifics:

(1) the order against which the appeal is taken;

(2) the grounds of appeal;

(3) the precise form of the order sought from the Court of Appeal;

(4) the list in which the appeal is to be set down.

The notice must be signed by the appellant. A practice direction also requires the notice to state that no notice of the hearing will be given but that the respondent is required to stay informed of the status of the case. The Court of Appeal may strike a notice that does not contain the required information but, more likely, the appellant will be permitted to amend the notice.

The requirement that the grounds for the appeal be set forth in the notice creates the most problems. The question always arises as to how specific the notice must be. The court has indicated that grounds should be stated shortly and simply and that particulars are not required. The most significant effect of the statement of the grounds for appeal is that a ground not set forth in the notice may not be argued at the hearing without permission from the court. This requires the appellant and his legal advisors to think out very quickly the basis for the appeal, perhaps before the transcript of testimony is prepared. It is, however, permissable to indicate at the end of the notice that the appellant reserves the right to add additional grounds when the transcript is available, but such a statement does not obviate the necessity for obtaining permission for the amendment of the notice after the appeal has been included on the List of Forthcoming Appeals. The notice may be amended in any respect without permission before that time.

Once a proper notice of appeal has been prepared, it must be served on all parties in the trial court "who are directly affected by the appeal."[2] A party is directly affected by the appeal if the order entered by the Court of Appeal will have an adverse effect on the party. An example is when two defendants are held jointly liable and only one defendant appeals, and there is a right of contribution between them. A reversal of the order as to the defendant who appeals will eliminate the right of the other defendant to contribution. Because of this possibility, the other defendant must be served with a copy of the notice of appeal. If the appeal is from a county court, the registrar of that court must also be served.

Service must take place within four weeks of the date on which the order appealed from was "sealed or otherwise perfected."[3] Prior to 1986 the important date was the date of entry in a book kept by the trial court.[4] It is possible, however, to seek an extension of time in which to serve the notice of appeal. This can be obtained from the trial court if filed before the expiration of the original 28 day period. Thereafter, it can be obtained only from the Court of Appeal. There is no limit on when the application can be filed and thus no limit on the effective length of the extension. The factors taken into account in ruling on an application for an extension have been judicially developed; they are not set forth in the rule. They include the length of delay, the reasons for the delay, the arguable nature of the appeal, and the prejudice to the opposing party.[5]

The next step is to have the appeal "set down," that is lodged in the Civil Appeals Office. This must be done within seven days of the service of the notice of appeal. In order for an appeal to be set down, the appellant must cause to be delivered to the Civil Appeals Office the following documents:

(1) a copy of the sealed order that is the subject of the appeal;

(2) two copies of the notice of appeal, one of which is accompanied by the appeal fee or endorsed as paid by the clerk of the Chancery Division who actually receives the money, and the other endorsed with a certificate of service by the appellant that a copy of the notice has been served on named parties, and

(3) a list of exhibits (which can be filed later with the bundle of documents if not presently available).

When these documents are received by the Civil Appeals Office, they are reviewed for compliance with Order 59, including whether the service of the notice of appeal and the lodging of the documents were timely. If there is any defect, other than nonpayment of the fee, the person filing them is notified and the papers put in a pending file. If not, the notice of appeal is stamped with the date received and an appeal file is created. Actual receipt by the Civil Appeals Office determines the lodging date; not when the documents are put in the mail. The appeal is then processed as described in section A 8 b, *infra*.

If leave to appeal is required, some preliminary steps must be followed. If the trial court can grant leave, an application for leave to appeal must first be made to it. If it denies leave, or if only the Court of Appeals can grant it, the application is made by filing a "Notice of *ex parte* Application" in the Court of Appeal. The notice is nothing more than a statement of the nature of the application. It must be accompanied by a copy of the order sought to be appealed, a copy of the order of the trial court refusing leave to appeal, an affidavit setting forth the grounds for appeal, and the filing fee. The application must be filed within seven days of the refusal by the trial court of the same application. It is then included on the application list and an associate is assigned the responsibility to ensure that the applicant lodges the required documents. Within 10 days of the setting down, the applicant must lodge three complete sets of the relevant documents in the case including the pleadings and a note or transcript of the reasoned judgment of the trial court, plus a copy of the proposed notice of appeal. The application is summarized by an associate. The summary and all of the original papers are referred to a single Court of Appeal judge. The judge may deny the application or order it set down for hearing. If the latter, notice is then given to the opposing party. The application is argued orally before a single Court of Appeal judge with both parties present. At the end of the hearing, the judge rules immediately on whether to grant it or not, usually with a brief statement of reasons.

There are two significant features to this procedure. The first is the *ex parte* nature of the application and its initial consideration. There is no notice of the filing of the application given to the other parties. The second is that whatever ruling is made on the application there is no appeal from it by any party. The discretion of the Court of Appeal judge is absolute in ruling on the application.

The application is treated differently if it is filed after the expiration of the 28 day appeal period. In that case the application must be joined with an application for extension of time in which to lodge the application seeking leave to appeal. In this situation, notice of the two applications is given to the other parties who are then entitled to be heard on both motions at the same hearing. If a timely application is granted, the appellant has an automatic seven days in which to serve the notice of appeal. If the application was untimely and an extension of time is granted, then the application must be lodged within what ever time the judge establishes.

b. Respondent's Notice

Once a notice of appeal is set down, the appellant must give notice of that fact to the respondent. If the respondent intends to do something other than defend the order on the grounds given by the trial court, the respondent must lodge a respondent's notice. A respondent can argue for affirmance on different grounds, seek a variance in the order, or take a cross appeal. A cross appeal is used only when the respondent is seeking relief on a cause of action different from that at issue on the main appeal, or wishes to challenge the jurisdiction of the trial court. The respondent's notice must include the text of the proposed order sought from the Court of Appeal in either of the latter two situations. The respondent must serve the notice on the appellant and the other parties directly affected by it within 21 days of the service of the notices of appeal and lodge it with the Civil Appeals Office within two days of service.

4. Relief Pending Appeal

The taking of an appeal does not automatically have any effect upon the order appealed from or the execution of it. A stay can be granted by the trial court or a single judge of the Court of Appeal. Absent special circumstances, the application must first be made to the trial court and only if refused is relief sought in the Court of Appeal. There is no right to a stay; the grant of a stay is always in the discretion of the judge even when the order is for money only.

The guiding principle underlying the system is that the litigant who prevailed in the trial court should not be denied the benefit of the order except under certain circumstances. Unless the appeal would be moot if a stay were not granted or unless the appellant would suffer harm for which damages would not be adequate compensation, the order should not be stayed. If the order is for money, a stay will be granted only if the appellant can show that the respondent probably could not repay the money if the award is reversed or substantially reduced. A decision of a single judge on an application can be appealed to a full panel. An application for an injunction pending appeal is handled in the same manner.

Another type of relief pending appeal that can be obtained is security for costs. If the appeal is denied the respondent is usually awarded its costs on appeal. Ordinarily the only circumstances in which such security for costs is granted are when it is uncertain that the appellant is financially able to pay the costs, if the appellant is not a resident of the U.K., or if the appeal is frivolous or vexatious. Security for costs may be highly significant because of the rule that costs include the fees of the solicitor and counsel. These applications are heard by the Registrar.

5. Bundles

It is the obligation of the appellant, not the clerk of the trial court, to lodge the documents required for the appeal, referred to as bundles, in the Court of Appeal. The appellant must lodge three or two copies of the documents (depending upon the number of judges who will hear the appeal) with the Civil Appeals Office within 14 days of the appeal appearing on the List of Forthcoming Appeals (this list is discussed in section A 8 b, *infra*). The documents required to be filed are:

(1) the notice of appeal;

(2) respondent's notice;

(3) the order appealed;

(4) the pleadings;

(5) the reasoned judgment of the trial court;

(6) relevant portions of the transcript of evidence or, if none is available, of the judge's notes of evidence;

(7) the list of exhibits or schedule of evidence;

(8) relevant affidavits or exhibits admitted into evidence.

If there was an official reporter who made shorthand notes of the evidence, the appellant is obliged to order the required number of copies of the transcript (2 or 3) and to make arrangements to pay for them. Only orginals may be filed. The appellant may not order one copy from the reporter, make photocopies of it, and file the photocopies. The reporter will then file the copies directly with the Civil Appeals Office. If there was no reporter present, the appellant must request the judge to make copies of the judge's notes of evidence. If there are no judge's notes, then the notes of the evidence prepared by counsel should be filed.

The documents in a bundle must be bound together and the pages numbered. When the bundle is received it is given to an associate to review for compliance with the rules and practice directions. If there is any defect, the appellant is contacted to remedy the defect. There is no requirement that a copy of the bundle be served on or sent to the respondent.

Delay in the lodging of the bundles has been a problem. This resulted in the issuance of a Practice Statement by the Master of the Rolls in 1986 indicating the need for appellants to begin assembling the bundles as soon as the notice of appeal is lodged. The Statement indicated that the time limits would be strictly enforced and failure to lodge a bundle would result in dismissal of the appeal. An application for an extension of time to lodge a bundle would not be granted if the reason for the extension were simply that the appellant did not begin assembling the documents soon enough.

If a bundle is not timely lodged a notice of the failure is sent by the Civil Appeals Office to the appellant. If there is no response to the notice the appeal is listed for dismissal. There is a hearing on the dismissal, but no notice of it is given to the respondent. The reason for not giving notice is to save the respondent the expense of attending the hearing.

6. Application Practice

During the course of an appeal it is often necessary to seek relief from the rules or statutes governing appeals or to request the exercise of discretion permitted by the rules. Three types of applications have previously been discussed -- an application for leave to appeal, an application for extension of time to serve a notice of appeal or application for leave to appeal, and an application for relief pending appeal. In addition, there are many other types of applications, some of which are heard by a panel of the Court of Appeal, some by a single judge, and some by the Registrar. Those heard by the Registrar include: extensions of time for compliance with most rules, including the service of the notice of appeal; security for costs; adduce further evidence; expedite the appeal; postpone the hearing on the appeal or an application; and any directions on the processing of an appeal.

A single judge will hear applications by way of appeal from any decision on an application by the Registrar as well as applications for leave to appeal, an extension of time to seek leave to appeal, and relief pending appeal.

A panel of the Court of Appeal will hear an application by way of appeal from a decision of a single judge on an application; for leave to apply for judicial review; to strike a notice of appeal for failure to lodge the notice; and a special application relating to a matrimonial cause.

As can be seen from above, the Registrar hears most applications with only a limited number reserved for a single judge or a panel.

There are two noteworthy aspects of the application practice. One, all applications, whether considered *ex parte* or on notice, are heard orally. This might be considered an aspect of the "comprehensive orality" of the English legal process, but in fact many of the applications are heard "in chambers." When a hearing is "in chambers," only the parties and their legal representatives are allowed to be present. Neither the public nor the news media may attend. Two, there is a right to appeal any decision made by the Registrar on an application, and a right to seek leave to appeal every decision of a single judge on an application other than an application for leave to appeal.

7. Briefs and Appendices

There are no briefs or appendices filed in the Court of Appeal. The only documents filed by counsel after the bundles are a skeleton argument and a chronology of events discussed in the next section.

8. Case Processing and Disposition Process

a. Case Processing

The case processing system begins with the lodging of the notice of appeal and accompanying documents with the Civil Appeals Office. At that time the processing of the appeal becomes the responsibility of the Registrar and the staff of the Civil Appeals Office.

The first step is to enter the appeal on one of the appeal lists. Previously an appeal was "listed" when it was entered in one of the list books maintained by the Court of Appeal's clerical staff. Actual books are no longer used, having been replaced by a computer; thus listing currently means entry on a list in the computer. The entry on a list is usually referred to as setting down, but technically the lodging of the required appeal documents constitutes setting down. There are a total of 25 lists divided by the courts and tribunals from which appeals can be taken to the Court of Appeal, (e.g. Chancery Division, county court), and for each court or tribunal subdivided by the nature of the order being appealed (e.g. Queen's Bench Division (Final and New Trial List), Family Division (Interlocutory List). The particular list named in the notice of appeal is used as a guide only; which list an appeal is put on is for the Registrar and his staff to determine. The significance of the list is two fold. One is that it may determine the order in which the appeal is heard, some lists having priority over others. The other is that it will have an effect on which judges will hear the appeal because an effort is made to have at least one who is a specialist in the general subject matter of the appeal as reflected by the list on which it is included.

When the proper list is identified, the appeal is given a number, the title of the case remaining the same as in the trial court. The appellant is then sent a letter notifying him that the appeal was set down, the date it was set down, and the listing number. Enclosed with the letter are four forms that solicit information about the appeal, and instructions. One of the forms, calling for the name of counsel and an estimate of the time that will be required for the oral hearing, is to be completed by the appellant and returned to the Civil Appeals Office. This document will be used later in scheduling the hearings. The appellant is required, within four days of the setting down of an appeal, to so notify the persons upon whom the notice of appeal was served, including specifying the list on which the appeal was set down.

When all of the internal processing steps have been completed, the appeal is put on the List of Forthcoming Appeals. The List is printed with the Daily Cause List, a document printed daily by government employees for all of the superior courts sitting in London as well as the law lords. Its primary function is to list the cases being heard that day (hence its title) but it also includes weekly the List of Forthcoming Appeals, a list of all of the appeals set down in the Court of Appeal. According to one authority, priority matters are included on the Forthcoming Appeals List within one week of setting down. For appeals that have no priority, it takes four to six weeks. The reason for this delay is not explained.

Publication in this list triggers the next two steps in the case processing system--the lodging of the bundle and the filing of counsel's estimate of the length of hearing. Both are supposed to occur within 14 days of the appeal appearing in the List of Forthcoming Appeals. Responsibility for seeing that the bundles and estimates are lodged lies in a section of the Civil Appeals Office. The staff monitor the lodging of bundles and estimates and if there is a delay, they check with the appellant to ascertain the problem. If there is no response to a reminder concerning the failure to lodge a bundle, the appeal will be listed for dismissal.

The appellant's counsel lodges his estimate of the length of the hearing within the 14 day limit. Respondent's counsel is required to review it immediately and if he disagrees with it, lodges his own.

When a bundle is lodged, it is sent to an associate to check for completeness. Any deficiency is called to the attention of the appellant. The principal difficulties arise with appeals from county courts where there is often no shorthand reporter present or no tape recording of the evidence. Frequently there is no record made of the judgment (statement of the judge in support of the order) even though it is necessary for the appeal. In such a case the judge must try to write one or the parties must recreate it out of their notes.

Prior to October, 1987, once the bundles were lodged the appeal was not eligible for a hearing date until it appeared on the Warned List. This was a separate list that was published with the Daily Cause List to indicate that the appeal was eligible to be listed for hearing. The Warned List was abolished in October, 1987, because it served no useful purpose.

Once a bundle is lodged and if there are no pending applications, the appeal is ready to be listed for hearing any time after the expiration of 14 days. When an appeal will be listed for hearing is subject to a number of factors. Of the 25 lists specified in the rules, only 11 are actually used, but even they do not control the timing of listing for hearing. Certain informal priorities have been established by the Master of the Rolls and the Registrar, who directly supervises the Listing Office. Highest priority is given to child custody, liberty of the subject, immigration, possession, some interlocutory matters, and election cases.[7] The appeals with the lowest priority are tort and contract cases from the Queen's Bench Division and county courts.

The development of the hearing list for any given day begins up to two months in advance. The listing is tentative, however, until the Registrar makes up a schedule for the term establishing the number of panels and assigning individual judges to sit on them. In assigning a particular appeal to a panel, the usual practice is to have at least one judge who is a specialist in the subject matter of the appeal.

The fixing of the hearing of any particular appeal is always a matter of negotiation between the Listing Office and the clerks of counsel. Usually no effort is made to list until a request is received from the solicitor of one of the parties. Telephone calls are then made to clerks of the counsel for each side to ascertain when their schedules are open, using the estimated length of oral argument submitted shortly after the setting down of the appeal as the basis for determining how much time to block out for the hearing. The overriding principle is, however, the consent of counsel. If either counsel objects to a particular hearing date, the appeal is not listed for that day.

Technically, prior to 1989, only appeals that were estimated to last longer than 5 days were given a fixed date for the hearing (termed a fixture) and all appeals with shorter time estimates given a "flexible fixture," that is, a hearing date within a range of dates. As part of the 1989 changes, this system was changed to give every appeal a fixed date for a hearing with the commitment that the appeal would be heard on that date or the next following sitting date.

A relatively recent innovation is the Short Warned List for "floater" appeals. These are appeals from a county court, the Queen's Bench Division, or some types of Chancery appeals that do not require a judge with specialized knowledge in the subject matter and have the same counsel on appeal as at trial. These are considered to be appeals for which counsel can prepare for overnight and thus can be scheduled as late as 3 p.m. on the previous day. The final schedule for the next day is sent to the printer at 3 p.m. each day for inclusion in the Daily Cause List. This list is printed at night and is posted early each morning in the Royal Courts of Justice.

The placement of an appeal on the Short Warned List has an effect on the filing of the skeleton argument and the chronology of events. At least three weeks notice is given of the placement of an appeal on this list with a date given when the appeal is "on call," that is, can be scheduled for hearing for the next day. For such cases, the skeleton argument discussed in the next subsection must be filed at least 10 days prior to the "on call" date.

Applications heard by a single judge are scheduled at least two days in advance if *ex parte* or seven days if the opposing party will be present. For these applications an associate will prepare a summary of the case for use by the judge. The Listing Office decides which judge will be assigned which applications. When there is an application for an extension of time to file an application for leave to appeal, both applications are heard at the same time with both parties being heard.

b. The Disposition Process

Three of the changes made since October, 1982, directly concern the manner in which the judges of the Court of Appeal consider and dispose of appeals--the filing of skeleton arguments and a written chronology of events and the prereading of these documents and those in the bundles.

All three of these changes modify the tradition of comprehensive orality because they enable the judges to prepare in advance for oral argument and to exclude from the oral hearing the reading at length from the bundles. The skeleton argument, first requested in 1983 and made mandatory in 1989, is intended to be something less than an American brief or even the printed case filed in the House of Lords. All it is intended to do is identify the issues raised on appeal, not argue them. It should identify the issues, and give citations including the precise pages without quotation to the principal authorities relied upon. For factual questions, the skeleton argument should give the basis on which the Court of Appeal can interfere with the factual finding with cross references to the relevant pages of the transcript as well as references to the documents in the bundles that are relevant to the issues. The document has no specified form. Prior to 1989 it should have been filed at least 24 hours before the hearing began, but was sometimes not filed until the start of the hearing. The submission of a skeleton prior to 1989 was requested but not required. In many cases one was not filed by one or both parties. Given its nature, it is prepared by counsel, not the solicitor.

A respondent is required to file a skeleton argument only in certain circumstances. If the respondent will only argue that the order appealed from was correct for the reasons and authorities given in the judgment, the respondent need only file a letter to that effect. If the respondent intends to rely on any authority or refer to any evidence not relied upon by the trial judge, then the respondent must file a skeleton argument.

Beginning in 1989, the skeleton argument not only was made mandatory but the time of its filing was moved up to four weeks prior to the scheduled hearing date. This early filing serves several purposes. It will permit the legal staff of the Court of Appeals to review it to determine whether the estimates of the length of the hearing are reasonable, and if not to permit an adjustment to be made in the time set aside for the hearing. The early preparation of the skeleton arguments is further designed to force counsel to consider the merits of their positions and thereby move up any discussions of settlement, avoiding the last minute settlement that does not permit another appeal to be heard in its place. The early filing will also assist the judges in their prereading for the oral hearing and permit the court's legal staff to prepare memoranda on the issues presented by the appeal for the use of the judges.

The written chronology, first mentioned in a 1985 Practice Note, is a separate document and includes only factual matters. Its filing was also made mandatory in 1989.

Prior to the 1982 changes, each judge of the Court of Appeal sat five days a week for 37 weeks of the year--that is for the entire time the court was in session. During this period there was little time for advance reading even if it were not thought to be inconsistent with the oral tradition. When the practice of pre-reading was adopted, the court modified the sitting schedule of each judge so that a judge would sit only four days per week, with the fifth day assigned to pre-reading and preparing reserved judgments.

The principal items read by the judges in advance are the notice of appeal, the respondent's notice, if any, the reasoned judgment of the trial judge, the chronology of events, and the skeleton arguments. The judge will also read any portion of the bundles the judge thinks to be particularly relevant as indicated in the skeleton argument. If the bundle exceeds 100 pages, counsel are requested to file copies of particularly relevant documents so that the judges can easily ascertain what should be pre-read. The pre-reading enables the presiding judge to announce at the beginning of the hearing that the judges have read those documents and are thus familiar with the facts and that the counsel can dispense with the reading from the record and proceed immediately to the argument on the issues. The practice is the same whether the appeal is heard by two or three judges.

Prior to 1989 counsel were also requested to file the day before the hearing a list of the cases they intend to refer to during the argument. This list permitted the ushers to collect the volumes in which the cases are published to have them ready for distribution to the judges as each case is discussed by counsel. The list was not intended for use by the judges in preparing for the hearing. Whether this list will continue to be required with the mandatory filing of skeleton arguments is not clear.

Oral hearings are heard only in the Royal Courts of Justice. They begin each day at 10:30 a.m. and last until 4:15 p.m. with a recess for lunch from 1:00 until 2:00 p.m. Use of the courtrooms is shared with the High Court, so the courtrooms used by the Court of Appeal will vary from day to day except for that of the Master of the Rolls who has a courtroom permanently assigned to him. There are usually six or seven panels sitting each day, some composed of three judges and others of two, depending upon the nature of the appeal. The judge senior in point of service is the presiding judge.

The courtrooms are essentially the same but vary in small details. They are not large, seating no more than fifty persons. The judges sit on a high bench. Immediately in front of the judges' bench is a smaller bench at which an associate and the shorthand reporter sit facing counsel and the others in attendance. At either side of the court officials' bench are small benches with writing surfaces for reporters of opinions and news media reporters. Facing the judges' bench are rows of seats for others attending the hearing. The first row which has only seats and no writing area, is occupied by parties representing themselves and reporters. The second row is reserved for Queen's Counsel, the third row for junior counsel, and the fourth row for solicitors and parties. These three rows have both seats and writing areas. The last rows, usually only two or three, are for the public.

When the judges enter, everyone stands. When the judges are at their seats they bow to those present and everyone except the public bows in return. Thereafter whenever any court official, counsel, or solicitor enters or leaves the court they bow to the judges. The judges, the associates, and counsel all wear gowns and wigs. Counsel refer to the judges as "My Lord" and to each other as "my learned friend."

At the beginning of the hearing the presiding judge will inform counsel that the judges have read the principal documents and understand the facts and that counsel need not review them in detail. Because pre-reading is of fairly recent origin, many counsel have not adjusted to the practice and proceed to review the facts. Sometimes, but not always, they can be discouraged from doing so by the presiding judge.

The opening argument is by counsel for the appellant. Usually most of the hearing consists of counsel reading lengthy excerpts from every case that might have some relevance to the appeal. As each appeal is taken up, the ushers will bring the appropriate volume to each judge, with the page marked if the ushers had advance notice of the cases cited. If the ushers do not have advance notice, everyone waits until copies of the particular volume are found and distributed to the judges. The judges will follow the reading of the case and interrupt to ask questions about particular passages or even direct counsel to other portions of the case and ask the relevance of them. The whole approach is one of exploration, deliberation, and consideration in which counsel and the judges participate. The judges candidly express their doubts about the points being made or the relevance of the cases cited by counsel. When counsel for the appellant has concluded, the same exercise is engaged in by respondent's counsel. At the conclusion of the respondent's argument, the appellant can then make a rebuttal argument.

The pace of the argument is unhurried unless the presiding judge takes a particularly active role in questioning counsel, and even that may have no effect. The oral tradition dictates that the judges must listen as long as counsel wants to speak. The result was that the hearings last several hours at a minimum, often last several days, and on occasion can go for several weeks. The median time for hearings in the Court of Appeal is slightly over one full day for three judge appeals, somewhat less for those heard by two judges, according to statistics compiled by the Civil Appeals Office. It remains to be seen whether the changes implemented in June, 1989, will result in limits being put on the length of the arguments of counsel.

When counsel have completed their arguments, the presiding judge will turn to each of the other judges and conduct a whispered conference. The presiding judge will then indicate whether judgment will be given immediately, after a short off the bench conference, or reserved.

If the judgments are given immediately or after a short conference they are *ex tempore*, that is given orally from the bench. The first judge to speak will review the procedural and factual history of the case and then discuss the application of the most relevant precedent and other authorities cited by counsel. Usually each of the other judges will give a separate judgment but may simply say "I agree." If the judges go off the bench for a short conference, they may return and then give an *ex tempore* judgment or they may announce that judgments will be handed down the next day or at some specified or unspecified date in the future. If the judgments are given the next day, they are usually *ex tempore*. If there is a lengthy delay, the judgments will almost always be written.

When judgment is reserved, the time taken is for further consideration of the bundles and the authorities discussed during the hearing. The judges almost never do any independant research. For a judgment given *ex tempore* the shorthand writer will transcribe it and give the judges an opportunity to review and correct it before it is filed in the Supreme Court library. Written reserved judgments are usually just announced and not read in open court, a change since 1982.

When an oral hearing is completed and there is an hour or more left in the day, the court will begin hearing the next appeal if counsel are present. This will usually be one of the "floater appeals" as described in section b, *supra*.

When judgments are rendered, either *ex tempore* or reserved, two matters will be taken up immediately. The first is that the successful party will always ask for its costs. In England these include fees for counsel and solicitors as well as other out of pocket expenses of the appeal. In the normal case the losing party will not oppose unless there is some peculiarity to the case. The second matter is that the losing party may also request leave to appeal to the House of Lords. The Court of Appeal can grant leave, but usually the court will refuse leave and tell the party if leave is to be granted it will be by the House of Lords. Even so, the large majority of the appeals from the Court of Appeal heard by the House of Lords are as a result of leave granted by the Court of Appeal.[8]

9. Order

When each judge on a panel gives a reasoned judgement on the appeal, the judge concludes by saying either that he would allow or deny the appeal. If in favor of a reversal of the order appealed from the judge would allow it; if in favor of affirmance the judge would deny the appeal. These reasoned judgments do not, however, have any direct effect on the order of the trial court. That requires an order of the Court of Appeal, drawn by the associate present in the courtroom when the judgments were delivered. There is no time limit on when this is done. The order when prepared by the associates is sealed and sent out to the parties and to the trial court. No member of the panel reviews it.

Once the order is sent out, the Court of Appeal has no power to alter its judgments (except for editing purposes) or the order based on them.

10. Appeal to the House of Lords[9]

If the losing party desires to seek further review in the House of Lords and has been denied leave to do so by the Court of Appeal it must seek leave from the House of Lords itself. There is no right to appeal to the House. The petition for leave to appeal must be lodged with the House of Lords Judicial Office within 30 days of the date the order of the Court of Appeal disposing of the appeal. The petition must include a statement of facts, points of law to be raised, and reasons why the petition should be granted. A copy of the order of the Court of Appeal that is the subject of the petition must accompany the petition, as must a certificate of service of the petition on the opposing parties.

The petition is referred to an Appeal Committee consisting of three law lords. An oral hearing on the petition is held if any member of the committee thinks that the petition has merit or at least has doubt that it has no merit. If a hearing is held the opposing parties are heard, but only one counsel may argue for each party. If leave is granted, the appellant must lodge a petition to appeal within three months of the date of the order of the Court of Appeal. Thereafter each party files a Printed Case, which can be described as a shortened version of an American brief, and an appendix containing the documents relevant to the appeal. These two documents must be lodged by the appellant within six weeks of the lodging of the petition to appeal, and the respondent's Printed Case is due 14 days thereafter. The appellant must then file 12 bound volumes that include the petition to appeal, the Printed Case of each party, and the Appendix.

Once the Printed Cases are filed, either party can request that the appeal be set for hearing. Appeals are heard before the Appellate Committee consisting of five law lords or other lords eligible to sit on it. These hearings are similar to those in the Court of Appeal except that the Committee sits at a committee table and the members do not wear robes.

The Appellate Committee does not give *ex tempore* judgments; all are reserved and written. They are formally called speeches and technically are reports to the full House of Lords.

B. United States

1. The Appealable Judgment

An appealable judgment must meet the definition of a final judgment or one of the exceptions to it, as discussed in section B 4 a of Chapter 1. It must also meet whatever formal requirements that have been established to turn a ruling by the judge into a judgment. Such requirements usually including reduction of the ruling to writing in a separate document, signing of the judgment by the judge, and the filing of the judgment with the clerk of the trial court. Most jurisdictions also require the fact of the filing of the judgment to be entered in the docket of the court, which is the formal record of the major events in each court proceeding. Recording a document or event in the court docket makes it a matter of public record and notice to the world.

2. Parties

The requirement that the party taking the appeal be aggrieved by the judgment is explored in section B 4 b of Chapter 1, *supra*. The status of the parties in the trial court when an appeal is taken is, at first glance, simple. The party who loses in the trial court takes the appeal and is known as the appellant. The winner in the trial court defends the appeal and is known as the appellee or, in some jurisdictions, the respondent. The proper designation is usually specified in the appellate rules of each jurisdiction.

There are, however, a number of factors that can complicate the matter. If both parties are aggrieved by the judgment and both appeal, the second appeal is termed a cross appeal. The first party appealing is the appellant and cross appellee and the second is the appellee and cross appellant.

The existence of multiple parties in the trial court adds further complications. If only one party appeals, all other parties are designated as appellees unless one or more of the other parties have the same interests as the original appellant and also take an appeal. In such a case, the subsequent appellants are known as appellants or co-appellants. If a party in the trial court does not participate in the appeal, that party has no status in the appellate court.

If a person who was not a party in the trial court believes that its legal interests are adversely affected by the judgment and no one who is a party with the same interests decides to appeal, the non party may seek to intervene in the proceeding in the trial court for the purpose of taking the appeal. This person is designated as intervenor in the trial court and appellant in the appellate court. A person may also intervene to defend the judgment as an appellee in the appellate court if the person's legal interests are benefited by the judgment and no one else with similar interests is participating as an appellee.

The right to appeal may be lost by either an aggrieved plaintiff or defendant. The plaintiff who is aggrieved by a judgment for less than what it sought as relief in the trial court is no longer considered aggrieved if it accepts the reduced amount from the defendant. Similarly, a defendant who pays a judgment voluntarily is considered to have acquiesced in the judgment. Payment is voluntary unless made pursuant to legal process such as a writ of execution.

3. Initiating and Perfecting the Appeal

a. The Notice of Appeal

The filing of a notice of appeal by a party aggrieved by the judgment initiates the appeal process.[10] The timely filing of a notice of appeal is the single most important step in the appellate process because it is considered necessary to give the appellate court jurisdiction to hear and determine the appeal.

There are three crucial elements to a notice of appeal--content, filing, and timeliness. A defect as to any one of the three may render a notice invalid, thereby defeating the appellate court's jurisdiction and requiring the dismissal of the appeal.

The content of the notice of appeal is specified by the appellate rules. Rule 3(c) of the Federal Rules of Appellate Procedure is typical. It requires that the notice include the name of the party taking the appeal, the judgment or part thereof appealed from, and the name of the court to which the appeal is taken. Notwithstanding the simplicity of the requirements, many notices of appeal do not include one or more of these requirements. The federal courts of appeals cases applying the rule rendered the requirements almost meaningless. The only test applied was that whatever document is filed must make the court and the other parties aware of an intention to appeal.

A 1988 decision of the Supreme Court holding invalid an appeal by a party not specifically named in the notice of appeal may, however, signal a change in this approach.[11] If there is only one appealable judgment and only one court to which the appeal can be taken, the absence of the required reference to either will probably not be treated as significant. Some courts, however, are more literal minded and tend to find invalid a notice of appeal that does not include all of the information specified by the rule, thereby destroying the validity of the appeal.

A notice of appeal must also be properly filed. Most appellate rules require the notice to be filed with the clerk of the trial court, although some mandate filing with the clerk of the appellate court, and a few even specify both courts. Filing is construed to mean that the document must be within the custody and control of the court clerk. It does not mean that the document must be stamped "filed," noted on the case docket, or placed in the case file. Filing with the trial judge or placing the notice in the mail does not, however, constitute filing with the clerk. Filing with the clerk of the appellate court rather than the clerk of the trial court is not an acceptable substitute in most jurisdictions. This stems from the fact that filing constitutes notice not only to the court and the parties but to the world, and filing in a place not specified in the rule may cause someone to act on the assumption no appeal has been taken. Notwithstanding this second justification for requiring that the filing only in the place specified in the rule, Federal Rule of Appellate Procedure 4(a)(1) was amended in 1979 to validate a notice of appeal mistakenly filed in the court of appeals, rather than the district court.

Just as important as where the notice of appeal is filed is when it is filed. The time in which a notice of appeal must be filed is usually specified in the statute establishing the right to appeal, but in a few jurisdictions including the federal courts the time period is established by court rule. A thirty day period is most common, but in some jurisdictions it is as long as sixty days. Because, as noted above, the timely filing of a notice of appeal is considered jurisdictional, the time for filing cannot be extended by the appellate court. This is true whether a valid notice is filed late or an invalid notice of appeal is timely filed. Some jurisdictions permit the trial court to extend the period for filing a notice of appeal, but the request for an extension must be made within a limited period, usually thirty days, after expiration of the original time period. The grounds for extension are typically excusable neglect or good cause, but in practice the only acceptable excuse is that the prospective appellant did not find out about entry of the appealable judgment through no fault of its own. The only certain basis for an extension is when the fault is that of court personnel.

If an appeal from an interlocutory order is allowed by statute or rule, a shorter time for taking the appeal is usually provided, ten days being the most common. If an interlocutory appeal is not taken when permitted, the order may still be reviewed upon appeal from the final judgment.

When the appeal time period begins to run is, of course, crucial.[12] The most common event that triggers the running of the time period is when the appealable judgment is entered, as is explained in section A 1, *supra*. The appeal time can be tolled by the filing of a motion in the trial court seeking either a new trial or an alteration of the judgment that was entered. When the motion is acted upon, a new appeal time period begins to run. This post trial motion itself must be timely filed to toll the appeal time period. Usually only ten days are allowed for the filing of such a motion.

In a few jurisdictions the crucial event is the service of the notice of appeal on the other parties in the case. This must occur within the appeal time period to make the appeal valid. Even when entry of the judgment is the determinative event, service is still required but the failure to serve does not destroy the jurisdiction of the appellate court. It does, however, permit the party not served to seek dismissal of the appeal as to that party.[13]

There is an acknowledged relationship between the simplicity of the content and filing requirements of the notice of appeal and the treatment of the filing of a timely notice of appeal as jurisdictional. The rule drafters wanted to avoid the dismissal of appeals for failure to comply with technical requirements for taking an appeal, so they made those requirements as few and as simple as possible. Notwithstanding this effort, the percentage of notices of appeal that do not meet even the minimal requirements of the appellate rules is surprisingly high, forcing appellate courts to choose between enforcement of the rules and the denial of a party's opportunity for appellate review. Most but not all appellate courts insist upon compliance with the procedural rules.

b. Cross Appeals

Many of the requirements for taking an appeal are also applicable to a cross appeal. A cross appeal is an appeal by the appellee who also seeks to challenge the final judgment. An appellee can defend the judgment on any ground for which there is support in the record, even if that ground was rejected by that court. If, however, the appellee wishes to modify the judgment so as to receive additional relief it must file a notice of appeal. In a few jurisdictions the appellee must also file a cross appeal if it wishes to support the judgment on a ground rejected by the trial court.

The requirements as to content and filing for the cross notice of appeal are the same as for the original notice of appeal but the timeliness requirements are slightly different. A cross appellant has the same time as the appellant or a fixed period after the initial notice of appeal is filed, usually fourteen days, whichever is longer. The additional period is given to permit a party who might not have appealed to decide whether to do so when the opposing party files a notice of appeal near the end of the original appeal time period.

c. Perfecting the Appeal

After the notice of appeal is filed, the appellant must take several additional steps to ensure that the appellate court will hear the appeal. Most jurisdictions impose some type of fee on the taking of an appeal. In the federal courts there is both a filing fee for the filing of a notice of appeal in the trial court and a docketing fee for docketing the case in the appellate court. Some jurisdictions also require a bond to be posted by the appellant. This guarantees that the appellee will be reimbursed for allowable costs on appeal if the appeal is unsuccessful. The amount of the bond is small, usually only $250.

The failure to comply with one of these requirements can result in dismissal of the appeal upon motion by the appellee, but the failure does not affect the jurisdiction of the appellate court. For this reason the court may ignore or waive the deficiency. What usually occurs is that when the appellee files a motion to dismiss for failure to comply with the requirements, the court gives the appellant a period of time within which to comply before it will dismiss the appeal, and this prompts the appellant to comply unless it has decided to abandon the appeal.

4. Relief Pending Appeal

When an appeal is taken, the question of the effect of the appeal on the judgment being appealed becomes significant. If the defendant appeals a judgment for the plaintiff and the judgment is thereby automatically stayed, there is no guarantee that the defendant-appellant will be able to comply with the judgment if it is affirmed by the appellate court. If there is no stay of the judgment, there is no guarantee that the *status quo* can be restored if the judgment is reversed by the appellate court. For these reasons a system for relief pending appeal has been developed.

The taking of an appeal does not itself stay the judgment. If the judgment is for money, there is a right to a stay upon a posting of a bond by the appellant to guarantee the payment of the judgment, appeal costs, and any damages resulting from the delay caused by the appeal including interest on the judgment. The amount of the bond is set by the trial court who is free to reduce or eliminate the bond requirement if there is no risk that the appellant will not be able to comply with the judgment if unsuccessful on appeal. The trial judge will also establish the form of the bond--cash, property, or bonding company.

The matter becomes more complicated when relief other than money is involved, such as ownership, possession or use of property, or performance or non-performance of an act. Whether or not the court should order the maintenance of the *status quo* while the appeal is pending is left up to the trial judge's discretion. Four factors have been developed for the judge to consider in deciding whether to grant the stay. They are:

(1) likelihood of success on appeal,

(2) harm to appellant if stay not granted,

(3) harm to appellee if stay is granted, and

(4) public interests involved.

There is a flexible relationship between the first factor and the other three. If the first is very strong, then the necessity for a showing of the other three is reduced, and vice versa.[14]

The importance of relief pending appeal in non monetary cases is demonstrated by the fact that if a stay is not granted the dispute may become moot, requiring dismissal of the appeal. For example, if the dispute involves the consumption or destruction of property or the publication of information, the point of the case may disappear if the event sought to be prevented occurs before the appeal is decided. The entire appeal may thus depend upon the prompt seeking of relief pending appeal.

5. Record on Appeal

The record on appeal is the *sine qua non* of appellate review because it is the only means by which the appellate court can ascertain whether the trial court committed reversible error. As noted in Chapter 1, section A 4 e *supra*, the existence of reversible error must be found for the appellate court to take any action other than to affirm the judgment. The only means it has to determine what occurred in the trial court in its search for reversible error is an examination of the record. Unless the appellant can show that an alleged error occurred by demonstrating the fact from the record, the appellate court is in no position to find the error, much less find that the error requires reversal of the judgment. The only alternatives are for the appellate court to conduct its own hearing on what occurred at trial or to retry the case *de novo*. The first is impractical and the second inconsistent with the American view of the function of appellate courts. The operating principle for American appellate courts is, consequently, if it is not in the record it did not happen.

There are two opposite views on what constitutes the record on appeal. One view, reflected in the Federal Rule of Appellate Procedure 10, is that the entire record in the trial court constitutes the record on appeal. This is true whether or not any particular item in the trial court record is included in the documents and transcript forwarded to the appellate court. Thus if any item is not originally included in the record, it can always be added later if needed. The other view is that the record on appeal consists only of those items from the trial record designated by the parties to be forwarded to the appellate court. If any item is not forwarded, it is treated as though it was never part of the record unless the record is formally amended as a result of a motion by one of the parties.

The portion of the record that consists of the transcript of the testimony at trial has been a major contributor to the delay in the appellate process and thus has been the focus of much attention in coping with the crisis of volume. Under the traditional system, the pace of the appellate process was left to the lawyers for the parties. They were responsible for ensuring that the record was transmitted to the appellate court. The transcript was not prepared until ordered by the lawyers, so it needed to be ordered early enough to be included with the rest of the record forwarded to the appellate court. This was to occur within a specified time period after the filing of the notice of appeal, usually 30 days. In practice, however, the transcript was almost never prepared on time for three principal reasons:

(1) the lawyers did not order it when they should have;

(2) if they ordered it they often failed to make the necessary arrangements to pay for it; and

(3) the court reporter was not able to prepare the transcript expeditiously because of the time the reporter spent in court and on earlier transcript orders.

The preparation of the transcript was not monitored by either the trial court or the appellate court. If a court reporter wanted an extension of time in which to prepare the transcript, he needed to request it from the trial court judge for whom the reporter worked every day and who would seldom deny the extension. Often it was not even requested. As a consequence the potential for delay was enormous, and this potential was often realized.

The solution most commonly adopted was to amend the appellate rules to emphasize the duty of the appellate lawyers to order the transcript and make arrangements to pay for it and, even more importantly, to give the appellate court the authority and responsibility to monitor the process and control extensions of time for preparation of the transcript. Today the transcript must be ordered simultaneously with or within ten days of the filing of the notice of appeal. The lawyer must certify that arrangements for payment have been made, and notice of the ordering must be given to the appellate court. If the court reporter is unable to complete the transcript within the required period (usually 30 days), the reporter must request an extension from the appellate court, giving reasons for the request. Federal Rules of Appellate Procedure 10(b) and 11(b) are representative of this approach, which has greatly alleviated the problem. Longer term solutions involve computer assisted transcription of the testimony but this has not developed as quickly as had been expected. More recently, the federal courts have authorized using video tapes of the trial as a substitute for the transcript on an experimental basis. Until a new system becomes the standard, however, it is essential that those involved in the recording of testimony in court recognize that the recording is not an end in itself.

The goal is to be able to prepare a transcript that can be used by lawyers and the appellate court if there is an appeal.

6. Motion Practice

Motions in an appellate court are of two principal types, substantive and procedural. Substantive motions are those that may result in a determination of the appeal on the merits or, if not on the merits, may result in a dismissal of the appeal. Procedural motions go merely to the processing of the appeal, the status of parties, relief pending appeal, among others. They may indirectly affect the outcome of the appeal but do not do so directly.

Substantive motions that go to the merits are decided by a three judge panel, usually upon recommendation of staff. Procedural motions will be determined by a single judge, or the clerk, or other staff member. The determination of who acts on various types of motion is made by local rule or internal procedure of the court and may or may not be publicly announced. Whether action is taken by a panel of judges, a single judge, or a staff member, the order on the motion is issued in the name of the court. Actions of a single judge or staff member may be reviewed by a motions or administrative panel, but this seldom occurs.

Motions must be in writing, and a response filed within a limited time, usually ten days. Only in the most extraordinary cases is oral argument held on a motion.

Two key elements of motion practice in a busy appellate court are to minimize the amount of judge time spent on motions and to prevent the filing of a motion from delaying consideration of the appeal on the merits. These goals are achieved by having procedural motions acted upon by a single judge upon recommendation of staff or by staff alone. Action is taken on the papers submitted without oral argument, and with little or no opportunity for reconsideration.

7. Briefs and Appendix

a. Briefs

The appellate rules govern all aspects of the brief--when it must be filed and served, form, length, structure, content, and even the color of the cover. The filing of the record in the appellate court triggers the running of the time in which the appellant's brief must be filed. In most jurisdictions the appellant has thirty to forty five days to file its brief and the appellee has the same or slightly shorter time. The appellant may also file a reply brief but within a much shorter period of time.

At one time briefs could be of unlimited length, but as the pressure of volume increased, courts began to impose page limitations. Limits of forty to fifty pages for the principal briefs are now common and requests to file longer briefs are seldom granted. The experience of courts with page limits is that they improve rather than detract from the quality of the briefs, even though their principal purpose was simply to cut down on the volume of paper the judges must read.

The structure and content of the brief is also carefully controlled. The principal sections of the brief are detailed in Chapter 3, section A 1--Statement of Issues, Statement of Case, Statement of Facts, Argument, and Conclusion. The rules also specify the content of each section.

The brief serves two principal functions. First, it provides the judges with the "what" of the appeal--information about the case including procedural history, facts developed at trial, issues raised by the appeal, and the facts and law that relate to those issues. It also provides the "why" of the resolution of the appeal--the views of the party submitting the brief on why the facts, the law, and justice require that the appeal be decided in its favor. Thus the brief is a document of both information and advocacy.

The importance of the brief in the American appellate process is best signified by what occurs if a party does not file a brief. For the appellant, it means that the appeal will be dismissed, thereby allowing enforcement of the trial court judgment. The appellant cannot simply omit a brief and rely on an oral presentation, or expect the court *sua sponte* to review the record to see if any error was committed. For the appellee there is some variation among jurisdictions as to the proper course of action to take if the appellee does not file a brief. In a few states, there is an automatic reversal of the judgment. Most jurisdictions, however, take the position that the judgment is entitled to a presumption of correctness and insist that the appellant show reversible error. A common sanction against the appellee is to deny it the opportunity to make an oral argument even if the appellant makes one.

Almost all authors of the many texts and innumerable articles on the principles of effective brief writing agree that the two most important characteristics are brevity and clarity. While they have always been virtues in brief writing, in the busy American appellate court of today they are absolutely essential. If a brief is unduly long or the writing is unclear, the ability of the brief to make an impression on the judge or to permit the judge to put much reliance on it in reaching a decision, is sharply reduced. The judge simply does not have the time to struggle with it, although he may assign the task to a law clerk or staff attorney. Candor is likewise essential. If the judge discovers that a brief contains misstatements or overstatements, or, worse, leaves out harmful but essential facts or contrary law, the court will totally lose confidence in the brief and it will play no part in the decision making process except to weaken the position of the party who filed it. Judge Albert Tate, Jr. of the United States Court of Appeals for the Fifth Circuit expressed this view in the following terms:

> The brief is a companion of the judge from before the oral argument until after the rehearing is denied, and it will be referred to or reread as often as necessary. The judge to whom the decision is assigned will continually consult the effective appellate brief--issue by issue and fact by fact--in his research and as he drafts the proposed opinion. Primarily on the basis of the briefs, each other judge of

the panel will decide to sign the proposed opinion or instead to dissent, concur, or suggest changes in it.

Even before the opinion is assigned and circulated, the participating judges all use primarily the briefs to prepare for oral argument and to reach a tentative conclusion for the opinion-assignment conference immediately following argument. After the opinion is issued, they again consult the briefs in deciding whether to grant a rehearing. At all stages, each participating judge relies largely upon the briefs when deciding whether to engage in independent research of the record or the law. . . .

In summary, the truly effective appellate brief, from the point of view of the court, is one quite similar to a superior law clerk's memorandum. It contains discussion and analysis and summary of all factual considerations and legal rationales necessary for the decision. Once the contents are verified, through the ready means furnished by accurate citation to the record and published material, the judge ideally should be able to dictate his opinion from the brief, including liberal paraphrasing or plagiarizing of its concise and accurate wording. In serving through his brief as a valued research assistant to the court, counsel has certainly aided the administration of appellate justice, whether his client wins or loses.

I have emphasized my concept of the appellate brief as chiefly a vehicle to enable the judge to understand quickly the issues and facts, disputed or not, of the appeal, and for him most readily to grasp the argument of counsel, in its strengths and weaknesses. I do not, however, imply that the brief's usefulness is negatived by its advocacy. By selection, emphasis, and articulation, counsel properly attempts to persuade the court of the correctness of his client's position, although (if he wishes his brief to be useful to and used by the court) he must do so accurately and with candor about the factual and legal data applicable to the issues of the case. The more clear, concise, complete, and coherent is the brief furnished for the court's use, the more certainly will the brief afford the court access not only to the legal materials furnished by it for decision, but also to counsel's persuasiveness in his brief's contention that the law and the facts demand that his client prevail.[15]

b. Appendix

In the era when all briefs were required to be printed and photocopying had yet to be invented, parties were also required to file a printed appendix that contained those portions of the appeal record the parties thought were necessary to support their positions. Because the original record was too bulky and there was only one copy of it, the judges were prevented from making easy use of it in preparing for oral argument, reaching a decision, or preparing and agreeing on an opinion. To overcome these difficulties, the appendix was required as a substitute for the record. It was printed in the same form as the brief and, if short enough, was part of the appellant's brief. When the photocopying process was developed to a stage where it could easily reproduce briefs and the record, the printing requirement for both was eliminated. Some courts, however, have gone so far as to eliminate the appendix entirely, content to rely only on the appeal record and photocopies of it. Other courts require an appendix, but one containing only the most relevant items from the record.

Whether or how much of an appendix is required depends upon whether the appendix is considered a substitute for the record or merely a more convenient means of access to it. Under the first approach, the court ignores the original record and relies exclusively on the appendix. If an essential item in the record is not in the appendix, it is treated as though it were not part of the record. Under the latter, the court treats the entire record as being before it, and thus the failure to include a portion of the record in the appendix is not fatal.

The appendix is usually filed with the appellant's brief, but may be filed as late as the last brief.

8. Case Processing and Disposition Process

a. Case Processing

Under the procedures in the federal courts and in a growing number of states, as soon as the notice is filed in the trial court, the clerk of the trial court is required to send to the clerk of the appellate court a copy of the notice and a copy of the docket entries of the case. Upon receipt, the clerk of the appellate court dockets the appeal, opens a case file, and gives the appeal a number. At this point control over the appeal is in the appellate court. The appellate court clerk notifies each party in the trial court of the fact of docketing the appeal, the title of the case in the appellate court, and the appeal number. With the filing of the notice of appeal, or within a specified number of days thereafter, the appellant must order in writing from the court reporter a transcript of those portions of the testimony the appellant thinks are relevant to the appeal. The reporter must then note on the order its receipt and the date on which the transcript is expected to be completed and file a copy with the clerk of the appellate court. If the transcript cannot be completed within thirty days of receipt of the order the reporter must request an extension from the appellate court.

Some appellate courts require the appellant to file a docketing statement either with the notice of appeal or within a limited period of time thereafter, usually not more than 21 days. The statement includes basic information about the appeal relating to jurisdiction of the appellate court, the nature of the appellate proceeding, the date of judgment being appealed and any post trial motions and rulings thereon, a brief statement of the case and of the facts, the issues raised by the appeal, and a statement as to why oral argument is necessary. This statement can be used for several purposes. First, it can be used as part of a conference program administered by the court to encourage the settlement of appeals or to limit the issues on appeal. Second, it can be used to determine briefing schedules, either longer or shorter than those established in the appellate rules, or whether oral argument should be held.

It can also be used to determine whether there are any jurisdictional defects that would require the dismissal of the appeal.

The essential part of case processing is the monitoring of the filing of the various documents with the appellate court including the docketing statements, record, transcript, briefs, appendix, responses to motions, and any other action required to be taken by the attorneys or parties. If a key item is not filed by the appellant, there is an automatic procedure for notification by the clerk of the default, a directive that the default be cured within a specified period of time, and a recital that the appeal will be dismissed or some other sanction imposed automatically without further notice. If the sanction is dismissal of the appeal, that is done by the clerk without any judicial action necessary.

The settlement conference is used by a growing number of appellate courts in an effort to dispose of appeals without the necessity for the filing of briefs or judicial action on the merits. It involves a court official, usually a staff attorney or a retired judge, initiating either an in person or telephone conference with the attorneys for the parties to explore the possibilities of settlement or agreement on the key issues to be decided. They are used primarily in particular types of appeals, such as those involving money judgments that are more susceptible to settlement. No pressure is brought on the parties to settle, and if there is no settlement the fact of the conference and the discussions in it are not revealed to the judges who decide the case.

The extent to which settlement conferences actually increase the rate of settlement has not been clearly established.[16] Nonetheless, courts that use them appear to find them worthwhile. To the extent that they do promote settlement, they permit the judge time that would have been devoted to that appeal to be spent on others and resolve appeals more quickly with a result satisfactory to the parties. There is no evidence that the procedure has caused an increase in the number of appeals. If the preparation of the briefs or the ultimate disposition of the appeal is delayed in the event no settlement results, then the procedure may not be worth the effort. Again, there is no clear statistical data to prove one effect rather than the other.

Another procedure that some courts have developed to expedite disposition of appeals is summary disposition. Under this procedure either party before or after the filing of briefs may file a motion seeking disposition of the appeal on the documents before the court. The result may be a dismissal of the appeal (usually on jurisdictional grounds or for some procedural defect), summary affirmance, or summary reversal. The court may also take similar action on its own motion without a request of a party. A summary disposition will occur only if the court is convinced, after an examination of the documents, that the resolution of the appeal is so clear that further efforts by the parties and by the court will not change the outcome. A key element in the summary procedure is that if summary disposition is denied, the consideration given to it must not delay the ultimate disposition of the case nor must it involve substantial judge time. This means that the filing of a motion for summary disposition must have no effect on the briefing schedule. It also means that most of the review of the record and other documents should be done by staff rather than the judges.

Some courts have also adopted an expedited appeal procedure. Under it, after a review of the documents including a docketing statement filed with or shortly after the notice of appeal, some cases will be assigned to a "fast track" with shortened briefs and shortened filing times and with no or only a very brief oral argument. This is done usually only on agreement of the parties or at their request. The idea is that the parties are willing to exchange full consideration after some delay for a speedy disposition after a more superficial consideration. This procedure has not gained wide acceptance because of the processing and scheduling complications it entails and the reluctance of at least one party to agree to it.

Almost every appellate court uses a screening process to decide whether to have oral argument in each appeal. This decision can be made by staff or a judge on the basis of a review of a docketing statement or briefs. The significance of this decision, the reason for it being made, and the standards on which it is made are discussed in the next section.

b. The Disposition Process

i) Submission on Briefs

If the court has decided to consider an appeal solely on the basis of the briefs without oral argument, the case is assigned to a three judge panel of the appellate court. In a few courts the judges are assigned permanently to one panel, but in most courts the judges rotate among the panels so that each judge sits with each other judge approximately the same number of times. Most appeals are assigned to panels in rotation, to avoid attempting to influence the outcome of the appeal. The assignment of the judges to a panel is done by the presiding judge, the court's administrator, or the clerk. The assignment of appeals to a panel is done by the clerk.

Appeals are assigned to a panel either in the order the appeals are docketed or in the order they are ready for submission, i.e., in the order the last brief is filed. The former is preferable, because it precludes any delay in the filing of the record or the briefs from having any effect on when the appeal is considered on the merits by a panel.

When an appeal is submitted on the briefs only to a panel for a decision on the merits, it may be accompanied by a recommendation from a staff attorney. If, in the screening process, a staff attorney has concluded that oral argument is not necessary, he may prepare a memorandum, a draft opinion, or both that is submitted to the panel with the briefs. In either event the briefs and record are reviewed by all of the judges on the panel and their law clerks. The judges then communicate their views on the disposition of the appeal either by a personal conference, a telephone conference, or a memorandum. When the judges are in agreement on the disposition, they will also decide whether an opinion should be written or the case disposed of by order. If an opinion is to be written, the appeal is assigned to one member of the panel to complete that task. If a staff attorney has prepared a draft opinion, it may be adopted by the panel. If not, the judge will prepare the opinion, using law clerks if that is the judge's practice.

When a draft opinion is prepared, it is circulated to the other two judges on the panel for their review. This can include anything from a cursory reading by the judge to an in depth checking of every word in it, including the cases cited and the record, by the judge and law clerks. The extent to which checks are made depends upon the significance of the opinion and the interest the judges have in the issues raised in the appeal and the resolutions of the issues in the opinion. Sometimes the other members of the panel will accept the opinion as drafted. More than likely they will suggest changes, either minor semantic changes or major revisions that go to the approach taken, or in some cases, the result.

Once the text is accepted by at least two members of the panel, it will be given to the clerk's office for filing. When filed, a copy is sent to the lawyer for each party, the news media, and to the reporter of decisions or, if the court does not have one, directly to the publishers of the reports that contain the court's opinions. If an opinion is not to be published, a copy is sent only to the attorneys and to the media. The opinion is, however, first stamped with a notice that it is not for publication. One copy is included in the appellate court's file of the case and another is included in the record sent back to the trial court.

ii) Submission After Oral Argument

The same procedure is followed for appeals that are to be argued orally, but with some major exceptions. The appellate court clerk is notified when an appeal is screened for oral argument. The clerk makes up the calendar of cases to be heard in a particular week approximately thirty to sixty days in advance. The lawyers are then notified when their appeals are to be heard. A copy of the calendar is available to the news media and other interested persons. Usually a particular panel will hear oral arguments one week out of each four and will hear between twenty and twenty-five cases per week. If the court has more than three judges, the names of the judges who will sit on a particular panel are not released. The origins of this aspect of secrecy is not clear. The reason for it appears to be so that the lawyers cannot prepare their arguments to fit the particular judicial philosophies of the members of the panel. Identity of the panel members is always known in advance, of course, when the appellate court has only three members or when the entire court always sits *en banc*, as is the case with most supreme courts.

The preparation of a judge for an oral argument is somewhat different from the preparation for a conference to decide the appeal solely on the basis of the briefs.[17] The basic criterion for holding oral argument is that after a reading of the briefs the judges have questions about the facts or the law that they would like counsel to respond to before the judges decide the case. Preparation for oral argument is thus designed to isolate what is clear from what is unclear and to formulate the questions to be asked during the oral hearing. Often a law clerk or a staff attorney will prepare a bench memorandum for the judges to highlight the matters that are unclear.

The day before oral argument on an appeal each judge will review the briefs and the bench memoranda. On the morning of oral argument it is the practice in some courts for the judges to meet briefly to discuss the appeals to be heard that day and to ascertain if there is a consensus on the points to be pursued or even the precise questions to be asked.

The oral argument itself is a relatively structured proceeding. In length it does not exceed thirty minutes per side and is usually no more than fifteen or twenty minutes per side. The appellant speaks first, then the appellee, with the appellant having an opportunity for a short rebuttal, thus duplicating the order of the briefs. Given the advance preparation of the judges and the shortness of time, oral argument is essentially an opportunity for the judges to ask questions and the attorneys to answer them. The judges may be seeking information on the facts of the case or on the proper interpretation or application of particular statues, rules, or cases. The answers to these questions often involve advocacy at its best, because counsel will be forced by the questions to explain away adverse facts or law or the absence of helpful facts or law.

During the argument the lawyers refer to the judges as "Your Honor" or "Judge" or "Justice X" and to opposing counsel as "My opponent" or "Mr. X." The lawyers almost never speak directly to each other or interrupt the other's argument. The lawyers sit at tables facing the court and speak from a lectern placed between them. To ensure that the lawyers do not speak over their time limits, many lecterns are fitted with green, yellow and red lights to warn the lawyers when they are approaching or have reached their time limit. A clerk or the presiding judge keeps time and operates the lights. Courts and individual judges vary in how strictly they enforce the time limits.

After completion of all of the oral arguments scheduled for that day, the judges will hold a decision conference. They discuss each case and attempt to reach a tentative decision on the disposition of the appeal. One judge is then assigned the task of preparing an opinion. At this conference they may also discuss appeals that will be disposed of on the briefs alone without oral argument. In some courts the decision conference is not held until the end of the week when all of the week's appeals are discussed and a tentative decision made. Thereafter the opinion writing process is the same as for appeals on which there is no oral argument.[18]

9. Reconsideration

Once the opinion and judgment of the panel of the appellate court are filed, the losing party in most jurisdictions has the opportunity to request the panel or the entire appellate court to reconsider or modify the decision or opinion. The party has a limited period in which to request reconsideration, usually ten to fifteen days. The principal grounds for seeking reconsideration are a misunderstanding by the court of the facts as reflected in the opinion or an inconsistency between the decision and prior decisions of that court or a higher court. Reconsideration, like motions for new trials in the trial court, are seldom granted because they are essentially requests for the court to admit it made a mistake. In most appeals they are, consequently, a waste of time and little more than an opportunity for an unsuccessful litigant to delay the inevitable.

A rehearing *en banc* by the entire appellate court, is allowed in the federal courts of appeals and in some states when the initial decision is by a panel of fewer than all of the judges of the court. It is used primarily in law development cases when the opinion of the panel is not reflective of the views of a majority of the entire court and when the supreme court's own caseload may not permit it to review all of the cases in which it would be appropriate.[19] In all but the federal courts and a few of the largest states, an *en banc* procedure is not necessary because the supreme court is able to hear all appeals that involve substantial law development issues.

The request for a rehearing is made by a written motion. The opposing party has an opportunity to respond, usually within a ten day time limit. The papers are then circulated to the panel who decide informally whether to grant or deny the motion. There is never oral argument on the motion. For a request for a rehearing *en banc*, the motion and response are distributed to the entire court. If a majority votes in favor of rehearing, there is usually an oral argument but with the same briefs as originally filed.

10. Seeking Review in a Supreme Court

After, or instead of, seeking reconsideration in the intermediate appellate court (usually it is not a prerequisite) the losing party may then seek review in the supreme court of the jurisdiction. This usually must be sought within thirty days of the decision of the intermediate appellate court. In almost all jurisdictions review by the supreme court is discretionary in the supreme court but in some types of appeals, such as when a statute is declared unconstitutional, there is a right to it. The request is made by written motion or petition and is supported either by a memorandum or a brief. After the opposing party responds to the request, it is considered by the supreme court solely on the papers submitted without oral argument.

The criteria for the supreme court to grant the request are flexible. As noted in Chapter 1, section B 3, review is granted most often for appeals that involve law development. The most common reason for granting a request is when there is a conflict between decisions of intermediate appellate courts within the jurisdiction.[20] If the supreme court decides to hear the appeal it will call for additional briefs and almost always schedule oral argument. The procedures of the court for considering the briefs, hearing oral argument, and making a decision, and writing the opinion are essentially the same as for an intermediate appellate court.

Many jurisdictions have allowed some flexibility and permit the intermediate appellate court to be bypassed. The request for review goes directly to the supreme court. This can be done by the supreme court on its own motion, that of a party, or by the intermediate appellate court before it decides the appeal. Usually this occurs only in significant law development appeals that will inevitably go to the supreme court. A supreme court seldom accepts an appeal under a bypass procedure, however, because it prefers to have the benefit of consideration by the intermediate appellate court.

Compared to an intermediate appellate court, a supreme court decides relatively few appeals. The United States Supreme Court decides only between 150 and 200 appeals on the merits, and most state supreme courts in states with intermediate appellate courts decide even fewer. They spend most of their time deciding what appeals to hear and writing opinions on the appeals they do hear. They hear oral argument on almost every appeal and all of their opinions are published. They never, however, have oral argument on whether to accept or reject an appeal.

11. Issuance of Mandate

The final steps in the appellate process involve the clerk of the appellate court formally notifying the trial court of the judgment of the appellate court and returning the original record to the lower court. This occurs thirty days after the original decision of the appellate court or after any motion for rehearing or petition seeking review in the supreme court has been acted upon. The formal notification of the judgment is termed the mandate (or remittitur). The appellate court does not enforce its own judgment. Rather its judgment is recorded in the trial court and then the judgment is enforced by the trial court as its own judgment.

A statute or rule usually provides that the winner is entitled as part of the judgment of the appellate court to recover its costs and interest on the judgment during the pendency of the appeal. Costs include the direct expenses of the appeal such as filing fees, printing and mailing expenses, and the like. They do not include, however, attorney fees for the trial or the appeal unless a statute expressly so provides. This is known as the "American rule." Such statutes have been made applicable to a growing list of types of cases, particularly in the federal courts. Attorney fees or other monetary sanctions can also be awarded to the prevailing party if the court finds that the appeal was frivolous or carried on in bad faith.

C. Comparison

1. The Appealable Judgment or Order

In most American jurisdictions, for a judgment to be effective it must be written in a separate document, signed by the judge, filed with the clerk, and entered in the docket of the case. It is thus relatively easy to identify a document that purports to be a judgment. The problem is more complicated in the English system. Instead of an order being effective only upon entry, as was the situation prior to 1986, it is effective when announced. Subsequently, the order is reduced to writing and is variously referred to as being filed, entered, or sealed. Further confusion is added by rule 4 of Order 59 which provides that the appeal time begins to run when an order is sealed or otherwise perfected. It is unclear whether filing or entry or both are necessary, at least for appeal purposes. Attempting to establish an effective date for an order different from the date on which the order is effective for appeal purposes can easily create confusion for the unwary solicitor. This is less of a problem in England than it might be, however, because of the ability of the Court of Appeal to grant an extension of time for taking an appeal even after the appeal time has expired.

2. Parties

There are two principal differences between England and the United States concerning a person's status as a party in the appellate court. In the United States, a person who is not formally a party in the trial court but who claims to be aggrieved by a judgment or order must first intervene in the trial court to acquire status as a party. Only if that status is granted can the party appeal the judgment. The party can, of course, appeal the denial of the petition to intervene. In England, on the other hand, only the potential to have been named a party is required to permit a person to appeal. This makes any dispute as to the right of a person to appeal a matter for resolution by the Court of Appeal. The United States approach is that all such questions should be resolved at the trial level with the development of a record. Action of the appellate court is required only if there is a challenge to the ruling of the trial court. The American approach appears preferable from the standpoint of saving the time of the appellate court, the superior ability of the trial court to make a record, and the greater familiarity of the trial judge with the facts of the case. This procedure also puts the burden of going forward on the person who claims party status, rather than on an opposing party.

The other major difference is the ability of the Court of Appeal to permit a notice of appeal to be served on a person who was not a party in the trial court. That person thereby becomes a party in the Court of Appeal and relief can be granted against the person. This power is consistent with the status of the proceeding in the Court of Appeal as a rehearing, but in view of the fact that the court itself treats the proceeding as an appeal and is bound by the record developed in the trial court, it is highly unlikely that the court will bring in a new party and develop the factual record necessary to grant relief against that party. In some circumstances this may be a useful power, but this will occur so seldom that it does not appear to be of great significance.

3. Initiating and Perfecting the Appeal

a. The Notice of Appeal

Both the United States and England use a notice of appeal to initiate the appellate process. The similarities stop there, however, because there are major disparities in virtually everything else. In England the formal structure of the procedure is that the appeal is brought by motion, with the notice of appeal merely being notice of the motion. The appeal thus appears to be just another step in the same proceeding rather than the initiation of a proceeding in another court. The difficulty with the notice of motion characterization is that there is no motion that is filed, it is only the notice. In the United States the notice of appeal is more than a notice, it is the operative document for taking the appeal. It is, in effect, a statement by the appellant that says "I hereby appeal." The filing and serving of the document is what gives the court, the other parties, and the world notice that an appeal has been taken. Conceptually, the American approach more accurately reflects what is occurring, and for this reason is preferable. The practical difference, however, is minimal.

A more important variation lies in the fact that the operative act for taking an appeal in England is the service of the notice of appeal while in most jurisdictions in the United States it is the filing of the notice. Filing was chosen in the United States because it is easier to establish when it occurs and it is notice to the court and to the world. In the federal system and in many states, service of the notice becomes the responsibility of the clerk of the trial court and not of the appellant. This technique was chosen to minimize disputes over service and to ensure that everyone who should receive notice of the filing does receive it.

There is also a difference in where the notice is filed. In England it is the Court of Appeal, in the United States it is the trial court. The latter choice was made to make it simpler for the appellant to take the appeal. The assumption is that the party seeking to appeal is familiar with filing papers in the trial court and is less likely to make a mistake when taking the appeal. The English practice creates no difficulties for cases tried in the Royal Courts of Justice in London, but the same cannot be said for cases tried in other cities, either before the High Court or a county court, or in any of the tribunals over which the Court of Appeal has jurisdiction. Many American jurisdictions at one time followed the English practice but abandoned it for the reasons stated above.

Of all of the differences, however, the one that has the greatest impact on the person taking the appeal is the content of the notice of appeal. The American notice requires only formalities--the name of the person taking the appeal, the date of the judgment appealed from, and the court to which the appeal is taken. The English notice requires much more substance--the specifics of the order appealed from, the grounds of appeal, the precise order sought from the Court of Appeal, and the list on which the appeal is to be set down. Setting out the grounds of appeal is the most burdensome. The appellant must think through the basis for the appeal at a preliminary stage before having the full record and is subsequently bound by those grounds and cannot raise additional ones. The basis for this requirement is to inform the respondent as early as possible what are the issues that it will have to face in defending the order. The best explanation for these differences probably lies in the fact that the American notice of appeal is considered to be a jurisdiction invoking document. Unless a proper notice of appeal is timely filed, the appellate court cannot hear the appeal.[21] Under these circumstances, the American approach is to make the document itself and its filing as simple as possible to prevent the dismissal of appeals for want of jurisdiction. The English approach, however, appears to treat the notice of appeal as simply another pleading in a continuous proceeding. Defects in it can always be cured at a later date (with permission of the court) and thus requiring more substance should not create major difficulties.

This approach is carried through to the timeliness of the notice of appeal. The American treatment of the notice of appeal means that the time for filing a notice of appeal cannot be extended except in the most narrow circumstances, only for a very short time beyond the original date, and only by the trial court. Under the English approach, however, the time can be extended in the same manner as the time for filing any other pleading. The United States treats the time limit on taking an appeal as an unwaivable statute of limitations. The English view, however, treats it as just another time requirement that can be waived at any time, even long after this original appeal period has expired and for whatever reason the Court of Appeal thinks is appropriate.

Which approach is preferable depends upon whether a higher value is placed on the termination of litigation or on resolving a particular dispute properly. The American view leans toward the former, but at the same time makes it as easy as possible to initiate a challenge to the outcome in the lower court. The English view, on the other hand, sees the correct result as having the higher value, even though making it more difficult to initiate the challenge. While valid arguments can be made on either side, the better view is to favor the interests of the successful party, the courts, and the public in concluding litigation. The unsuccessful party in the trial court should have the right to have the decision of the trial court reviewed in an appellate court, but the opportunity to seek that review should be very short and the ability of the courts to extend the time very limited. Shortening the time for taking an appeal, as has been done in both England and the United States, is not effective if an extension of time can be sought and granted long after the appeal time has expired and without any limitation on the reasons for granting an extension. It is far preferable to cut off the appeal period early, and allow the trial court to set aside the judgment for any major defect such as fraud. Restricting the opportunities for a delayed appeal is particularly important in England where the authority of the Court of Appeal is so broad.

There are advantages to having some detailed information about each appeal early in the appellate process. This can be used by the opposing party to ascertain what the appeal is about and by the court staff to assist in the processing of the case. Some American courts have required docketing statements for this purpose and have found them useful. These statements are filed shortly after the notice of appeal and are not binding in the sense that a party is not foreclosed from raising an issue not mentioned in the docketing statement. The requiring of such a statement would be very compatible with the existing procedure now followed by the Civil Appeals Office when a notice of appeal is filed. The combination of a simple notice of appeal plus a docketing statement is preferable to the more complicated notice of appeal because of the treatment of the notice of appeal as a pleading and the complications involved when it is not timely filed, is defective, or must be amended.

Service of the notice of appeal is made in England on those parties in the trial court who "may be affected by the appeal." In the United States it is made on all parties in the trial court. The American rule is better because the appellant may not be able or may not be the best person to determine who may be affected by the appeal. If all parties are served, then each party can determine for itself whether to participate in the appeal as a respondent or appellee.

The determination of when the appeal time begins to run is not uniform in the two systems. In England it is from the date on which the order is "sealed or otherwise perfected" while in the United States it is from the date of entry of the judgment on the docket book kept by the trial court clerk. Prior to 1986, the English rule was the same as the United States.[22] It is difficult to see the advantage in the English rule. Order 42 of the Supreme Court rules relating to judgments makes only incidental reference to sealing. Rule 5 of that order makes entry the key event. More confusing is rule 3 of Order 42 which provides that an order is effective from the day of its date, not the date of its entry or the date it is sealed. The combination of Orders 42 and 59 creates confusion as to when the appeal time starts to run. If sealing is the significant event, then it is difficult to ascertain when it occurs unless some record is made of the fact of sealing in a court record available to the public. What else constitutes perfecting is unclear. The American rule requires a judgment signed by the judge, then entry of that judgment in an official record of the trial court. The rule starts the running of the appeal time from the date of that entry. The latter event is preferable because of the certainty it gives. Any party or interested person can easily ascertain when the appeal period begins, and even more importantly, when it ends.

The processing of the notice of appeal in the English and American appellate courts is essentially the same. One obvious but insubstantial distinction is the maintenance of the many different lists in the English Court of Appeal. Whatever may have been the justification for the orginal development of the lists, they serve little purpose today. To the extent that certain appeals are given priority status, this can be reflected in the computer entry for the appeal. The same is true for the nature of the appeal to assist in assigning judges to the panel to hear the case. For these same reasons, it is not necessary to require that the appropriate list be designated in the notice of appeal. It is the obligation of the appellant to notify the parties who were served of the setting down of the appeal. This is better done by the appellate court clerk's office, as is done in the United States, to ensure prompt and uniform notice to all parties in the trial court.

b. Cross Appeal and Respondent's Notice

If the winning party in the trial court intends only to defend the judgment on the rationale of the trial court, the party need file no response to the notice of appeal in either the United States or England. If the party wishes to change the judgment or order being appealed, it must file a document so indicating in both countries -- a notice of cross appeal in the United States or a respondent's notice in England. In the latter country, however, a respondent's notice is labeled a cross appeal only if the respondent is seeking relief on a cause of action different from the subject of the original appeal. If variance in the order is sought on the same cause of action, then a simple respondent's notice is filed. A similar notice is required if the respondent intends to support the order being appealed on grounds different from the one relied upon by the trial court.

Putting a different label on an effort by the respondent to vary the order appealed from based on whether the relief sought on a different cause of action seems an unnecessary complication. It is unlikely, however, to cause any substantial harm. The last noted variation between the two systems can probably be explained by the fact that no briefs are filed in England. A respondent's notice is thus the only way that the appellant can be appraised of the basis on which the respondent will make its argument. With a skeleton argument now required, this justification is no longer valid.

4. Relief Pending Appeal

England and the United States differ in three respects concerning relief pending appeal. One major difference is when the judgment is for money only. In the United States there is an automatic right to a stay, subject only to the posting of security in an amount set by local rule by the court for each case. In England, however, the philosophy is strongly against depriving the prevailing party in the trial court of the benefits of the order in its favor. The result is a rule that a stay is granted only if it can be shown that the appellant will suffer some harm in the event the order is reversed. As to money damages, this means that security will be required only if the appellant can show that the respondent will be unlikely to repay the money in the event of a reversal.

The English rule appears to make more sense. It prevents an appeal being taken solely for the purpose of delay in paying the damage award but allows flexibility to protect all parties.

The second difference--in England an appellant may be required to post security for costs--arises out of the fact that appeal costs are usually small in the United States because they do not include legal fees as they do in England.

The third difference concerns who has the primary duty to grant relief pending appeal. In the United States it is the trial judge while in England it is a judge of the Court of Appeal or the Registrar. The American rule is preferable because the trial judge is much more familiar with the circumstances of each party and can more easily assess the need for the relief.

5. Records and Bundles

Other than in terminology, the crucial distinction between the two systems lies in who has the responsibility for preparing and filing in the appellate court the relevant documents from the trial court. The English rule puts this responsibility on the appellant. The United States used to follow the same practice. It was discovered, however, that counsel for the appellants were notoriously inefficient in getting the documents transmitted from the trial court to the appellate court. Just as important, the documents were in the possession of the trial court clerk who, as a practical matter, forwarded them to the appellate court. A recognition of these facts led appellate courts in the United States to transfer the obligation for compiling and transmitting the record from the appellant to the clerk of the trial court.

The 1986 Practice Statement of the Master of the Rolls indicates that the Court of Appeal has the same problem with delay in having the bundles filed as did American appellate courts. Placing the responsibility on the trial clerks worked in the United States and should also be effective in England.

Delay in the preparation of transcripts of testimony was long a problem in the United States but has largely been resolved by several measures. First was to ensure early ordering of the transcript by the appellant's attorney. The second was to require that the court reporter rather than the appellant request an extension of time. The third was to place in the appellate court the authority over the granting of extensions. There is no apparent difficulty with transcripts prepared by stenographers in England, but there is a major problem in obtaining the notes of evidence prepared by judges as well as the reasoned judgments of the trial judge when no stenographer was present. Measures similar to those in the United States for ensuring prompt preparation of transcripts by court reporters would likely solve the problem of obtaining the notes and judgments of the judges, i.e., place the responsibility on the solicitor to request them (with a copy of the request to the Court of Appeals) within a limited period of time and then place the responsibility on the judge to prepare and file them.

In England, if bundles are not lodged in the Civil Appeals Office in a timely manner, a notice is sent to the appellant. If no response to the notice is forthcoming, an *ex parte* hearing is held on whether to dismiss the appeal. In the United States, the appeal would be dismissed automatically by the clerk of the appellate court. When a party does not respond to a notice from the court, there seems little point in having a hearing. The notice should make it clear, of course, that failure to respond to the notice within a specified period of time will result in the appeal being dismissed without further notice. If there is a hearing, however, it should not be *ex parte*. One of the principal factors that ought to be considered when deciding whether to dismiss the appeal is what harm the delay has caused the respondent. That can only be known if the respondent is given notice of the hearing and an opportunity to present its position. Handling all of this on the basis of memoranda to the court rather than by oral hearing would, of course, greatly simplify the matter.

6. Application and Motion Practice

One of the clearest examples of the contrast between the oral tradition in England and the written tradition in the United States is the manner in which applications or motions are considered. In England all applications are the subject of an oral hearing, while in the United States they are almost always disposed of on written submissions only. On the other hand, almost all motions in the United States are ruled upon by one or more judges, while the Registrar acts on most applications in the Court of Appeal.

Whatever the justification for conducting an oral hearing on the merits of each appeal, they surely are not relevant to applications if the efficient use of judicial time is of any significance.

Giving authority to the Registrar for ruling on most applications is far superior to the pre-1982 practice of having them heard by a panel of judges. Much of this advantage is lost however, by allowing an appeal of right from the decision of the Registrar to a single judge, and the right to seek application for leave to appeal from any decision on an application by a single judge (except an application for leave to appeal). As can be seen, the opportunities to consume the time of the judges are virtually endless. The better way to proceed is to treat each application as having been ruled upon by the court with no opportunity to appeal from the Registrar to a single judge or from a single judge to a three judge panel. At most there should be an opportunity to seek reconsideration of any decision, with the request being considered on the written papers only by a motions panel. To devote any more resources to applications is simply to distract the judges from their essential role of ruling on the substantive merits of appeals. To this end, the rules should not spell out who rules on particular types of applications; that should be left to the internal procedures of the court and be subject to change as circumstances dictate.

7. Briefs and Appendices

The relative merits of the oral tradition with no briefs and the written tradition with them are discussed in Chapter 3, *supra*.

8. Case Management and Internal Operating Procedures

a. The Philosophy of Case Management

The idea of active case management for appellate courts developed in the United States in the 1960's as a response to the crisis of volume. That philosophy came to England in the early 1980's but independantly of the American experience. The philosophy has not come to full acceptance in England, however, because of the overriding influences of the oral tradition. This influence is still felt in two major respects -- the scheduling of an appeal for oral hearing is still done primarily at the initiative of counsel, and the length and pace of the oral hearing is largely within the control of counsel. The March, 1989, Practice Direction indicates, however, that the latter may be changed. In sharp contrast, the determination of when (and whether) appeals are to be argued orally is solely within the control of the appellate court in the United States, as are the length and pace of the oral hearing.

b. Case Processing

Since the appointment of the Registrar and the creation of the Civil Appeals Office, monitoring the progress of appeals has begun, but only in a limited way, given the fact that the only items required to be filed are the bundles and the forms sent to the appellant. A review is made periodically of the appeals that have been pending for a substantial period of time after the bundle was filed without a request for a hearing on the merits. Monitoring is much more active in the United States because of the greater number of documents that are filed. If the Court of Appeal does require additional items be lodged, monitoring compliance with due dates is essential, as is a system for the automatic imposition of known sanctions.

It also does little good if, when a sanction is imposed, an application to lift the sanction will generate an oral hearing and a grant of the request.

Most of the techniques of case processing other than case monitoring--docketing statements, settlement conferences, summary dispositions, and expedited appeals have not been attempted or even discussed in England. The obvious reason is because they may be thought to be incompatible with the oral tradition. As discussed in Chapter 3, changes in that tradition should be made. If they are, then the Court of Appeal should attempt to use the techniques the Americans have found useful. The control over the length of oral argument allows certainty in the scheduling of oral arguments in the United States. The development of the schedule for each period of oral argument is extremely simple--the clerk's office merely schedules appeals in accordance with whatever order the court uses (usually in the order the record or last brief is filed). Attorneys receive approximately one month's notice of the argument date.

The unlimited length of the English oral hearing has made it virtually impossible to anticipate how long the hearings will last. The hearings have been scheduled in accordance with the estimates given by counsel shortly after the appeal was set down. Sometimes the hearing lasts longer than the estimates and this can create problems for the appeals scheduled to be heard next. The difficulty that arises most often is that the hearing may not last quite as long as estimated, so the panel hearing the appeal has dead time unless the hearing on another appeal can be scheduled on short notice. It is for this reason that the "floaters" were developed. While this does allow better use of the judges' time, it plays havoc with the schedules of the barristers involved. The entire process makes the life of the listing staff most hectic. The closest analogies to the listing office are the clerk's office in a trial court with a master calendar or a bookmaker's office. Telephones ring incessantly and a constant series of emergencies occur as appeals settle, barristers are unavailable, or a high priority appeal must be heard immediately. That the system works as well as it does is a tribute to the competence of the staff.

In recognition of these problems, the Master of the Rolls in his 1988 annual review proposed the addition to the court staff of several legally trained persons who would be responsible for reviewing the relevant documents and setting the length of the hearing for each appeal. The adoption of the proposal in the March, 1989, Practice Direction is a major step in giving the court control over the time of its judges. Objections to the time allotment, however, should not give the opportunity for another appeal and another oral hearing. If counsel think the time is too short, review of staff's decision should be in accordance with the procedure recommended in subsection 6, *supra*, for the review of actions on applications.

Another technique that could be attempted within the confines of the oral tradition is the settlement conference. This would be particularly appropriate for the types of appeals that have the lowest priority for scheduling for oral hearings--tort and contract cases from the Queen's Bench Division and the county courts, and because of the easy access to the legal representatives of the parties in London.

c. The Disposition Process

The dramatic differences in the disposition process under the two systems are compared in Chapter 3, section C *supra*.

9. Order and Mandate

The procedure under which the order of the Court of Appeal and the mandate of an American appellate court are prepared are essentially the same. One difference, that may effect when the ultimate termination of the dispute occurs, is that there is no formal time limit in England on when the order is prepared and sent out, whereas in the United States it must be completed within a fixed period of time. Obviously requiring that it may be done within a specific time period prevents any unnecessary delay.

10. Reconsideration

There is no procedure for seeking reconsideration in the English Court of Appeal either before the original panel or the court *en banc*. Most American intermediate appellate courts still allow for one or the other or both. Neither is necessary in England and should not be allowed in the United States if the supreme court of the jurisdiction has the capacity to reconcile disagreements between different divisions of the intermediate appellate court and perform its law development role as is the situation in all but a few states.

11. Seeking Review in the Supreme Court of the House of Lords.

The Appellate Committee of the House of Lords and a supreme court in an American jurisdiction with an intermediate appellate court perform much the same function in much the same way. The most significant similarity is that the jurisdiction of each is almost entirely discretionary. There are, however, some major ways in which they differ. First, the Court of Appeal as well as the Appeal Committee of the House of Lords can grant leave to appeal. In American jurisdictions, only the highest court itself can decide whether to hear an appeal. It seems inappropriate that an inferior court can dictate what appeals a superior court must hear. The highest court of a jurisdiction should be the sole arbiter of what appeals it hears and decides. For a court with discretionary jurisdiction, deciding what cases to hear is almost as important exercise of a court's power as deciding the merits of the cases it does hear. It is significant that most of the appeals heard by the House of Lords are allowed by the Court of Appeal rather than by the Appeal Committee.

Second, the Appeal Committee of the House of Lords hears oral argument on whether it should hear an appeal. This again is a demonstration of the influence of the oral tradition, but is clearly an unwise use of judicial time. Setting forth the reasons why the law, as developed by a decision of the Court of Appeal, is incorrect and why the House of Lords should review the decision can be done just as well or even better in writing. Third, the procedures for getting an appeal heard by the Appellate Committee are far more complicated than seeking review by a supreme court in the United States, with no apparent justification. Fourth, the flexibility in the membership of the Appellate Committee from case to case has no counterpart in the United States. It introduces an element of uncertainty that should not exist in the highest court of a nation because it means that what the law is may turn upon who is assigned to sit on a particular appeal. It also permits the suspicion, if not the actuality, of predetermining the result by the choice of which law lords or other persons eligible to sit do so.

ENDNOTES

1. The material in this chapter is based on Supreme Court Act 1981; Order 59 of the Rules of the Supreme Court; *Supreme Court Practice* (The White Book) Order 59 (1988); 37 Halsbury's Laws of England ¶ 677-709 (4th ed. 1982) 5 Atkin's *Court Forms, Appeals* ¶ 65-95 (2d ed. 1984); interviews with the Master of the Rolls, Registrar John Adams and the staff of the Court of Appeal Civil Appeals Office, and the author's personal observations.

2. Order 59 v.3 (5).

3. Order 59, v.4 (1)

4. Supreme Court Practice 1988 note 59/4/2.

5. *C.M. Van Stillevoldt BV v. El Carriers Inc.*, [1983] 1 All E.R. 699, 704 C.A.

6. Atkin's *Court Forms, supra* note 1 at ¶ 78 note 2.

7. Id at ¶ 90, note 2.

8. L. Blom-Cooper & G. Drewery, *Final Appeal* 132 (1972) shows that from 1952-68, of 366 leaves to appeal to the House of Lords in cases, 286 were granted by the Court of Appeal and 80 by the Appeal Committee of the House of Lords. The statutes published annually by the Lord Chancellor's Department do not include data on this question.

9. The procedures for appeals to the House of Lords are governed by Standing Orders of the House of Lords, the Administration of Justice Act 1969 as amended by the Administration of Justice Act 1977 and the Supreme Court Act 1981. See generally Atkin's *Court Forms, supra* note 1 at ¶37-64. For a fuller description of the appellate process in the House of Lords see L. Blom-Cooper & G. Drewry, *supra* note 8.

10. The process described in this chapter is representative of many if not most American appellate courts, but certainly not all. There is a great variation between appellate courts in different jurisdictions and even within the same jurisdiciton. Further, no one court would exactly follow each step in the process as set forth here. In a few jurisdictions, for example, service

of the notice of appeal rather than its filing, is the crucial act in initiating an appeal.

11. *Torres v. Oakland Scavenger Co.*, 108 S.Ct. 2405 (1988).

12. Cases wrestling with the problem of when the appeal time begins to run are collected in the annual cumulative supplement to R. Martineau, *Modern Appellate Practice-Federal and State Civil Appeals* § 6.5 (1983).

13. Federal Rule of Appellate Procedure 3(a) expressly provides that "[f]ailure of an appellant to take any step other than the timely filing of a notice of appeal does not affect the validity of the appeal, but is grounds only for such action as the court of appeals deems appropriate, which may include dismissal of the appeal." Many states have similar provisions.

14. *Washington Met. Area Transit Com'n. v. Holiday Tours,* Inc., 559 F.2d 841 (1977).

15. Tate, *The Art of Brief Writing: What a Judge Wants to Read*, 4 Litigation 11, 13-15 (Winter, 1978).

16. For a critical assessment of settlement conferences, see Goldman, *The Appellate Settlement Conference: An Effective Procedural Reform?* 2 State Ct. J. 3 (Winter, 1978). See also Steelman and Goldman, *Preargument Settlement Conferences in State Appellate Courts,* 10 State Court J. 4 (Fall, 1986). A more positive evaluation is found in Kaufman, *Must Every Appeal Run the Gamut? The Civil Appeals Management Plan,* 95 Yale L. J. 755 (1986).

17. Chief Justice Rehnquist tells how he prepares for oral argument in W. Rehnquist, *The Supreme Court* 271-73 (1987). U.S. Circuit Judge Frank Coffin does likewise in F. Coffin, *The Ways of a Judge* 81-108 (1980).

18. The various types of judicial conferences are discussed in R. Leflar, *Internal Operating Procedures of Appellate Courts* 27-59 (1976).

19. For an excellent review of the use of *en banc* rehearings in the federal courts of appeals, see Solimine, *Ideology and En Banc Review,* 67 North Carolina L. Rev. 29 (1988).

20. Rule 10 of the Rules of the United States Supreme Court states that it will grant review "only when there are special and important reasons therefor." It then lists three types of decisions that it will likely consider, but states a caveat that the list is not controlling nor the limits of the court's discretion.

21. In *Torres v. Oakland Scavenger Co.*, 108 S. Ct. 2405 (1988) the United States Supreme Court demonstrated the necessity for compliance with the formal requirements of the notice of appeal by holding that a notice of appeal that referred to one party by name and other parties as "et al" did not preserve the right of appeal for any party not specifically named.

22. Supreme Court Practice 1988 ¶ 59/4/2.

Chapter 6   The Future of Appellate Justice in England and the United States

A. Summary of Similarities and Differences

1. Structure and Function

The English and American systems of appellate justice are alike in many ways, but dramatically different in others. The structures are essentially the same, with appeals going from the trial court to an intermediate appellate court to a supreme court. The principal function of the intermediate appellate courts in each system is error correction, notwithstanding the formal classification of the English appeal as a rehearing, with law development the primary task of the highest court. The principles of appellate review in both countries are also quite similar in demanding that only an aggrieved party can appeal and only final judgments or orders or interlocutory orders that may cause irreparable harm can be appealed as of right. The standards of review in each jurisdiction are almost identical, again in spite of the rehearing status of the proceeding in the English Court of Appeal. Doctrines of harmless error and restricting review to issues presented in the lower court are similarly applicable in both systems, although the latter rule is observed more faithfully in England than in the United States.

There are two areas in which the systems differ sharply and appear to be growing more widely apart--the right to appeal and the size of the reviewing panel in the intermediate appellate court. Notwithstanding the crisis of volume in American appellate courts, there has been no acceptance of proposals to require that a review of the merits of an appeal from a final judgment be subject to a preliminary finding of worthiness by a single judge or a panel of judges. Such a requirement has been imposed in England to some types of final orders, and legislation is currently pending to extend this procedure to all classes of final orders. A major expansion will occur even without this legislation by the transfer of much of the jurisdiction of the High Court to the county courts unless a change in Order 59 is made. Compounding the problem is the fact that the responsibility for deciding whether to grant leave to appeal has been placed in the unreviewable discretion of a single judge.

The second major difference lies in the size of the reviewing panel. It is a premise of the American system that an intermediate appellate court should always sit in panels of no less than three because of the internal dynamics of a panel of that size. In the English Court of Appeal today approximately half of the appeals heard on the merits are decided by two judge panels. Again, this will increase with the transfer of jurisdiction from the High Court to the county court.

2. Personnel

The personnel of appellate review in England and the United States are similar in involving lawyers, judges, and staff, but the similarities are at best superficial in almost every respect.

The most well known difference between the two countries is the division of the legal profession in England into two branches, solicitors and barristers, with only the barristers having the right of audience in appellate courts. In the United States, each state has an undivided legal profession and any lawyer admitted to practice in any jurisdiction can practice in any court in that jurisdiction, including the appellate courts. The academic education of English barristers and solicitors and American lawyers is quite different. The former is undergraduate and not required for admission to the bar or qualifying as a solicitor while the latter is graduate and mandatory. In England, however, the academic training is followed by one year of vocational training and a one year pupillage for barristers while for solicitors it is one year vocational and three years apprenticeship. Civil procedure is at best an elective course in England while required in the United States. American law schools are required to offer skills courses. Skills have been no part of a barrister's training in England, even in the vocational stage, but will be in the future. The proposals of the Lord Chancellor to expand the rights of audience of solicitors and change other practices of barristers will have little or no effect on the quality of appellate advocacy.

The only similarity between the two systems concerns appellate litigation--in neither have the knowledge and skills required of an appellate litigator given much attention. This situation is changing in the United States but not in England.

With respect to judges, the combination of formal and informal requirements to hold judicial office in the English system puts only the most highly qualified barristers on the High Court and only experienced High Court judges on the Court of Appeal. By contrast professional qualifications are often not significant in the United States, particularly in states that elect their judges.

Another significant variation between the two systems concern the staff who serve the appellate courts. In the United States, each appellate judge has at least one legal assistant and one secretary appointed and supervised by the judge. The remainder of the staff, including both legal and clerical, are appointed and supervised by personnel responsible only to the judges. In England, on the other hand, the judges have no personal staff other than clerks who generally perform services of a personal nature rather than legal or secretarial. Court staff are employees of the executive branch appointed and supervised by persons in that branch. Only the judges who are presidents of divisions of the Supreme Court, including the Court of Appeals, have secretaries and they are appointed by the Lord Chancellor, as is the Registrar of Civil Appeals who, until 1989, was the only legally trained person on the staff of the Civil Division of the Court of Appeal.

Complete reliance is placed on counsel to bring the relevant facts and law to the attention of the judges. The decision made in 1989 to add legally trained staff to the Court of Appeal represents a major change in this approach, although there is no suggestion they will play any role in helping the judges on the merits of the appeals.

The most fundamental differences between the two systems are in the manner in which appeals are presented to the appellate courts and the opinions or judgments prepared by the judges. These differences can best be summarized in describing the English system as based on the oral tradition and the American system on the written tradition.

3. The Oral and Written Traditions

Under the oral tradition in its pure form, all of the material considered by the judges--facts, law, and the arguments of counsel based on them--must be presented to the judges in open court. Immediately following is the oral rendition of the decision of each judge and the judge's reasons in support of it. Both are based solely on what was presented by counsel, with no independent research by the judges. The oral tradition means that an observer in the courtroom can see and hear the entire decision making process and be exposed to all of the factors that go into it. The observer can literally observe the judges making up their minds.

The American system, on the other hand, involves primary reliance on written presentations by counsel with either a short or no oral argument, followed by a written opinion prepared by one of the judges after such additional research as the judges consider necessary, and with all of the judges joining in the one opinion.

Publication of judgments and opinions also vary widely. In the United States in each jurisdiction there is at least one series of reports that includes all of the opinions designated for publication by each appellate court of the jurisdiction. In England, on the other hand, only a small percentage of the judgments of the Court of Appeals are published in general series reports, none of which are devoted exclusively to the judgments of the Court of Appeal. In addition, the judges of the Court of Appeal play no part in the publication decision.

4. Caseload Growth and Responses to It

Both systems have had increases in caseloads since the early 1960's, but the growth in the United States has been far greater. Each system has responded in various ways to this increase, including the addition of new judges and, in the United States, the creation of intermediate appellate courts in states where they did not previously exist. Since 1961 the federal courts of appeals have tripled the number of dispositions on the merits per judge with only a marginal increase in the median time span from the filing of the notice of appeal to the termination in the appellate court. In England during the same period, the per judge disposition rate has decreased rather than increased, while the median time is almost half again as long as the Americans.

There are a number of reasons for these developments. For the Americans, restricting the right to appeal or reducing the size of the appellate panel were not options to be considered. If anything, making it easier and cheaper to appeal was one of the goals of the appellate system. For the appellate courts, their principal option was to increase the productivity of each judge. This they did through the use of staff, particularly legal, disposition without oral argument or sharply restricting the length of oral argument, writing less than full opinions intended for publication or eliminating the opinion entirely, settlement conferences, summary dispositions, and a variety of other measures.

Beginning in 1982 the English Court of Appeal has also attempted to improve productivity by instituting the prereading of some portions of the bundles and initially requesting but not requiring skeleton arguments and chronologies of events from counsel. These efforts were not successful, however, because when oral hearings were scheduled and how long they lasted were still within the control of counsel. Changes made in 1989 that require the submission of skeleton arguments four weeks in advance of the oral hearing, the appointment of legal staff to review them, adjustment of the estimates made by counsel of the length of the oral hearing, and greater advance preparation by the judges, give the best hope that the length of the oral hearing may be shortened with a consequent increase in the number of dispositions on the merits per judge.

5. The Civil Appeals Process

The civil appeals process in the two systems is similar in many respects, but there are fundamental variations, many of which are attributable to the differences between the oral and written traditions.

Major variations in the process begin with the content of the notice of appeal, its jurisdictional nature, the significance of service, and the ability to obtain an extension of time for taking an appeal. The United States emphasizes finality, while England emphasizes the opportunity to seek review. Once an appeal is filed, most American appellate courts exercise active case management to ensure that appeals are disposed of as quickly as possible. In England, the idea of active case management is only beginning to take hold. The scheduling of cases for oral argument has always been in accordance with internal court procedures without consultation with counsel in the United States, while in England it is not only at the convenience of counsel but at counsel's initiative. The length of the oral hearing has traditionally been in the sole control of counsel in England, while in the United States appellate courts have been setting limits on its duration for over one hundred years.

Nothing distinguishes the two systems more than the process for the disposition of cases and preparation of statements of reasons in support of decisions. In England the oral hearing, decision conference, and the preparation and rendering of the decisions and the reasons to support it are all combined in a single public proceeding. In the United States, on the other hand, each of these steps is done separately, with only the short oral hearing conducted in public.

B. The Future of Appellate Justice

In attempting to assess the future of appellate justice in England and the United States, there must first be an understanding of the essentials of any system of appellate justice for it to be both efficient and effective. These essentials flow from the two principal functions of appellate review -- error correction and law development, that is review to benefit the litigants individually as well as to serve society in general. To achieve these ends, appellate review should include:

1. a right to appeal a final judgment
2. to a panel of three judges that
3. after such consideration of the views of the parties as the complexity of the case dictates
4. render a decision supported by a written statement of reasons
5. which if precedent setting is published
6. with published opinions easily available to interested persons,
7. all without undue expense or delay to the litigants.

The appellate process in any particular jurisdiction will invariably include many other features imposed by statute, rule, or tradition. One or more of these features may be important in specific cases or types of cases, and may be more important to certain participants in the appellate process. These other features must always, however, be treated as subordinate to the essential features and never be allowed to displace any of the essential features.

1. England

The system of appellate justice in England is currently in a state of transition. For a century after the passage of the Judicature Acts of 1873-75, the system remained essentially the same. To the extent that there were changes, particularly in caseload, they were easily handled by simply adding more judges to the Court of Appeal. It was inevitable, however, in light of economic and social changes in England, that the demand for appellate justice would grow to such an extent that the mere addition of new judges would not prove an adequate remedy. After a point, adding new judges itself created additional problems.

Since 1982 there has been a recognition that it was no longer acceptable to continue to do things the way they had always been done simply for the sake of adherence to tradition. Many changes were made in the appellate process, but they did not appear to have any helpful effect on the pace of the process or on the nature of the consideration given by the judges to individual cases. Two of the changes, in fact, have an adverse effect -- requiring leave to appeal in certain types of cases and having them heard by two rather than three judge panels.

Before there can be substantial improvement in the English system, there must be a recognition that the oral tradition, whatever its merits at the trial level, is neither efficient nor effective at the appellate level. Preservation of this tradition, which should be recognized as only a means to achieve appellate justice and not an end in itself, should not be used as a justification for restricting the right of appeal or for changing the essential nature of the reviewing panel by reducing its size to less than three. Such changes adversely affect both the extent to which appellate justice is available to litigants and the quality of the justice received by them.

The major premise of the oral tradition is the skill of the English barrister as an oral advocate. This premise is not justified by the education or training of the barrister either at university or in the vocational education training before or during pupillage. It is likewise not justified by their performance in the Court of Appeal, as observed by the author and others. There is no appellate bar and thus no specialists in appellate advocacy.

The English system does not recognize appellate litigation as demanding either specialized knowledge or skills. The changes in the vocational training of barristers implemented in 1989 do not mention appellate advocacy. Neither do any of the reports of papers developed in connection with the Government's efforts to reform the legal profession and the delivery of legal services. The reality is that the skills of a trial advocate bear little relationship to those of an appellate advocate. It is not surprising, consequently, that the average English barrister is no more competent in an appellate setting than his American counterpart. The effect of this inadequacy on English appellate justice, however, is far greater than in the United States. This is because the English system relies almost entirely on the oral skills of the barrister, while the American system does not.

It is obvious that the oral tradition, notwithstanding the strength of the belief in its virtues, cannot remain unaltered, immune to the pressures of caseload and the technology of the computer age. Some changes have already been made in it and more are properly in the offing. Sir Jack Jacob has predicted in his 1986 Hamlyn lecture that the English legal process of the future will be a combination of oral and written procedures. This should be particularly true in the appellate courts where all of the relevant information--the facts as represented in the record and the law as found in statutes and judicial opinions--is already in written form before the judges consider it. The only major questions left open are how the views of the parties on the relationship of this written data to the issues in the case should be presented to and considered by the judges, how the judges should prepare their judgments on these issues, and how all of this material should be made available to the public. When viewed from this perspective, the task of developing solutions to the crisis of volume should not be unduly difficult, particularly in view of the relatively small caseload of the Court of Appeal.

Central to a solution to the problem of increasing the productivity of English Court of Appeal is the recognition of the relationship between the number of appeals that can be heard orally and the number of appeals that can be decided on the merits. If an oral hearing is held on every appeal, then the ratio between them is one to one. This means that to increase productivity the length of the oral hearing must be reduced or some appeals decided without oral hearing, or both. The tradition in the English Court of Appeal has been that every appeal decided on the merits is heard orally, and that the timing and the length of the oral hearing are solely within the control of counsel. Under such a procedure, how the judges spend their time is controlled by counsel and thus the number of cases they can dispose of--their productivity--is controlled by counsel. The only way to change this is for the court to take control of its own schedule by determining for itself how long the oral hearing should last and when it should occur. The March, 1989, Practice Direction would appear to reflect the adoption of this view by the Court of Appeal.

The shortening of the oral hearing is similarly dependent upon requiring counsel to submit in advance their versions of the issues and the facts and the authorities upon which they rely so that the oral hearing can be limited to their arguments as to why the facts and the law require the court to rule in their client's favor. Again, the March, 1989, Practice Direction is a major step in achieving this goal.

The effectiveness and the accountability of the English system of appellate justice cannot equal that of the American system until it is recognized that the appellate process should be primarily a written one. This will give the judges a much greater opportunity to consider the facts, the law, and the arguments of counsel and to craft carefully their judgments. It will also provide interested persons the opportunity to study the judgments and the factual and legal bases for them, thereby enhancing public awareness of the law, critical analysis of it, and accountability of the system to the public it serves.

2. United States

The appellate justice system in the United States is facing somewhat different problems than the English system, but they stem from the same problem--the volume of cases. American appellate courts faced the crisis of volume much sooner than did England. They responded more quickly because the pressures were greater, the written tradition permitted greater flexibility in developing new procedures and techniques, and Americans are simply not as dedicated to tradition as the English.

The result is that the number of appeals disposed of on the merits per judge has increased dramatically. Most of the changes have not adversely affected the essentials of appellate justice except when appellate courts have abandoned preparing a written statement of reasons in support of their decisions. A written statement is essential for two reasons--as a guarantee that the decision is carefully thought through and as a means of accountability both to the litigants in the case and to the legal public.

A major difficulty has arisen with regard to opinions that are designated by the court not to be published in the official or semi-official reports. In some instances these opinions are precedential and should be published. The greater problem is, however, that these unpublished opinions are included in computer based systems and various specialized unofficial reporters. Such limited publication creates problems of unequal access by litigants in other cases.

An even greater problem exists in larger jurisdictions in which the total number of cases being decided at the intermediate level is far too many to permit the supreme court to resolve all conflicts between different panels of the intermediate appellate court or to exercise its law development function in all of the cases in which it should. When these conditions occur, there should be created at the intermediate level the capacity to resolve conflicts and develop the law until the supreme court decides to act.[1]

There are other things that the intermediate appellate courts can do to reduce their workload. Elimination of "doing justice" as a function of appellate courts separate from error correction and law development, strict enforcement of the final judgment rule, refusal to consider new issues on appeal, hearing oral argument only when the judges have questions to ask of counsel that cannot better be answered in writing and only when they think it will help them reach a decision, insistence upon a higher level of competence by appellate litigators, and assignment of additional functions to professional staff can all do much to ensure that the time and energies of the appellate judges are not wasted on matters not essential to appellate justice.

Even if all of these recommended techniques are used, however, there is still a serious question whether those American intermediate appellate courts with the highest caseloads can continue to perform their function in accordance with the essentials of appellate justice. Several thoughtful federal appellate judges, Frank Coffin of the First Circuit,[2] Irving Kaufman of the Second Circuit,[3] and Howard Markey of the Federal Circuit,[4] have recently pointed to the harmful effects on appellate justice of too many judges deciding too many cases. Their concerns are well taken. Such concerns have led some to propose solutions that have already been utilized in England--greater reliance on oral rather than written processes, reduction of panel size, and eliminating the right of appeal. The author's examination of how those procedures actually work in the English system, as demonstrated in this book, clearly shows that each of them adds nothing to the efficiency of the English process and at the same time substantially detracts from its effectiveness in providing the essentials of appellate justices. Just as significantly, neither American appellate judges nor American lawyers have accepted any of these proposals as useful solutions to the problems confronting American appellate courts.

Another proposal, made recently by an American Bar Association committee and by a federal commission,[5] resurrects the often rejected idea of having specialist judges handle specific categories of cases based on subject matter, e.g. tax, criminal, administrative. Whether or not the proposal is cast in terms of specialist judges rather than specialist courts the concept is essentially the same--that experts can provide greater uniformity and greater efficiency than generalists. This approach to appellate justice was fully considered when the American Bar Association's Standards for Court Organization were drafted in the mid 1970's. Section 1.13 states that "appellate courts of specialized subject matter jurisdiction should not be established." In the Commentary to this section, it states certain principles for organizing an appellate court. "The *first* principle is that appellate courts of specialized subject-matter jurisdiction should not be established." (Emphasis supplied.) The principal reason given in that "the appellate court function of developing the law cannot be performed in a coherent and consistent way if divisions compel the law's fabric to be made in a decisional patchwork."

There are other reasons that are just as compelling. The first is that in many cases issues cannot be so neatly isolated. Cases that may involve a specialized area also may involve other areas that are appropriately the task of another panel. Procedural questions, of course, can arise in any case, as can questions of a constitutional nature. A more practical consideration is the dislike of most appellate judges to be limited to only certain types of cases. A steady diet of any particular type of case will, for most judges, make a difficult job even worse. There are times when a certain inefficiency is desirable,[6] and this is one of them. The experience with assigning English Court of Appeal judges to sit in the Criminal Division is instructive. Each judge's assignment is limited to three weeks. When the author asked why the time period was so short, the simple explanation was that the judges could not stand it for any longer than that. For these reasons, the specialist panel idea should not be viewed as a useful remedy for the future.[7]

The American appellate judges have an enviable record in coping with the crisis of volume. The pressures of caseload are almost certain to be even greater in the future. By continuing to focus on the essentials of appellate review they can continue to modify the appellate process to permit them to perform the awesome task society has assigned to them both efficiently and effectively.

ENDNOTES

1. The Institute of Judicial Administration recently annouced a study of interpanel conflicts on state intermediate appellate courts. 22 I.J.A. Report 8 Nos. 1-2 (1990).

2. Coffin, *Grace Under Pressure: A Call for Judicial Self-Help,* 50 Ohio St. L.J. 399 (1989).

3. Kaufman, *New Remedies for the Next Century of Judicial Reform: Time as the Greatest Innovator,* 57 Fordham L. Rev. 253 (1988).

4. Markey, *On the Present Deterioration of the Federal Appellate Process: Never Another Learned Hand,* 33 South Dakota L. Rev. 371 (1988).

5. ABA Standing Committee on Federal Judicial Improvements 29-33 (1989); Federal Courts Study Committee, Final Report 69-72, 120-121 (1990).

6. Gross, *The American Advantage: The Value of Inefficient Litigation,* 85 Michigan L. Rev. 734 (1987).

7. For an excellent debate on the necessity for substituting subject matter courts for regional courts see Hellman, *Jumboism and Jurisprudence: The Theory and Practice of Precedent in the Large Appellate Court,* 56 U. of Chicago L. Rev. 541 (1989) (against the proposal) and Meador, *A Challenge to Judicial Architecture: Modifying the Regional Design of the U.S. Courts of Appeals,* 56 U. of Chicago L. Rev. 603 (1989) (favoring the proposal). Judge James Oakes of the U.S. Court of Appeals for the Second Circuit also challenges the premise that inconsistency in decisions between the various circuit courts of appeals is out of control or necessarily bad in Oakes, *Grace Notes on "Grace Under Pressure,"* 50 Ohio St. L. J. 701, 712-13 (1989). For a report of a similar debate concerning the three divisions of the High Court see Note, The *Divisions of the High Court,* 8 Civil Justice Q. 4 (1989).

Appendix A Summary of Recommendations

In Chapters 1-5 and particularly in the comparison section of each chapter, the strengths and weaknesses and the major differences of each system were identified and analyzed. The relative advantages of each system's approach as to each difference were discussed and a conclusion reached as to which was preferable. Each of these conclusions constitutes a recommendation for a change in the American or English system of appellate justice. The major recommendations for changes in each system are summarized below.

1. England

a. Structure and Function

1) Establish by statute the right to appeal to the Court of Appeal from the final order of a court and make appeals from any non final order subject to leave to appeal.

2) Take away the power of the Supreme Court Rules Committee to restrict the right to appeal a final order.

3) Require that an application for leave to appeal be decided by a three judge panel, not a single judge.

4) Establish general criteria for the granting of applications for leave to appeal.

5) Eliminate the *ex parte* filing and initial consideration of an application for leave to appeal.

6) Eliminate the authority of the trial judge to grant leave to appeal.

7) Make the distinction between final and interlocutory orders turn on the relief granted, not the relief sought.

8) Take away from the Supreme Court Rules Committee the power to define what is a final order and what is an interlocutory order.

9) Place in the trial judge authority to grant party status by a non party for purposes of appeal.

b. Personnel of Appellate Review

1) Require civil procedure, appellate procedure, and trial advocacy be a part of the legal education of every barrister and solicitor and appellate advocacy of every barrister.

2) Require continuing legal education in appellate litigation.

3) Place authority in the courts over the staff serving the courts including appointment, promotion, discharge, and compensation.

4) Provide each appellate judge with a minimum of one legally trained assistant and one secretary.

c. The Oral Tradition

1) Place in selected libraries copies of the bundle, skeleton arguments, and judgments for every appeal terminated on the merits.

2) Restrict the oral hearing to advocacy.

3) Impose time limits on the length of the oral hearing.

4) Issue a single written judgment of the court on each appeal decided on the merits.

5) Place authority in the judges on the panel issuing a judgment to decide whether it should be published.

6) Include every judgment selected for publication in at least one series of reports along with the speeches of the Appellate Committee of the House of Lords.

7) Prohibit the citation of judgments not published in the general series.

d. Coping With Increased Caseloads

Require that each appeal decided on the merits be decided by a three judge panel.

e. The Civil Appeals Process

1) Require that an order of a trial court to be effective be reduced to writing on a separate document, signed by the judge, filed with the clerk of the trial court, and the fact of filing entered in the court docket.

2) Establish the date of entry of the appellate order as the date on which the appeal time begins to run.

3) Make the filing of the notice of appeal rather than its service the act that initiates the appeal process.

4) Simplify the content of the notice of appeal, limiting its content to a recital of the fact of taking the appeal, the name of the party appealing, the court to which the appeal is taken, and the order being appealed.

5) If additional information about the appeal is desired, the parties may be required to file a docketing statement.

6) Severely limit the circumstances under which an extension of time to file an appeal can be granted and the time in which it can be sought.

7) Place responsibility for granting relief pending appeal on the trial judge.

8) Place responsibility for assembling and forwarding the bundles on the trial court clerk rather than on the appellant.

9) Place responsibility on the solicitor to request of the transcript of testimony the notes of evidence and of the judgment, and on the reporter and the judge to prepare them.

10) Eliminate the need for a hearing on the dismissal of an appeal for failure to file the bundle or any other required document in a timely manner.

11) Eliminate oral hearings on applications.

12) Consider the use of settlement conferences, summary dispositions, and expedited appeals.

13) Require the filing of the order of the Court of Appeal disposing of an appeal within a limited period of time.

14) Allow only a panel of the law lords to grant leave to appeal to the House of Lords.

15) Eliminate the oral hearing on applications for leave to appeal to the House of Lords.

16) Simplify the procedures for seeking leave to appeal to the House of Lords.

2. United States

a. Structure and Function

1) Eliminate the concept that one function of an appellate court is to "do justice" between the parties independent of the functions of error correction and law development.

2) Eliminate the confusion over the final judgment rule and the temptation to create exceptions to it by making only final judgments appealable as of right and all interlocutory orders appealable in the discretion of the appellate court.

3) Strictly adhere to the requirement that an issue be presented to the trial court before it can be raised in the appellate court.

4) Establish a mechanism within the intermediate appellate court for resolving conflicts between panels and performing a law development function in jurisdictions in which the intermediate appeallate court decides too many cases to permit the supreme court to perform these functions in every case in which it is appropriate.

b. Personnel of Appellate Review

1) Recognize that appellate litigation requires special knowledge and skills and encourage the teaching of them in law school and continuing legal education programs.

2) Change judicial selection procedures so that appellate judges are chosen on the basis of their professional and personal qualifications rather than for political reasons.

3) Delegate to professional staff all decisions that do not go to deciding appeals on the merits.

c. Coping With Increased Caseloads

Require a written statement of reasons for the disposition on the merits of every appeal, even if the statement is not published.

d. The Civil Appeals Process

1) Enforce strictly the requirements concerning the content and filing of the notice of appeal.

2) Permit the staying of the effectiveness of a money judgment only when there is a reasonable question as to the ability of the appellee to repay the money in the event of a reversal.

3) Eliminate reconsideration in the intermediate appellate court if the supreme court has sufficient time to perform the law development function for the jurisdiction.

4) Enforce non publication rules against computer based systems and other non official reports.

Appendix B The Oral Tradition in Practice — 5 Case Studies

Introduction

An essential feature of the author's study of appellate justice in England was to observe a substantial number of oral hearings in the Court of Appeal, supplemented by witnessing several hearings each in the House of Lords, The Inner House of the Court of Session of Scotland, and the Criminal Division of the Court of Appeal. It was thought that it would be helpful to the readers in understanding the appellate process in England to have detailed descriptions of a selected number of appeals in the Court of Appeal. To this end the listing office of the Civil Appeals Office was requested to select five appeals that would be representative of the nature of the appeals that are heard by the Court of Appeal and that would give the author an exposure to a range of counsel from very junior barristers to senior Queen's Counsel. The five case studies included in this chapter are the result. In view of the critical comments made on the performance of some of the barristers involved in the appeals, it is important to note that the appeals were selected in advance by someone other than the author.

Each case study includes a procedural and factual history of the case in the trial court and in the Court of Appeal, some of the notes the author made while in court observing the oral arguments, and a summary of the judgments rendered on the appeal. Following the report of each appeal the author has added his personal observations on what can be learned from the particular appeal as it reflects on the ability of the Court of Appeal to perform its error correction and law development functions efficiently and effectively.

It is noteworthy from the standpoint of the academic researcher that but for the assistance of the Master of the Rolls and the staff of the Civil Appeals Office, these case studies would not have been possible. Copies of the bundles and the skeleton arguments are not retained by the Court of Appeal and were in these appeals only at the request of the author and only with the permission of the solicitors for the parties. Permission of the solicitors was required because the bundles, even though they were filed with the Court, are considered to be the property of the person who filed them. Skeleton arguments are given to the judges and they do not retain them. Copies of the judgments as taken down by the court reporters must be purchased from the shorthand writers association or may be read in the Supreme Court Library but may not be copied there absent special permission. They are, however, available on computer based systems.

RE "C" A Minor

Before:
The Master of the Rolls,
Lord Justice Neill, and
Sir Roualeyn Cumming-Bruce.
Hearing Date: October 3, 1987
Judgments Rendered: October 14, 1987
Reported: The (London) Times, October 16, 1987

Facts and Procedural History

This was an appeal from an order of the Portsmouth County Court, rendered on May 13, 1987, dismissing an application made by the county for an order freeing a twelve year-old boy for adoption, and also dismissing applications made by the boy's natural mother seeking revocation of the care order he was then under and a resumption of access leading to a transfer of custody to her.

On October 17, 1985, the Hampshire County Council Social Services Department (HSS) applied to the Portsmouth County Court for an order freeing a brother and a sister--a ten year-old boy and a thirteen year-old girl--for adoption by their foster parents, with whom they had lived since January, 1982. The childrens' natural mother refused to consent to the adoption, and Hampshire County requested the court to dispense with her consent on the grounds that she had persistently failed without reasonable cause to discharge her parental duties, and that she was withholding her consent unreasonably.

The freeing application came before the court for directions on January 31, 1986, and a hearing date was set for April 3, 1986. At that hearing the mother made known her intention to file her own application for revocation of the matrimonial care order--issued by the court in October, 1981 and which had removed the children from her custody--and for the return of the children to her care. Because she had not yet been granted legal aid, the court adjourned the hearing until June 4, 1986, when both cross-applications were scheduled to be heard. The mother filed her application for revocation of the care order on May 16, 1986, seeking alternatively an order for access leading eventually to a transfer of custody. Hearings on the applications began as scheduled on the 4th of June and continued for nearly a year, punctuated by five adjournments, three of which lasted as long as two months.

During the course of these proceedings, the girl had several court-approved meetings with her mother, and in early 1987 expressed a desire to be reunited with her. On March 10, 1987, the application to free her for adoption was formally abandoned; the court revoked the care order and returned custody of the girl to her natural mother. The boy, however, remained adamantly opposed to even access visits by his natural family, and expressed his desire to remain with his foster parents.

The judgment on the application to free him for adoption was finally rendered on May 15, 1987. The judge set forth the facts of the case as he had found them based on lengthy testimony, twenty-one affidavits submitted by both parties, medical reports by three psychiatrists, and three reports by the court-appointed guardian *ad litem*. In 1977 the Portsmouth County Court had found the mother to be a "somewhat haphazard provider" and made supervision orders on her five children. Pursuant to an order of the court made on October 16, 1981, the mother surrendered three of her children who were received into a council observation and assessment centre. In December, 1981, the two youngest children were introduced to their foster parents; that placement was confirmed in January, 1982.

After foster placement, access to the two children was reduced to a minimum; access was terminated altogether in December, 1983, after a public confrontation between the natural family and the social worker who accompanied the children during visits.

In his judgement the judge stated the grounds on which (HSS) sought dispensation:

1) that the mother was withholding her consent unreasonably;

2) that she had persistently failed without reasonable cause to discharge her parental duties;

3) that she had abandoned the boy, and; 4) that she had neglected him.

The judge held that the allegations of neglect and abandonment required that a criminal standard ("leaving the child to its fate") be met in order to be sustained. He concluded that the mother's conduct had never risen to this standard, and so dismissed these grounds for dispensation after a full review of each.

Turning to the question of the reasonableness of the mother's refusal to consent to the adoption, the court stated that the answer turned on whether the mother's applications for custody or immediate access could succeed, and whether there was a "realistic prospect of access" at any time before the boy turned eighteen. If either of her applications could be granted, her withholding of consent could not be deemed unreasonable. The prospect of access in the future, or lack thereof, would not be dispositive, but would bear on the question of whether a reasonable person in the mother's position would refuse consent to adoption.

Considering the psychiatric evidence, which strongly suggested that the boy should continue to live with his foster parents, and the boy's own rejection of his natural family, the judge concluded that it would be "disastrous" for the boy to return to live with his mother. He therefore dismissed the mother's application for custody. For much the same reasons, and for the benefit of the boy's sense of security within his foster parents' home, the judge dismissed the mother's application for immediate access. Finally, the judge noted that the likelihood of access in the future was much harder to ascertain, but concluded from the evidence that there was a "very real possibility" that the boy would want to see his natural family in later adolescence.

In considering the reasonableness of the mother's refusal to consent, the judge concluded that a reasonable person in her position "would have to be endowed with a knowledge of the alternatives to adoption and in particular custodianship." He further stated that a reasonable person in the mother's position would have to "ask herself whether the custodianship with its disadvantages as well as its advantages might not be a better solution to [the boy's] position than adoption." The judge was willing to give only slight weight to the custodianship alternative, however, since no application for such an order had actually been made.

The judge delineated six factors which a reasonable person would consider when deciding whether to consent to the adoption. Taking all of these matters into account, the judge found that the mother had not unreasonably withheld her consent to the adoption period. Accordingly, on May 13, 1987, the judge ordered the freeing application dismissed and that the care order which the boy was currently under be continued.

On June 10, 1987, Hampshire County filed a notice of appeal from the Portsmouth County Court's order. The first ground given for the appeal was that the judge failed to consider a number of matters when making the determination of the reasonableness of withholding consent.

The notice of appeal also contended that the judge misdirected himself when he factored the custodianship alternative into the reasonableness calculus--after already dismissing the mother's applications for custody and access--and that he wrongly disregarded the paramount importance of the child's welfare when determining an application for custodianship.

Furthermore, Hampshire County claimed that the judge ignored the authority in *Re S (a minor), Times* December 31, 1986 (C.A.), in which the Court of Appeal held that "unless a court was satisfied that a custodianship order would offer the child a greater benefit than adoption would do, the court should not on an application for adoption give further consideration to custodianship." The final ground given for the appeal was that having found that the interests of the boy were best served by his remaining with his foster parents, the judge wrongly held that the possibility of future access was a basis on which the mother could reasonably refuse consent to a freeing order.

Upon service of the notice of appeal, solicitors for the mother immediately applied on her behalf for an extension of Legal Aid so they could prepare a response; the extension was granted on June 26, 1987. A respondent's notice of reply was served on the July 2, the last day for doing so. On July 13, solicitors for the mother were informed that the copy of the respondent's notice sent to the Civil Appeals Office was ineffective because it was not accompanied by the required fee, nor did it include an endorsement of service. After the fee was paid, the Civil Appeals Office informed counsel that the respondent's notice would be set down provided Hampshire County consented to this being done out of time. Consent was refused by letter on July 23. Solicitors for the mother responded on September 10 by applying to the Registrar of Civil Appeals for leave to submit the respondent's notice out of time. The application was granted on September 29; time for submitting the Respondent's notice was extended until October 1, and Hampshire County was ordered to pay the costs of the application.

In the Respondent's notice, the mother contended that the order of the Portsmouth County Court should stand for the reasons given by the judge, and that in reaching his decision the judge did not accede the bounds of his discretion. The mother replied to the grounds for the appeal point by point. In a cross-appeal, the mother requested that the judge's order be varied to allow for a program of access, eventually to lead to a transfer of custody. Alternatively, the mother requested, in the event the appeal was allowed, that there be a retrial on the freeing application and on the application for access to the boy's natural family, on the ground that she had been prejudiced by the judge's disclosure of psychiatric evidence which had been compiled in support of her case in the county court.

Neither counsel submitted a skeleton argument to the Court of Appeal, but counsel for Hampshire County had prepared for the court a summary of the history of the proceedings in the court below.

Oral Hearing

The hearing opened at 2:05 p.m. with the Master of the Rolls announcing that the judges had read the papers in the bundles. He expressed his concern over the delay in the proceedings in the trial court. He asked why no transcript was ordered in the case. Counsel for the appellant explained that the appeal was limited to the point that the trial court erred by taking an improper factor into account in making his decision. The MR stated that the findings of fact of the trial judge would have to be accepted in the absence of the transcript. Counsel for the respondent expressed surprise that a transcript was not ordered. The MR then noted the lack of skeleton arguments. He also commented that the absence of the transcript affected the cross appeal.

Counsel for appellant then began her arguments. A major problem arose when she challenged a portion of the trial judge's order because she could not find the exact language in the judgment even though she spent a great deal of time looking for it. She was unable to cite any provision in a statute that supported her position.

Much of the time was spent with the judges asking counsel why the appeal was taken without ordering a transcript. She attempted to explain that the county was concerned with the precedent of the trial court's decision that consent adoption could be refused because of the possibility of custodianship in the future when it had been denied in the pending proceeding.

She concluded at 3:47 p.m.

Counsel for the guardian *ad litem* was asked if he had anything to say and he did not.

At 3:51 counsel for the respondent began his argument. The MR immediately asked what was the status of the cross appeal. At 3:56 court recessed so counsel could confer with his client. At 4:00 the court reconvened. The respondent's counsel indicated that his client wanted to withdraw the cross appeal but wanted to express concern about the possibility of seeking access in the future.

At 4:03 the MR announced that judgment would be reserved until the next day.

At 10:50 a.m. on October 14, the Court announced its judgments.

Judgments

Sir Roualeyn Cumming-Bruce delivered the first judgment for the Court of Appeal. After framing the issues of the appeal and giving a brief overview of the facts, Sir Roualeyn turned to the procedural history of the case, which he identified as "a matter of grave concern." He went on to say: "For a contested application to free for adoption to take eighteen months from the institution of the application to the date of judgment is a serious matter, and particularly serious having regard to the age of the two children the subject of the application." He continued by saying that the protracted proceedings of the case demonstrated "the sorry consequences of attempts to fit in a rather long case concerning the future and custody and care of children into the dispatch of other business in the County Court." Although he no longer considered himself sufficiently familiar with the business of the County Court to prescribe a remedy, he nevertheless felt it his duty to "draw attention to the very unfortunate consequence that the children and the parties were subjected to [by] this very protracted delay."

Turning to the appeal, Sir Roualeyn noted that no transcript of testimony had been put before the Court of Appeal; consequently, the facts found by the judge, as set forth in his judgment, constituted the factual basis of submissions on this appeal. From these findings, he was "unable to detect any issue of law raised by the submissions made on behalf of [Hampshire County]." He cited *Re W* [1971] A.C. 682 for the appropriate legal test ("What would a hypothetical parent endowed with the capacity to be reasonable decide to do when faced with a request for consent?"), and turned to the grounds of appeal, which could be conveniently made the framework of the submissions to the Court. He then considered each of the eight matters which Hampshire County submitted the trial judge disregarded as relevant to the decision of the hypothetical parent. As to each, he concluded that when read as a whole, the judgment clearly indicated that each of these matters had been given due consideration. These submissions were all grounded in the faulty assumption that when the judge made his aforementioned summary, "he thought it would be read as an exhaustive statement of all the matters which he had already, in other passages of his judgment, shown that he regarded as relevant to the decision of the hypothetical parent." A fair reading of the entire judgment indicated otherwise, and he held that these alleged misdirections were "wholly without foundation."

Regarding the possibility of custodianship, he agreed with the trial judge that it was a factor of only slight weight, but insisted that "it certainly is a factor that a sensible hypothetical reasonable parent would consider as one of the factors which might well properly affect the decision whether to consent to adoption." He thus held that Hampshire County had wholly failed to make out the submission that there was any misdirection in that part of the judgment which dealt with the application for an order for freedom to adopt.

Sir Roualeyn next turned to the mother's cross-appeal. At the end of the argument, the judges had indicated that they did not wish to hear counsel for the mother. Counsel correctly inferred from this that the Court had found no misdirection, and further that the trial judge's denial of the mother's applications for access and transfer of custody would also not be disturbed. As to the possibility of the mother seeking access in the future, Lord Cumming-Bruce pointed out that in his judgment, the trial judge had acknowledged the possibility that circumstances could change enough to permit new applications for access and transfer of custody to be made at some future date. Sir Roualeyn therefore declared that "if such a change of circumstance did take place nothing that I have said should be taken to prejudice the mother in seeking to persuade the court of the existence of such a change of circumstances." For these reasons, he held that the appeal should be dismissed and, the mother not pursuing her cross-appeal, that should be dismissed as well.

In a very short opinion, Lord Justice Neill also spoke of his anxiety about the timetable of this case, but conceded that at the very least the matter had been thoroughly investigated and fully dealt with by the trial judge. For the reasons explained by Sir Roualeyn, Lord Justice Neill agreed that there was no basis for interfering with the decision of the trial judge. The Lord Justice also praised counsel's wisdom in withdrawing the cross-appeal, and agreed that its dismissal should not be allowed to prejudice any future application for access which the mother might wish to make when appropriate.

The Master of the Rolls agreed that the appeal and cross-appeal should be dismissed. He stressed his agreement with the holding that the withdrawal of the cross-appeal should not prejudice any future application for access made by the mother, since the trial judge had found that a change in circumstances sufficient to justify such an application was a real possibility. The MR strongly doubted, however, that circumstances could so change that custody would be awarded to the mother. He drew this distinction between custody and access because he did not wish there "to be a feeling of insecurity either on the part of the foster parents or of [the boy] himself in the remaining six years or so of his minority."

The MR also wished to clarify what had been decided about the making of a custodianship order by the Court of Appeal in *Re M (a minor)* [1987] 1 W.L.R 162, [1987] 1 F.L.R. 465 and in *Re W (a minor)* C.A. transcript June 12, 1987 (the latter case had been brought to the MR's attention after argument by a law reporter). After a brief review of those judgments, the MR stated that in the instant appeal that the judge correctly appreciated that the prospective adopters had made no application for custodianship, but considered with equal propriety the possibility that the making of such an order might be appropriate in the future. The making of an order freeing the boy for adoption would have foreclosed that possibility, provided it was followed by an adoption order.

The MR also made clear his concern with the lack of continuity in the hearing of this application, as well as the length of time over which the hearing was spread. He stated that this lack of continuity of hearing seemed inherent in the present system of listing in the county courts, and expressed his hope "that those who are responsible for listing in the county courts will take urgent steps to institute a new listing system which will eliminate such 'stop-go' hearings and will not await the inevitable conclusion of the Civil Justice Review Body that this should be done." The MR agreed with Sir Roualeyn Cumming-Bruce that the delay in this case was particularly serious because it involved children: "It is a major blemish on the system of the Administration of Justice by the County Courts in this country, and I hope that it will not be perpetuated for a day longer than is absolutely necessary."

Observations

This case was a classic demonstration of the inadequacies of the English appellate system. A defective respondent's notice, an unwarranted opposition to an application for extension of time, failure by the appellant to order the transcript of testimony, failure of the respondent-cross appellant to know that the transcript had not been ordered, no skeleton arguments, withdrawal of a cross appeal in the middle of the oral hearing, two unprepared barristers, an appeal based on a legal issue that had not been thought through prior to the oral hearing, inability during the hearing to locate the precise portion of the trial judge's judgment being challenged, failure to recognize the standard of review, principal reliance by the appellant on a decision published only in a newspaper, and oral arguments by counsel who had no knowledge of the principles of public speaking were all present in this one appeal. Justice may have been done in this case, but if it was done, it was in spite of and not a result of the performance of the legal representatives, both solicitors and barristers.

DAVID THOMAS BRAY
(H.M. Inspector of Taxes)
V. PETER MAURICE BEST

Before:
Lord Justices May, Balcombe, and Woolf.
Hearing Dates: October 6 and 8, 1987
Judgments Rendered: October 30, 1987
Reported: [1988] 2 Aller 105, [1988]
1 WLR 784, [1988] STC 103

Facts and Procedural History

This was an appeal by a taxpayer of an order of the Chancery Division dated January 20, 1986 which overturned a commissioner's decision discharging tax assessments for a twenty-year period and assessing taxes only for 1978/79.

The taxpayer was employed by a company from fiscal year 1958/59 to April 1, 1979 (in fiscal year 1978/79), when he and all of the company's other employees were transferred to the employ of company's parent organization. In anticipation of that transfer, the trustees of two trusts which had been established for the benefit of the company's employees acted to begin winding-up the trusts in order to distribute their net assets to the intended beneficiaries. In the course of the next fiscal year, 1979/80, the taxpayer became entitled, pursuant to the exercise of discretion vested in the trustees of the two trusts, to amounts from both trusts totalling 18,111 pounds.

The taxpayer accepted income tax liability with respect to these payments for the year of assessment 1978/79, but only to the extent required by Section 187 of the Income and Corporation Taxes Act 1970, i.e. the amount in excess of 10,000 pounds, 8,111 pounds. Inland Revenue, however, claimed that the entire amount, 18,111 pounds, constituted emoluments from the taxpayer's employment within the meaning of Section 181(1), Schedule E of the 1970 Act, which taxes "any emoluments for the taxable period" from any office or employment. Section 183(1) defines the expression "emoluments" as including "all salaries, fees, wages, perquisites and profits whatsoever." Section 526(5) defines "chargeable period" as "an accounting period of a company or a year of assessment."

Inland Revenue made twenty-one assessments (one for each year from 1958/59 through 1978/79) against the taxpayer, apportioning the trust payments as income received over the entire period of his employment with the company. The taxpayer appealed these assessments to the Special Commissioners, and his case was heard by a single commissioner. The judgment of the Commissioner was set out in writing in a reserved decision given on February 16, 1984. The Commissioner accepted the taxpayer's appeal as a test case, the trustees having made similar allocations to over 750 other persons. The Commissioner held that none of the assessments made were well founded, and that a single assessment for the year 1978/79 would be equally unfounded.

The quantum of accepted tax liability under Section 187 of the 1970 Act for the year 1978/79 was not agreed between the parties until July, 1984. On August 2, 1984, in accord with his reserved decision, the commissioner formally determined all of the appeals before him by discharging the assessments for the years 1958/59 to 1978/79 inclusive, and by reducing Mr. Best's assessment for the year 1978/79 under § 187 to the agreed figure of 8,111 pounds.

The Inspector of Taxes immediately declared his dissatisfaction with this determination, and on August 6 required the Commissioners to state a case for the opinion of the High Court pursuant to the Taxes Management Act 1970, Section 56.

The Inspector's appeal from the Commissioner's decision was heard by the Chancery Division on December 12 and 13, 1985, and judgment was rendered on January 20, 1986. The first issue was whether the payments received from the trusts were emoluments from the taxpayer's employment with the company. The judge stated that this was "a question of fact upon which the decision of the Special Commissioner is final unless it can be shown . . . that the true and only possible conclusion from the primary facts found by the Special Commissioner is to the contrary . . . " The judge found the authorities relied on by the Inspector in this regard unpersuasive, and found no reason to upset the Commissioner's finding on this point.

The judge turned next to the second question for decision: "namely, given that the payments in question are emoluments arising from the taxpayer's employment by the company, is it possible to attribute a year or years of assessment to such payments?" The judge was sympathetic to the Commissioner's opinion that the answer was no, but found counsel for the Crown's "simple submission that this conclusion is indefensible wholly convincing." "If paid for service as an employee," continued the judge,

> It must be paid in respect of some period of service, whether that be a definable special period or whether, on the other hand, the payments have to be regarded as spread over the whole period of service of the employee. Of course, having regard to the precise facts of this case it may be (and, indeed, I think, it is) extremely difficult to say in respect of precisely what period of service these payments were made . . . but that they must be attributed to some is, in my view, inescapable.

The judge held that the question of apportionment was an issue of fact, and accordingly ordered, on January 20, 1986, that the matter be remitted to the Special Commissioners to decide "over what period the additional emoluments must be deemed to have been earned, and how they are to be apportioned over the various financial years in that period."

The taxpayer lodged a notice of appeal from the Chancery Court's decision in the Court of Appeal on March 6, 1986. The stated grounds for the appeal were that the judge was wrong in sustaining the Commissioner's conclusion that the trust payments were emoluments of the taxpayers former employment, and that the judge was wrong in holding that these alleged emoluments were chargeable to any period or periods within the meaning of Case 1 of Schedule E.

The taxpayer abandoned the first ground of appeal in his skeleton argument submitted to the Court of Appeal. The taxpayer's "fundamental submission" in his skeleton argument was that the 18,111 pounds was not liable to tax because of a principle of United Kingdom tax law known as the "source doctrine," which provides that to be taxable, "a receipt must not only be income within one of the charging Schedules and Cases; the taxpayer must also possess the source of income in the tax year to which the income is properly attributable." The taxpayer now conceded that the amounts paid to him in the distribution year 1979/80 were emoluments which arose from his employment with the company. But they were income only of the distribution year, and because the taxpayer no longer had the source in that year, they were not liable to tax. The taxpayer cited a number of authorities to support his proposition.

Counsel for the Crown also submitted a skeleton argument on behalf of the Inspector of Taxes, and insisted therein that the Inspector was entitled to succeed on the question of apportionment, both in principle and on the authorities. "Logically," argued the Inspector, "since employment cannot exist save during a period, an emolument from the employment must be an emolument for all or some part of that period." The Inspector further argued that it could not have been Parliament's intention to allow tax avoidance through Section 181: "If the taxpayer is right, then tax can be avoided on emoluments, if they are paid after 5 April after termination of the relevant employment and are not expressed to be emoluments for any specific part of the period of employment."

Oral Hearing

The oral hearing began at 10:30 a.m. on Tuesday, October 6, 1987. Both sides had filed skelton arguments.

There was a total of five barristers and five solicitors in court.

Counsel for the appellant opened by identifying counsel for each side. He informed the court that this was a test case.

He proceeded to recite the procedural history of the case. The presiding judge informed counsel that the judges had read the papers and that it would not be necessary to recite the facts in detail. He asked how long the hearing would last. Counsel responded that he anticipated it would take one full day.

The presiding judge identified the key issue in the case. Counsel pointed out the key statutory provisions. He had had copies made of the original act and the amended act and distributed copies to the judges. Counsel proceeded to read the relevant portions of the statute and then summarized its requirements. Their challenge is to the applicability of only one of the requirements.

Counsel first argued from the language of the statute and from the facts of the case, referring quite often to the skeleton argument he had submitted to the court. After discussing the relevance of some prior cases, he distributed to the judges copies of one case decided by the House of Lords. He read from various portions of the speeches and of the printed cases submitted to the House by counsel in that case to show what had actually been decided.

He then read from other prior cases, giving the facts of the cases and reading from the judgments. He stated that he is doing so not because he thinks the cases are relevant but because they relied upon by the respondent.

Counsel acknowledged that his problem is that none of the earlier cases support his position. He proceeded to read the judgment of the trial court. The presiding judge interrupted, saying that the judges had read it. Counsel then identified the key part of the judgment and attempted to demonstrate why it was incorrect.

Counsel next distributed copies of judgments in several prior cases to the judges and proceeded to read from them. After that he discussed cases cited in his skeleton argument, he attempted to show how they are not relevant. He read a very lengthy head note from one of the cases.

At one point he noted that in 1986 the Treasury took the exact opposite position in another case than the one it was taking in this case, and that in each case the Treasury position was accepted.

The hearing recessed at 12:54 p.m. and reconvened at 2:11 p.m. with counsel for the appellant continuing his argument. He reviewed prior cases, reading at length from them, then explaining the meaning of the cases. Quite often during this portion of the hearing counsel stated that he did not want to take up too much of the judges' time with one thing or another--but always did.

He concluded his argument at 3:15 p.m. From 3:15 to 3:25 p.m. a co-counsel argues. He wanted to distribute copies of a case to the judges but cannot locate the copies.

At 3:25 p.m. counsel for the respondent began his argument.

He first set forth some of the facts of the case, reviewed the finding of facts by the trial judge, and read from one of the key documents in the case. At one point he looked for something in his notes but could not find it after spending at least five minutes looking for it. He made what he called a semantic and logical argument, offering three alternatives for allocation of the payments to particular years. When pressed by the judges for which of the alternatives he favored, he refused to choose one, saying it is up to the judges to decide which was correct, but that one of them had to be.

The hearing recessed at 4:12 p.m., to be resumed on Thursday, October 8. On that date the hearing resumed at 10:30 a.m.

Before respondent's counsel could continue his argument, appellant's counsel brought a new case to the attention of the court.

Respondent's argument resumed at 11:02 a.m. with a careful review of the facts in an earlier case. There was an extensive exchange between counsel and the judges on whether that case turned on a question of law or of facts.

Counsel next reviewed all of the cases cited by the appellant and distinguished them. He then reviewed the judgments of the commissioner and the trial judge. His last statement was to correct a mistake in his skeleton argument. He concluded at 11:38 a.m.

The appellant's counsel made his rebuttal, with the primary discussion by him and the judges on what was the rule of law established in each of the cases cited and the *ratio decidendi* in each.

The hearing concluded at 1:10 p.m.

Judgments

The judgments were rendered on October 30, 1987. Lord Justice May delivered the first opinion of the court, and after a brief overview of the procedural history of the case, turned to the apportionment issue and the "source doctrine," Lord Justice May stated that the source doctrine was well-established by authority and was not being challenged by the Inland Revenue in this appeal. He then distinguished this appeal from the authorities cited by Inland Revenue to support its claim that where the period of the services for which emoluments have been received extends into two or more years, then a fair apportionment on all the facts is necessary, an argument designed to circumvent the source doctrine.

The Lord Justice next considered cases cited by the taxpayer "in which payments found to be emoluments from a taxpayer's employment were nevertheless held not to have been paid for service as an employee in that employment." In each case the payments were assessed once only in the year of receipt: it was never argued that they could or should be spread over a period of years in a fashion similar to that suggested by the judge. Lord Justice May thus stated that while these cases did not directly contradict the judge, he found it surprising that the point was not raised in these cases, since spreading the receipts over a period of years in these cases would have benefitted the respective taxpayers.

The Lord Justice was therefore of the opinion that "the learned judge's conclusion that an emolument from an employment must of necessity and as a matter of law be attributed to a period or periods of that employment is erroneous." The Commissioner had found no justification on the facts of this case for attributing all or any part of the relevant receipts to the year of assessment 1978/79, nor for apportioning them between the twenty-one years of his employment. "The Special Commissioner has in effect made a finding that the receipt of the relevant monies was attributable to the Distribution Year, but that as the taxpayer was not then employed, there was no source in that year, and thus no liability to tax." That finding generally should not be disturbed on appeal, and in any event the Lord Justice was satisfied that it was in accord with common sense.

Finally, Lord Justice May suggested that the correctness of the Commissioner's view could be tested by asking how any apportionment would be made if it had to be made--a very difficult process in this case, since the trustees had relied on no formula when they made the payments. "In this case," the Lord Justice summarized,

In the first instance the Revenue attributed the taxpayer's relevant receipt to the Distribution Year. When they appreciated their difficulty under the source doctrine they sought to apportion the receipt over the whole 21 years of the taxpayer's employment. In argument counsel for the Revenue sought to suggest that if this were incorrect, then the receipt should be attributable either to the eligibility periods under the respective trust deeds, or finally to the day when the trusts were terminated and the trustee's obligations to determine the various entitlements arose. However if the Revenue's first or second choice cannot be substantiated, I for my part would be averse to giving them a third, or possibly a fourth opportunity to get it right.

Accordingly, Lord Justice May held that the appeal should be allowed and the Commissioner's decision reinstated.

Lord Justice Balcombe agreed that the appeal should be allowed, since he was unable to accept the judge's opinion that "if a payment is made to an employee for services generally ... then that payment must be made in respect of some period of service." To the contrary, he argued that a payment for services generally "should be attributed to the year in which it is paid" unless facts point to a different conclusion. The findings of the Commissioner revealed no such facts in this case.

The Lord Justice also reasoned that if the Court was to order apportionment, it should be able to provide guidelines for doing so to the Commissioners; the facts of this case provided no basis for any such guidelines. The "widely differing possibilities" suggested by the Inland Revenue, none of which was obviously preferable to another, demonstrated to the Lord Justice the impossibility in this case of attributing the trust payments to any year of assessment other than that in which it was paid. "That is the year to which it prima facie attributable, and it is only the application of the 'source doctrine' which prevents it being assessed for that year."

Lord Justice Woolf concurred with his colleagues that the appeal should be allowed, but admitted that initially he thought the judge's view correct. He agreed that it was important to adopt a prima facie approach that an emolument is assessable for the year of assessment in which it is received unless there are grounds for attributing it to another period. He was inclined to believe, however, that the statutory language of the 1970 Act could support the view that "where . . . an emolument in respect of an employment is received in a year of assessment which commenced after the date of termination of that employment, this could be regarded in itself as being grounds for attributing the payment to an earlier year of assessment during which the employment existed, since what is being assessed is the emolument from that employment." The Lord Justice did not believe that the authorities cited in this case would bar such an approach. If the approach were correct, however, "then it is difficult to identify any scope for the application of the so-called 'source doctrine.'" Furthermore, he recognized the difficulties which would arise in attempting to apply the methods of apportionment proffered by Inland Revenue; this appeal had made clear that if the judge's decision was right, "absurd situations could arise in cases where, as here, there really is no material upon which a rational allocation of the payment can be made to an earlier chargeable period . . . during which the employment existed." The task would not merely be difficult, but would be "completely haphazard."

Lord Justice Woolf pointed out that fortunately, the Court was not compelled to uphold an approach "which would have such highly undesirable consequences." As the judgments of his colleagues had made clear, the earlier decisions on this subject, while not conclusive, were "wholly consistent with the conclusion reached by the Special Commissioner."

Observations

This case is noteworthy for several reasons. The number of lawyers present in the courtroom was high--a total of 10. The respondent was the Treasury and represented by one of the junior counsel for the Treasury who are to be considered the equivalent of the Queen's Counsel. Both sides had filed lengthy skeleton arguments, and their oral arguments followed them quite closely. Counsel also distributed copies of recent cases to the court during the course of the hearing. Counsel were well prepared on the issues, but did not always have complete mastery of their papers.

It was clear from the beginning that the judges were knowledgeable about the facts of the case and had read the papers. Notwithstanding this, both the appellant and the respondent reviewed the details of the facts at length. It was also clear that the judges understood what the key issue was because the presiding judge so informed counsel at the beginning of the argument. Notwithstanding this, both counsel made their arguments as though the judges knew nothing about the case.

During the course of the argument the author observed in his notes that respondent's counsel made a fatal error by presenting to the court three alternatives for interpreting the statute that would permit the payments in question to be subject to the tax, but failing to select one of them as the one the respondent thought was the correct interpretation. Even in response to a direct request from the court, he refused to do so, answering that the court could pick any one it chose. This made the position of the respondent to be one of "We don't care how you interpret the statute so long as we can collect the tax." The court obviously did not want to be put in that position. It appeared to the author that the case was lost at that point and nothing else that was said made much difference. The court obviously wanted the position of the Treasury on which interpretation was the correct one and was not happy with the unwillingness of counsel to take a position. Counsel would have been far better off had he given the court what it wanted--a preferred interpretation and the rationale for it being the correct one. The judgments of the Court confirmed this contemporaneous observation.

THE QUEEN -v-
SECRETARY OF STATE FOR THE HOME DEPARTMENT
Ex Parte: ZALIHE HUSEYIN

Before:
The Master of the Rolls and
Lord Justices Neill and Gibson
Hearing Date: October 20, 1987
Judgments Rendered: October 30, 1987
Reported: The *Times* October 31, 1987

Facts and Procedural History

The Secretary of State appealed from a final order of the Queen's Bench Division, rendered April 15, 1987, quashing a deportation order issued against a foreign visitor who had overstayed her authorized time in the United Kingdom.

Zalihe Telbiz, a citizen of Cyprus, came to the U.K. on September 15, 1981, when she was granted leave to enter for one month as a visitor. The Home Office subsequently extended her leave until September 15, 1982, but Ms. Telbiz failed to depart on that date. Ms. Telbiz was eventually found, arrested, and charged with overstaying, to which she pled guilty in the Newham Magistrates' Court on October 26, 1983. In that court she produced an airline ticket to Cyprus dated November 4, 1983; consequently, the magistrates conditionally discharged her for twelve months, but encouraged her apparent desire to return to Cyprus by recommending her for deportation.

Instead of flying to Cyprus, Ms. Telbiz on the 4th of November married Ocal Huseyin, a British citizen by birth in the United Kingdom. Four days later, solicitors acting on Mrs. Huseyin's behalf applied to the Home Office for leave to remain in the United Kingdom indefinitely, on the basis that she was now the wife of a British citizen. Besides the timing of the marriage, certain discrepancies which arose during an Immigration Officer's interview of the couple cast additional doubt upon the legitimacy of their union. In light of these facts, the Home Office decided to act on the magistrates' recommendation to deport Mrs. Huseyin, and an order to that effect was issued by the Secretary of State on July 9, 1984, under authority of the Immigration Act of 1971. Various representations made by Mrs. Huseyin's solicitors failed to dissuade the Home Office from this decision. When the intercessions of her Member of Parliament proved ineffective as well, Mrs. Huseyin applied to the Queen's Bench Division for judicial review of her deportation order July 16, 1985. Leave was granted by a divisional court of the Queen's Bench Division on October 11, 1985, and Notice of Motion for Judicial Review was served on October 21, 1985. Her case, seeking declaratory relief that the deportation order was unlawful, was heard on April 14, 1987.

The divisional court issued a final judgment quashing the deportation order the following day, resting this decision on its construction of Section 1(5) of the Immigration Act of 1971. By the terms of Section 3(2), the 1971 Act empowered the Secretary of State to adopt rules to govern its administration, but the court held that this power was restricted by Section 1(5) of the Act, "where it is provided that Commonwealth citizens settled in the United Kingdom on 1st January 1973 [the Act's effective date], and their wives and children, are not by virtue of anything in the Rules any less free to come into and go from the United Kingdom than if the Act had not been passed."

The court found that under the terms of the Commonwealth Immigrants Act 1962, the Immigration Appeal Act 1969, and the pre-1973 Rules as set forth in Command Paper 4295, prior to 1973 the wife of a Commonwealth citizen born in the United

Kingdom could not be deported. Further, the 1971 Act, which extended considerably the categories of those liable to deportation, did not expressly refer to wives of Commonwealth citizens. This omission was reflected in the updated Rules promulgated in House of Commons 169 (HC 169). The court thus held that Mrs. Huseyin benefitted from the provisions of Section 1(5) because she was at present less free to enter and depart from the United Kingdom than if the 1971 Act had not been passed. She was therefore accorded the advantages of the earlier Rules, and the court directed that her deportation order be quashed.

Counsel for Mrs. Huseyin had also argued that she was qualified to remain in the United Kingdom by virtue of Rule 124 of HC 169, which in part provides: "A woman admitted in a temporary capacity who marries a man settled here should on application be given indefinite leave to remain." The Queen's Bench, however, held that the words "admitted in a temporary capacity" refer not to an historical event, but rather to a woman's legal status at the time of her marriage. This provision, unlike Section 1(5), thus afforded Mrs. Huseyin no protection, since she was, at the time of her marriage, an overstayer.

The Secretary of State lodged a notice of appeal from the court's judgment on May 12, 1985, on the grounds that the divisional court erred in law in holding that "any disadvantage vis-à-vis deportation to which [Mrs. Huseyin] was subject as compared with the position which would have applied to her before 1973 arose by virtue of anything in the Immigration Rules (HC 169)." Such disadvantage, contended the Secretary, arose only by reason of differences between relevant provisions of the Immigrants Act 1962 and the Immigrants Appeal Act 1969 on one hand, and the Immigration Act 1971 on the other. Mrs. Huseyin cross-appealed from that portion of the court's judgment which denied her the protection of Rule 124.

Counsel for the Home Office elaborated on the grounds given in the Notice of Appeal in a hand-written skeleton argument. The Home Office asserted that the Secretary's power to deport and an individual's liability to deportation are provided for in the Immigration Act 1971 itself, not in the Rules, which merely describe the statutory provisions in this regard. Since Section 1(5) applies not to the provisions of the Act itself, but only to the Rules, so the argument went, Section 1(5) had no direct application to the power to deport or liability to deportation. Under this analysis, the judge's comparison of the current Rules to earlier versions was irrelevant.

The Home Office also contended that *The Queen v. Immigration Appeal Tribunal Ex parte Ruhul*, a decision handed down by the Court of Appeal on July 31, 1987, several months after the judgment being appealed was rendered, was not good authority in the present case. The Secretary of State asserted that *Ruhul* concerned only rights of entry, not Section 1(5)'s effect on deportation, and so did not bind the Court of Appeal in the present case.

Additionally, the Home Office noted that Section 7 of the Act expressly provides exemption from deportation for certain Commonwealth citizens; if Parliament had intended Section 1(5) to restrict the Secretary of State's power to deport in the fashion held by the judge, Section 7 would have been superfluous. Finally, the Secretary stated that the language of Rule 124 clearly defines a woman's status at the time of her marriage; otherwise, the rule would provide alien women with a way around the immigration laws--a result Parliament could not have intended.

Oral Hearing

Court convened at 10:30 a.m. Just prior to the opening of court, counsel for the appellant filed a handwritten skeleton argument. Counsel for the respondent-cross appellant had previously filed a light page typewritten one.

Counsel for the appellant opened by apologizing for the late and informal skeleton argument. He explained that he had just gotten responsibility for the appeal the day before and thus did not have an opportunity to prepare it earlier.

Counsel stated that he wanted to waive an issue relating to the application of the statute to the case. The Master of the Rolls informed him that he did not think the issue could be waived because the Court could not ignore the statute. He suggested that counsel investigate the matter and counsel then asked his solicitors to do so.

Counsel began to review relevant portions of the immigration statute. He stated he would be brisk, but the MR asked him not to be too brisk. It then developed that the judges did not have a copy of the current immigration act so time was spent trying to find it. Ultimately, a clerk was sent to find it.

Counsel referred to the administrative rules upon which the trial judge relied in making his ruling. It was discovered that the judges did not have copies of the rules, but they were found quoted in the judgment of the trial judge.

Counsel in his argument cited the Ruhul case. He had copies of the report of the judgments as published in the *Times* and distributed them to the judges. Counsel read at length from the judgment, and then tried to distinguish it.

At 12:38 p.m. a recess was taken so that counsel could consult with his solicitor. At 12:44 the court was reconvened. Counsel stated that he realized that he was mistaken as to his argument and that he must now make the opposite argument.

The MR stated that he was not sure the point should be abandoned, and asked whether the Court would not have to rule in accordance with the statute no matter what argument was made by the appellant.

One of the judges suggested a basis for not applying the statute to the respondent. Counsel argued against the point, but the MR raised the question about the application of the act to children.

Luncheon recess was from 12:54 until 2:02. Counsel makes additional arguments, and concluded at 2:15 p.m.

Counsel for respondent argued that the Court should not decide the case on an issue not relied on by the appellant. He next argued why his client was protected by the statute and why the rules did not require his client's deportation. His argument concluded at 2:54 p.m. at which time counsel for the appellant made a rebuttal. During the rebuttal it again developed that the Court did not have copies of the relevant rules. His rebuttal concluded at 3:07 p.m. at which time the MR announced that judgment was reserved. No time for the announcement of the judgments was given.

Judgments

Sir John Donaldson, Master of the Rolls, held that the appeal should be dismissed based on the court's recent decision in *Ruhul*. The Court in that case considered the meaning of Section 1(5) in relation to Section 2(2) of the Commonwealth Immigrants Act 1968, which exempted from the Secretary of State's general power to refuse admission certain "privileged categories" of persons, including the wives of Commonwealth citizens resident in the United Kingdom. The Court in *Ruhul* held that Section 1(5) "imposed (i) a mandatory obligation on the Secretary of State to include in the rules appropriate provisions to reflect the previous statutory rights of [persons to whom Section 2(2) of the 1962 Act applied] to be given leave to enter and to give them equivalent protection and (ii) a negative obligation on him not to derogate from those rights in framing new rules."

The MR further noted that Section 6(2) of the 1962 Act likewise immunized wives of men born in the United Kingdom from deportation, and held that according to the *Ruhul* court's construction of Section 1(5), the current Rules were required to provide "that the Secretary of State would not exercise any of his powers to deport and, consequently, to refuse admission if doing so would infringe the statutory rights of persons to whom section 2(2) and 6(2) of the 1962 Act had previously applied."

The Master of the Rolls reached this conclusion reluctantly, noting that any woman could escape deportation simply by entering into an "immigration marriage," however insincere. So reluctant was he, in fact, that he considered a point not argued in *Ruhul* and expressly disavowed by the Secretary of State in the present case, *i.e.*, "whether the application of Section 1(5) was not limited to Commonwealth citizens settled in this country on 1st January 1973 and those who were their wives or children at that date." The MR abandoned this line of reasoning upon his conclusion that Parliament did not intend to discriminate between children born before and after January, 1973, or against the wives of widowers who remarried after that date.

Because the MR based his judgment on the Court's interpretation of Section 1(5), he declined to offer an opinion of the Queen's Bench's construction of Rule 124.

Lord Justice Neill agreed that the appeal should be dismissed, also citing the court's decision in *Ruhul*. From that decision the Lord Justice extracted the proposition "that the Secretary of State was obliged when framing HC 169 to include provisions which gave persons such as [Mrs. Huseyin] equivalent protection in that which they would have enjoyed under the Commonwealth Immigrants Acts 1962 and 1968 if the 1971 Act had never been passed." The Lord Justice conceded that such persons might become liable to deportation under the 1971 Act itself, but insisted that in setting out new Rules, the Secretary of State should have included a provision to protect [Mrs. Huseyin] and persons similarly situated from deportation, since she would have been immune from deportation under the Commonwealth Immigrants Act 1962.

Lord Justice Neill expressed reservations similar to those of the MR in reaching his decision on the Secretary's appeal, but could see no alternative but to dismiss. And like the Master of the Rolls, he also refrained from giving any interpretation of the language of Rule 124.

Lord Justice Gibson concurred with his colleagues that the appeal should be dismissed. In reaching this result, he did admit to being impressed by the submission made for the Secretary, that Section 7 of the 1971 Act, titled "Exemption From Deportation For Certain Existing Residents," includes no reference to the type of exemption claimed by Mrs. Huseyin. But the Lord Justice maintained that neither this omission, nor the language of Sections 1(5) and 3(2), indicated that Parliament intended the Rules referred to in Section 1(5) to restrict only the regulatory powers of the Secretary of State with respect to entry into and stay in the United Kingdom; the scope of Section 1(5) logically included Rules governing deportation as well. Lord Justice Gibson held that Section 1(5) required that the immunity from deportation which Mrs. Huseyin would have enjoyed prior to 1973 be secured by appropriate provision in the Rules.

Observations

This appeal demonstrated the difficulties that can arise when counsel is briefed only a short time before the oral hearing. Counsel for the appellant was obviously unprepared on the facts, but even more so on the law. To start out trying to concede a point and being told by the court that it may not be able to ignore it, then arguing for almost two hours, then stating that the argument was wrong and he will have to argue the opposite makes a mockery of the appellate process. Counsel for the respondent, on the other hand, was extremely well prepared on both the facts and the law and filed an effective skeleton argument. He made his points clearly, succinctly, and without repetition. It is significant that his argument listed only 39 minutes.

If only a private dispute between private parties had been involved it would have been bad enough, but when a significant question of statutory law is at stake, the Court should not be limited to the points made by counsel. This case was a classic one in which the oral tradition failed, and the judges should be able to research the law on their own. In the American system this would be done by law clerks and the judges. The English system does not now provide for overcoming the deficiencies of counsel. If the wrong decision were reached in this case, it would be a perfect occasion for the application of the doctrine of *"per incuriam"* as described in Chapter 1, section B 2, *supra*. In this case the oral tradition and the adversary system broke down because while one counsel was knowledgeable and prepared, the other was not.

SLAZENGERS LIMITED v. SEASPEED FERRIES INTERNATIONAL LIMITED

Before:
Lord Justices Dillon and Bingham
Hearing Dates: October 27-28, 1987
Judgments Rendered: October 28, 1987
Reported: [1987] 3 ALL ER 967; [1988] 1 WLR 221; [1987] 1 Lloyd's Rep 36.

Facts and Procedural History

This was an interlocutory appeal from an order made on 20 March 1987, for security for costs made by the Commercial Court (part of the Queen's Bench Division) against the foreign plaintiffs in a cargo damages action.

On May 20, 1977, the *Seaspeed Dora,* a roll-on/roll off cargo ship, sailed for the port of Jeddah, Saudi Arabia, loaded with cargo she had taken aboard at Rotterdam, Felixstowe, and Antwerp. She berthed at Jeddah on the first of June, and as a result of an unfortunate sequence of events during unloading operations that day, the vessel capsized and sank with a substantial portion of her cargo still on board.

In the spring of 1978 three actions were brought against Seaspeed Ferries International Ltd., of Liberia, the owner of the vessel, for damages for breach of contract. Writs were issued against Seaspeed on 30 May 1978, 31 May 1978, and 22 August 1978. Solicitors for Seaspeed accepted service of these writs on 22 June 1978, 20 June 1978, and 4 September 1978, respectively. These actions, which represented the claims of some 116 plaintiffs--as shippers or consignees of the lost cargo--against Seaspeed, were consolidated by an order of the Commercial Court on 3 June 1981. The actions were actually brought in the names of the plaintiffs by underwriters claiming by subrogation. A total of 76 claims were brought under 71 bills of lading. Of these plaintiffs, approximately 50 or 51 were normally resident outside of the jurisdiction; the remainder were English. The foreign plaintiffs were predominantly the shippers and consignees of the cargo loaded at Antwerp and Rotterdam.

In March, 1982, solicitors representing Seaspeed enquired of the plaintiffs' solicitors--through correspondence--whether their foreign clients would agree to provide security for costs. The solicitors for the plaintiffs indicated that they would not, calling attention to Rules of the Supreme Court Order 23, Rule 1-3/3, which states in part: "No order [for security for costs] will be made if there are co-plaintiffs resident in England." In February, 1986, Seaspeed's solicitors again raised the issue of security for costs, and requested in the alternative an undertaking that the plaintiffs accepted that any one of the English plaintiffs would be individually and wholly liable for any order for costs which might be made in favor of Seaspeed. Solicitors for the plaintiffs indicated that their clients remained unwilling to oblige the request for security, and were unable to give such an undertaking as suggested. In early March, 1987, Seaspeed applied to the Commercial Court for an order for security for costs under Order 23, Rule 1. Trial was scheduled to begin during the first working week of January, 1988, and was expected to last eight weeks.[1]

Upon hearing Seaspeed's application on 20 March 1987, the judge for the court decided to make an order inconsistent with the proposition stated in Supreme Court Practice 1985

---

[1] In his judgment for the Court of Appeal, Lord Justice Dillon anticipated that the primary issues at trial would be: "whether [Seaspeed is] liable, whether they are entitled to limit their liability and what the effect is of package limitation of liability under the Hague Rules relevant to the particular contracts of carriage."

23/1/3/3. Applying the old authorities cited by the White Book in support of this proposition the judge drew the following conclusions. First, the issue to be decided involved a matter of practice, not of law. Second, if any rigid rule of practice dictates that no order for security will be issued against a foreign plaintiff when there is an English co-plaintiff, that rule applies only in cases where all plaintiffs will be held jointly and severally liable for any order for costs that may be awarded to the defendant at the conclusion of the trial. Third, such an order might be made only where all of the plaintiffs rely on the same cause of action.

In this case, the judge determined, no two plaintiffs had an identical cause of action, even though their claims all turned on the common question of causation, and even though many pairs of them sued on the same bill of lading. And given the wide discretion trial courts have in apportioning costs, the judge found that it would be nearly impossible to predict accurately any particular outcome with reference to costs--an order holding one plaintiff wholly liable was far from inevitable, even unlikely. The judge thus concluded that it would be inappropriate to deprive Seaspeed of security based on the assumption that one or more English plaintiffs would be ordered to pay all of those costs attributable to the foreign plaintiffs. So also would it be incorrect to order the foreign plaintiffs to pay security sufficient to cover all of Seaspeed's anticipated costs. Accordingly, the judge made an order for security in favor of Seaspeed, but only to the extent necessary to cover the potential liability of the foreign plaintiffs for Seaspeed's costs. The foreign plaintiff was thus ordered to pay as security 50/115ths of Seaspeed's estimated costs of 250,000, pounds to be apportioned, if necessary, equally between each of them. The plaintiffs applied to the Court of Appeal for leave to appeal from this order of the Commercial Court on 14 May 1987, and were granted leave on 16 July 1987; notice of appeal was filed five days later.

The grounds given for the appeal in the notice of appeal were: First, that the judge erred in law by departing from the basic principle that if English and foreign plaintiffs are jointly and severally liable for costs, no security should be ordered against the foreign plaintiffs since the defendant can look to the English plaintiffs for satisfaction; second, that the judge erred in law by apportioning security by "head count" rather than by the correct legal test, which requires defendants to establish that there will be issues of fact or law unique to foreign plaintiffs such that there is a real likelihood of the defendants obtaining orders for costs against foreign plaintiffs alone; third, that in correctly determining the impracticability of predicting how costs might be finally awarded, the judge erred in law by failing to find that Seaspeed had not met its above-mentioned burden of proof; fourth, that the judge erred in law in finding that one or more English plaintiffs would not be liable for all costs in the event that Seaspeed prevailed at trial.

Both parties submitted skeleton arguments to the Court of Appeal.

Seaspeed claimed in its skeleton argument that courts have unfettered discretion to order costs against anyone, and may apportion costs in a fashion which does not leave one plaintiff liable for the entire amount. They argued that per capita apportionment is the fairest basis for any order for costs; no court could reasonably hold Slazengers Ltd., with a claim for 1,624, solely liable for costs totaling 250,000 pounds. Seaspeed also claimed that the order was just; without security, they may have to sue persons in Saudi Arabia to recover their costs. Furthermore, the English insurers, the real parties in interest, were merely taking advantage of the foreign status of the insured to avoid exposure to costs. Seaspeed concluded their skeleton argument by saying that any inflexible rule prohibiting orders for security in cases like this was superseded by the flexibility of 0.23, r. 1.

Oral Hearing

The hearing began at 11:47 a.m. The presiding judge announced that the judges had read the papers and the skeleton arguments filed by parties. As soon as that was said, the respondent submitted a new bundle of documents to the court.

Counsel for the appellant immediately began his argument on the law. At one point the presiding judge suggested that all of the cases cited by the appellant were lower court cases and not binding precedent. Counsel ignored the difficulty raised by the judge. Counsel cited the 1901 Supreme Court Practice Book and distributed copies to the judges.

Court recessed for lunch from 1:07 p.m. until 2:09. Counsel for the appellant resumed, making a whole range of arguments. At one point, counsel read his argument.

Lord Dillon suggested that the trial judge was just exercising his discretion, but counsel did not pick up on the point. His argument concluded at 3:08 p.m. at which time counsel for the respondent began his argument. He stated that his issues were listed in his skeleton argument but the presiding judge noted that the judges had not read the cases. Counsel reviewed the historical background of the rule that the trial judge had refused to apply. Counsel did not make the point of what harm would result if the trial judge's ruling were allowed to stand. Finally, one of the judges asked that question.

At the end of the day's hearing, counsel for the respondent was told to ascertain how many foreign claims there were and the amount of each. Court recessed at 4:12 p.m. It reconvened at 10:37 a.m. the next day. Counsel for the respondent had prepared a list with the information requested and gave it to the court. The judges asked some questions about it and the percentage of foreign claims of the total was calculated in court.

Counsel continued to review the historical development of the rule. At one point he discussed a decision of the House of Lords rendered earlier in the year. One of the judges asked what the order in that case had provided. Counsel did not know so the judge told him where the speeches in the appeal were published and that the information was contained in the published report. Counsel began to repeat himself. The judges pointed this out to him and tried to prevent him from being repetitive.

Counsel then began to discuss the cases cited by the appellant. Primarily he read from his skeleton argument but with some expansions. As to one of his arguments, the presiding judge stated that it was not relevant but counsel was not able to clarify the point to show that it was relevant. He then attempted to state the standard of review of the exercise of discretion by the trial judge, but the presiding judge cut him off by saying that the court was familiar with the standard.

He concluded his argument at 11:38 a.m. and the appellant began his rebuttal. He repeated the points made in his opening argument. At 11:47 the court recessed to consider its decision. It reconvened at 11:56 a.m., and the judgments were rendered.

Judgments

Lord Justice Dillon began by noting that, until recently, the practice followed by the courts in awarding security was not laid out in detail in the Rules of the Supreme Court, but rested on the general practice of the courts before the Judicature Act 1873. Although the practice, and its certain exceptions, were once applied rigidly, the Lord Justice stated that the language of Order 23, rule 1 indicates that courts now enjoy a very wide discretion in ordering security. He left no doubt that the rule grants to courts the discretionary jurisdiction to order security in cases involving both foreign and English plaintiffs, if the court considers it just to do so in light of all relevant circumstances. He thus agreed with the Commercial Court judge that the proposition of 0.23, r.1-3/3 is not unequivocally binding, but must be qualified by the general discretion conferred by 0.23, r.1.

Furthermore, Lord Justice Dillon noted that under a recent decision of the House of Lords, *Aiden Shipping Co. Ltd. v. Interbulk Ltd.* [1986] 1 A.C. 965, courts enjoy the discretionary power--in cases involving multiple plaintiffs--to apportion costs against each of the unsuccessful parties, rather than make a general order for costs against the plaintiffs as a group. "If therefore," stated the Lord Justice, "the case in which security is sought, where there are some English plaintiffs and some foreign plaintiffs, was a case where there was a realistic possibility that the court at the trial might make an order if the plaintiffs failed, ordering each to bear an aliquot share of the costs, an order such as [the judge] made . . . would be . . . highly appropriate."

The circumstance of this underwriters' action, however, admitted no likelihood of an order for costs being made against the foreign consignees but not against the English shippers, since the two had joined in the action to cover the question of title to sue. Having chosen to join together, both would be subject to an order for costs, not just the foreign consignees. Nor did the Lord Justice accept the proposition, suggested by Seaspeed in the court below, that instead of using a head-count, some limited security might be imposed on the foreign plaintiffs by reference to the value of those claims not represented by any English plaintiff, or by reference to that portion of trial time likely to be devoted to separate issues relating only to individual foreign plaintiffs, versus issues common to all the plaintiffs. The complexity of the pending litigation militated against using either alternative scheme to calculate the costs which could be attributable to the foreign plaintiffs.

Lord Justice Dillon reiterated that this was an underwriters' action in which the plaintiffs had chosen to stand together, and that if they failed wholly or in part at trial, the English and foreign plaintiffs would both be subject to any order for costs. Furthermore, no suggestion had been made that the

English plaintiffs, with or without the support of their underwriters, would not be able to satisfy any order for costs that might be made. The Lord Justice thus concluded that while the judge correctly decided that he was not limited by the inflexible rule as stated in the Supreme Court Practice, the form of the order for security was inappropriate to the circumstances of this action, and held that the appeal should be allowed and the order set aside.

Lord Justice Bingham agreed that in ordering security, judges enjoy wide discretion that should not be fettered by any inflexible rule, and was satisfied that the judge's order in this case was neither bad in principle nor the result of legal misdirection. Accordingly, that order could be challenged only on the familiar grounds that the judge considered factors that he should not have taken account of in making his decision, or that he failed to consider factors that he should have taken account of, or that his decision was "plainly wrong."

The Lord Justice suggested that if it were reasonably foreseeable that each foreign plaintiff in this case would be ordered to pay a proportionate part of Seaspeed's costs, and if it were reasonably likely that there would be no fund in the jurisdiction against which such an order could be enforced, the judge's order could not be shown to be wrong, and would be beyond challenge. But while an apportioned order for costs was not without precedent, such an order was virtually unheard of in the Commercial Court, and would be intrinsically unlikely at the conclusion of this case. Furthermore, counsel for the plaintiffs submitted that such an order would not be made, and accepted the proposition that an order made against the plaintiffs generally could be enforced *in toto* against any plaintiff. Seaspeed would not ask for an apportioned order, and in light of the plaintiffs' submissions, no court would conceivably grant a future request for such an order to the prejudice of Seaspeed.

Lord Justice Bingham next pointed out that the claims in this case were substantially brought by underwriters, a majority of whom were Lloyd's syndicates, and that there was every reason to believe that ample funds existed within the jurisdiction to satisfy any order for costs. Additionally, neither the solicitors for Seaspeed nor the plaintiffs, both of whom had extensive experience with this type of action, could cite precedent for an apportioned order in this type of case, or in which there had been any difficulty in obtaining payment of costs ordered against plaintiffs generally.

Although the novelty of the order was not dispositive, Lord Justice Bingham voiced his opinion that the practice described in the Supreme Court Practice is well-established and should be followed unless reason is shown for departing from it. The Lord Justice declined to interfere with the order simply on the grounds that the judge failed to take into account the unlikelihood of an apportioned order being made at the conclusion of the trial, but he was persuaded by the plaintiffs' argument that the judge failed to take account of a significant matter, namely the presence of insurers and the existence of sufficient funds within the jurisdiction against which an order for costs could be satisfied. These factors made it virtually certain that there would be no problem enforcing an order for costs. The Lord Justice thus held that in exercising its discretion afresh, the Court should allow the appeal and set aside the judge's order, since it was unnecessary for the reasonable protection of Seaspeed.

Observations

During the hearing the author made the following notes: "Style puts one to sleep" and "He argues with agonizing slowness--almost painful to listen to" and "Nothing in argument could not be said as well or better in writing."

The most remarkable aspect of this case was the amount of time that was spent getting to this preliminary stage of the litigation. The ship had sunk in 1977. The actions that were filed were consolidated in 1981. It was not until the summer of 1987 that a preliminarily matter such as the posting of security by foreign plaintiffs was decided. The wheels of justice grind slowly, but their case appears to be taking it to the extreme.

HARRODS LIMITED v. SCHWARTZ-SACKIN & CO. LTD.

Before:
Lord Justices Dillon and Bingham
Hearing Date: November 3, 1987
Judgments Rendered: November 4, 1987
Reported: Case Not Reported

Facts and Procedural History

This was an appeal from an interlocutory injunction restraining an art dealer from advertising its former relationship with Harrods Department Store.

In June of 1970, Schwartz-Sackin & Co. Ltd. entered into a concession agreement to operate the Fine Art Department of the Harrods Department store in Knightsbridge area of London. As concessionaires, Schwartz-Sackin was authorized to sell its goods through Harrods Fine Art Department, making use of Harrods' facilities and reputation, but were obliged to operate the department without reference to its own name or trademark. In return, Harrods received a 27% commission on Schwartz-Sackin sales made within its store. This arrangement continued through a succession of contract renewals, the last of which was signed on June 1, 1980.

On May 1, 1984, Harrods notified Schwartz-Sackin that in view of the latter's recent sales performance, the department store's board of directors had determined to terminate the concession agreement effective May 1, 1985, in accordance with the relevant provision of the contract. Clause 3(iii) provided: "This agreement may be terminated at any time by either party giving to the other twelve months notice in writing in advance of termination but no such notice may be given so as to result in termination earlier than 31 May 1985." In January, 1985, Schwartz-Sackin informed Harrods, under advice of counsel, of its intent to establish its business in the Knightsbridge area. Schwartz-Sackin further stated that this new business would "proclaim itself as and advertise the fact that Schwartz-Sackin & Co. Ltd. were, for 15 years, the Fine Art Department of Harrods, or some similar wording," and that this information would be circulated to its former customers, along with its new address, after the 31st of May. Schwartz-Sackin also indicated in this letter its desire that Harrods give an "unqualified assurance" that the latter would not use "confidential information relating to the running of the Fine Art Department," including the type and prices of its best selling goods, and the names and addresses of its customers. Schwartz-Sackin further vented its displeasure with the encroachment of other Harrods departments into the Fine Art Department's area of specialty, in violation of the concession agreement, for which it desired compensation.

Shortly thereafter, Harrods replied and expressed its opinion that the use of its name as envisioned by Schwartz-Sackin would contravene clause 2(b) of the concession agreement, whereby Schwartz-Sackin agreed "to seek to give the impression to the customers that the business carried on in the department is an integral part of the store." Harrods also threatened to veto any unauthorized use of its name by virtue of clause 2(p), by which Schwartz-Sackin agreed "not to advertise or to indicate its association with Harrods or to use Harrods' name directly or by inference in its advertising without obtaining Harrods' prior permission to do so." Additionally, Harrods denied that it had granted to Schwartz-Sackin the exclusive right to sell particular merchandise in its store, imputing that Schwartz-Sackin may in fact have garnered valuable commercial knowledge from Harrods' second hand department, and so denied that any compensation was due.

Solicitors for Schwartz-Sackin responded on the 5th of March, contending that clauses 2(b) and 2(p) were co-terminus with the concession agreement itself, which would expire according to Harrod's own wishes on the 31st of May. It was also their opinion that a court would imply Schwartz-Sackin's exclusive right to sell particular merchandise. Three weeks later, Harrods countered that the clauses in question were not limited to the period of the agreement, that any commercial information relating to the operation of the Fine Art Department as the property not of Schwartz-Sackin, but of Harrods, and that no term of exclusivity would be implied. Furthermore, Harrods insisted that Schwartz-Sackin provide undertakings that it would not "refer to themselves as having been connected either with Harrods or its Fine Art Department," that it would not "retain, use or divulge any list of customers of the Harrods Fine Art Department," that it would not "seek to use for their own benefit any goodwill which is vested in Harrods Fine Art Department," and that it would not "use or divulge any confidential information belonging to Harrods." Were these undertakings not forthcoming, warned Harrods, it would apply to the High Court for "immediate and appropriate interlocutory injunctive relief."

After a fruitless exchange of letters between solicitors for the parties, Harrods on the 30th of May again pressed Schwartz-Sackin for an undertaking that it would in no way "refer to themselves for any advertising or promotional purposes as having been connected either with Harrods or its Fine Art Department or communicate in any way whatsoever with any customer of Harrods or its Fine Art Department." Schwartz-Sackin remained intransigent, and Harrods served a Notice of Motion upon it in the Chancery Division of the High Court on June 11, 1985.

Harrods moved for an order that Schwartz-Sackin be restrained, pending judgment, from:

(1) advertising to potential customers that it had been associated with Harrods, or in any way acting in breach of clause 2(p);

(2) representing that it had operated or was known as Harrods Fine Art Department, or otherwise passing itself off as having been part of Harrods; and

(3) infringing Harrods' registered trademarks by using the mark "Harrods" in the course of selling any goods within the scope of those registrations "in such a manner as to import a reference to [Harrods]."

The writ issued against Schwartz-Sackin was registered in the Chancery Chambers on June 28, 1985, and replicated in the statement of claim the same request for injunctive relief as presented in the Notice of Motion. In addition, the statement of claim included requests for orders that Schwartz-Sackin not "circulate customers whose names or addresses [they] learned in operating the Fine Art Department" at Harrods without authorization, and for "the delivery up or destruction or obliteration upon oath of any advertising material or stationery the use of which in the course of trade would be a breach of the foregoing injunction."

In its defence dated June 5, 1985, Schwartz-Sackin maintained that clauses 2(b) and 2(p) were not binding after the termination of the concession agreement, or alternatively, if they did so bind, that they were void as an unreasonable restraint of trade contrary to public policy. It also denied that it possessed any confidential information regarding Harrods' business or customers. Schwartz-Sackin also counter-claimed that Harrods, in breach of implied contractual duties, vetoed the sale of certain items and used Schwartz-Sackin's trade analyses to complete with the Fine Art Department.

The Notice of Motion was amended on November 8, 1985, and the motion came before a judge of the Chancery Division on the 11th. In his judgment that was rendered the same day, the judge dismissed three of the four grounds which counsel for Harrods put forward for an injunction.

Harrods principal ground was based on clause 2(p) of the contract. The judge found most persuasive Harrods' contention that their reasons for including clause 2(p) in the concession agreement continued to apply after its termination. These purposes were derived by the judge from an affidavit submitted by the managing director of Harrods, and included:

(1) Harrods' desire that the concession remain a part of their store, to prevent its degeneration "into a mere bazaar consisting of numerous traders operating independently under one roof"--a concern also illustrated by clause 2(b);

(2) to prevent the prestige conferred upon the concessionaires from being used to sell merchandise outside of Harrods;

(3) to prevent the use of Harrods name and reputation in circumstances beyond the store's control.

The judge agreed that these purposes behind Harrods inclusion of clause 2(p) continued to apply after termination. The judge further held that the balance of convenience favored an injunction restraining Schwartz-Sackin from breaching clause 2(p) pending trial or further order.

Schwartz-Sackin appealed as of right, and its notice of appeal was served on December 17, 1985. The ground first given for the appeal was that the judge of the Chancery Division wrongly construed clause 2(p) as surviving termination of the contract. As their second ground for appeal, Schwartz-Sackin claimed that the judge alternatively erred "in concluding that there was an arguable case for enforcing [clause 2(p)] as reasonable notwithstanding that it is an unlimited restraint of trade clause, with particular regard to the fact that it is perpetual."

Schwartz-Sackin finally contended that in concluding that the balance of convenience favored the grant of the injunction, the judge erred.

Schwartz-Sackin filed a skeleton argument that declared that they sought "only the right to tell the truth, namely that for 15 years they operated the Fine Art Department of Harrods," and then briefly restated their position.

Schwartz-Sackin's skeleton argument also restated its position that clause 2(p) would unreasonably restrain trade if enforced, because the prohibition was unlimited as to both space and time.

Harrods served a Respondent's Notice on December 3, 1985, and reiterated its belief that the acts restrained by the injunction would constitute trademark infringement, passing-off, and unlawful use of goodwill. Harrods also contended that the balance of convenience favored an injunction because any need that Schwartz-Sackin previously had to inform third parties of its former connections with Harrods had been greatly reduced by the letters sent to customers, agents, and dealers.

Harrods also filed a skeleton argument in which it stressed that the Court of Appeal should not interfere with the lower court's discretion in granting the injunction, since clause 2(p) could arguably be construed as surviving termination of the contract. Harrods also restated its commercial interest in sustaining the injunction, as well as their opinion that Schwartz-Sackin had the burden of showing that Clause 2(p) was limited to the contractual period, among other arguments. Harrods denied responsibility for the delay of the hearing of the appeal or hearing over the merits in the trial court and suggested that since two years had passed, the matter would be better dealt with at trial. On May 21, 1987, solicitors for Harrods had notified Schwartz-Sackin's solicitors that they intended to set the matter down for trial the *following* week, upon expiration of the time for Notice of Intention to Proceed. Harrods also noted its awareness that Schwartz-Sackin was working to fix a date for the hearing of the appeal from the interlocutory injunction. Harrods suggested that the appeal would cause unnecessary expense and that the issue could more conveniently be disposed of at trial.

Oral Hearing

The oral hearing began at 10:35 a.m. There was a Queen's Counsel and a junior counsel representing each party. Both sides had filed skeleton arguments.

The presiding judge first stated that the judges had read the papers so a review of the facts by counsel was not necessary.

Counsel for the appellant made an effective opening in one sentence--he stated that what the case was about was whether the appellant could simply tell the truth.

The presiding judge immediately asked why this case had been pending so long without being tried. Counsel for the respondent read a list of dates provided by his clerk on the contacts between the clerk and the clerk for the defendant. There had been no contact between the clerks from January, 1986, to February, 1987. Counsel for both parties agreed that the case would be tried in January, 1988.

Counsel explained the details of the contract between the parties and the terms of the injunction. At 10:55 a.m. counsel began arguing the relevant law. At 11:25 a.m. counsel stated that he had made his primary submissions, then began making minor supporting arguments. In making these arguments he read passages from a case suggested by opposing counsel. After he did so opposing counsel pointed out why it was not relevant. The presiding judge distinguished the case on another ground. After making minor arguments that were not well received by the court, he returned to his principal argument based on the terms of the contract.

At this point the presiding judge asked why the court should intervene at this point since the case was so close to being tried. Counsel responded that the interpretation of the contract by the court would be binding at the trial. The presiding judge commented that an appeal from the final judgment would be a three judge panel and that that fact may make a difference (but he did not indicate what the difference would be).

The appellant concluded at 12:20 p.m. and the respondent immediately began his argument. Counsel first pointed out that the respondent did not want to proceed with the appeal but preferred to go to trial on the merits. Lord Justice Bingham stated that the respondent was partially to blame because it did not press for a early trial.

Counsel argued that at trial the plaintiff wants to introduce evidence on the "factual matrix" of the contract. Lord Justice Bingham suggested that this could be done by affidavit. Counsel then attempted to show why the contract was not unreasonable. During this portion of the argument he read from an old case and the appellant's counsel asked him to read additional portions of it, which he did.

The court recessed at 1:00 p.m. and reconvened at 2:08 p.m. Before argument resumed the presiding judge announced that during the recess he had checked with the listing office to ascertain the reason for the delay in listing the hearing in this case. The case had been put on the warned list in 1986. The listing office informed him that it was the practice of that office not to list cases for hearing until counsel for both sides requested it. Respondent's counsel stated that he thought it was up to the clerk of the appellant's counsel to contact the clerk of the respondent's counsel to have the case listed for hearing. The presiding judge complained that the system wasn't working when an interlocutory appeal was not heard until the case is ready to be tried on the merits, particularly when the trial itself was delayed over a year.

Counsel for the respondent resumed his argument, attempting to distinguish the cases cited by the appellant.

The argument wandered back and forth between the meaning of the language of the contract and when parole evidence is admissible to explain the terms of a contract. Counsel began repeating the arguments he made in the morning. At 3:37 p.m. he concluded his argument and the appellant began a rebuttal of the cases cited by the respondent. To the author it did not appear that these cases were relevant or needed rebuttal.

At 3:54 p.m. counsel for the appellant concluded. The court recessed to consider its judgments and at 4:10 p.m. announced it would deliver its judgments at 10:30 a.m. the next day, which it did.

Judgments

In his *ex tempore* judgment Lord Justice Dillon first reviewed the background of the case and the terms of the concession agreement, then outlined the issues to be decided. Concerning the duration of clause 2(p), construction of that provision depended on "what the common intention or purpose of both parties was in entering into the agreement." That intention, stated the Lord Justice, was to be "found objectively from the words of the agreement itself and such evidence of the surrounding circumstances as in properly admissible," excluding evidence given by either party concerning its subjective intentions in entering into the agreement or clause 2(p) in particular. Nor was it relevant to consider, as the judge in the court below apparently did, "merely what Harrods intended and what Harrods would have said if questioned by an officious bystander." The Lord Justice declared that the second question raised, whether clause 2(p) was unenforceable as an unreasonable restraint of trade, was ancillary to the question of construction.

It was also noted in these preliminary remarks that counsel for Harrods was not raising the passing-off issue on appeal, and also that the trademark claim had been abandoned.

Before turning to its merits, Lord Justice Dillon offered some comments on the "unfortunate procedural history of this appeal and ... the progress of the action." After noting current public complaints about delays in litigation, the Lord Justice identified this case as "a textbook example in some ways of how highly undesirable delays can be brought about." When the appeal was set down in January, 1986, the Civil Appeals Office only took an interventionist part in certain limited types of cases, such as those involving minors and immigration. At that time it was the clerks of counsel engaged for the appeal, especially those of counsel for the appellants, who bore the primary responsibility for arranging with the office a convenient date for the hearing of the appeal. "And as happens all too often," mused Lord Dillon, "the clerks preferred the convenience of their principals in relation to other cases to the interests of the clients in this particular case."

A year passed before anything was done to set a date for the hearing; in February, 1987, clerks for both parties met for the first time in the Civil Appeals Office, where they were told to find a mutually agreeable date. It was mid-August before they agreed to fix the date for the present hearing in November. Lord Justice Dillon declared that this interlocutory appeal could and should have been heard before Easter of 1986, and would have but for the attitude counsel permitted their clerks to take.

The Lord Justice also criticized Harrods, who having got their injunction, was in no hurry to get on for trial. Because they had failed to take any step in the action for over twelve months, it was not until late April, 1987, that they gave a month's notice of intention to proceed, expiring toward the end of May. Notwithstanding that delay, the action was set down for hearing in the Chancery Division in June, 1987, which was before the appeal had been given a date for hearing, and was likely to come on for trial early in the 1988 term. Again, but for delay, the action should have been heard at the beginning of 1987, if not the end of 1986. Lord Justice Dillon recognized that the appeal was brought before the Court at a very late stage, but stated that it still had to be heard and decided.

Lord Justice Dillon stated that the appeal could only succeed if the court determined that on the question of construction

Harrods could not succeed at trial because clause 2(p) terminated when the contract came to an end. "On that footing there is not a serious case to be tried," said the Lord Justice, "and of course on interlocutory applications the court very often does decide questions of construction because the court has the full argument on construction before it and nothing [would] be gained by deferring that question to re-argument at the trial."

Lord Dillon stated that the true construction of clause 2(p) was not a matter of general law but of the particular document involved; "the only possible question mark arises in relation to the matter of extrinsic evidence." In this regard, he quoted at length from *Reardon Smith Line v. Yngvar Hansen-Tangen*, [1976] 3 ALL ER 570, [1976] 1 WLR 989 (H.L.) in support of his proposition that in construing commercial contracts, "facts known to one party may be proved as part of the matrix of events, but it is the purpose of both parties and the common object of both parties that is to be sought as it would appear objectively to a reasonable man."

The Lord Justice then reviewed the affidavit evidence Harrods submitted in the lower court regarding its purpose in including clause 2(p) in the contract, and concluded that behind the store's stated reasons was concern over a possible breach of confidence. But Lord Dillon pointed out that if the object of clause 2(p) was to prevent public disclosure of concessions at Harrods, the prohibition would have applied with regard to all concessions; nothing in the agreement prevented Schwartz-Sackin from disclosing the presence of concessions other than its own. Nor was it likely that Harrods could make a better case at trial; the factual matrix of the case was fully presented in the affidavit evidence already submitted, some of which may not even have been admissible.

Lord Justice Dillon concluded that there was nothing "in the matrix of events out of which the agreement arose which warrant[ed] giving an extended construction or an extended duration to clause 2(p)." Nor was it proper to consider Harrods' reasons for clause 2(p) or what it would have said "if questioned by an officious bystander." He concluded that the basis on which Harrods launched its action did not support its claim. The Lord Justice thus held that the appeal should be allowed and the injunction set aside.

Lord Justice Bingham agreed that the appeal should be allowed. In delivering his judgment, the Lord Justice first considered the restraint of trade question. He concluded that if treated as a perpetual covenant, clause 2(p) would impose a restraint, if only minor, on Schwartz-Sackin's freedom to trade, and would therefore "be prima facie unenforceable at common law unless shown to be reasonable with reference to the interests of the parties concerned and of the public." The determination of reasonableness, however, would depend on the trial judge's assessment of evidence; the question could not be resolved on affidavit or an appeal.

Turning to the "crucial issue on this appeal"--construction of clause 2(p)--Lord Bingham stated that the first difficulty faced by Harrods was that clause 2(p) contained no language regarding the duration of the covenant, but such language could have easily been included when it was drafted. Second, even when looking at the whole agreement for the intended duration of the covenant, Lord Justice Bingham determined that most of the terms referred "to the manner in which the concession department [was] to be operated and [had] no possible application to a period when [Schwartz-Sackin was] not operating a concession department." Although some clauses--such as those dealing with settlement of customer complaints, indemnification, and accounting--could become effective after termination, Lord Bingham could not find "in any of these clauses or in the agreement as a whole anything to suggest that clause 2(p) should be read in the way for which [Harrods] contends."

Nor could Harrods case be made more persuasively at trial; the Lord Justice found the factual matrix of the case "very far from complex," and adequately described in the affidavit evidence before the court. In point of fact, much of that evidence dealt not with the factual matrix, but with reasons Harrods had for wanting the court to adopt its interpretation of clause 2(p). The trial judge had been "lured into paying attention to inadmissable evidence of what [Harrods] would have wanted instead of eliciting the joint intentions of the parties from the language they jointly used."

Lord Justice Bingham defended the rule requiring objective construction of the language of a written agreement as one that "ensures that the court gives effect to the parties' own contemporaneous bargain rather than to their *ex post facto* statements as to what they intended or would with the benefit of hindsight have intended," since "the agreement may represent the only overlapping area of [their] interest[s]." The court did not know, "quite rightly," whether the duration of clause 2(p) had even been discussed between Harrods and Schwartz-Sackin prior to the consummation of the agreement; if the issue had been raised, the intentions of the two parties clearly could have been quite different. "Where the agreement itself is silent," stated Lord Bingham, "there is simply no way of knowing how such a difference would have been resolved." Such deficiencies in the wording of an agreement, however, "cannot be made up by inadmissable evidence of one party's subjective intentions introduced in the guise of evidence to describe the factual matrix of the agreement."

Lord Justice Bingham declared that Harrods' "construction of clause 2(p) must be either right or wrong. It cannot be arguable, and it cannot in my opinion be affected by oral evidence." He concluded that it was wrong, and held that the appeal must be allowed and the injunction discharged.

Like Lord Justice Dillon, Lord Bingham also expressed concern over the timing of the appeal, particulary because of the imminence of the trial. He stated that most of the blame for the delay belonged to Schwartz-Sackin, and suggested that this might be relevant on any application to enforce Harrods' cross-undertaking in damages. But that issue was not before the court, and thus the Lord Justice expressed no opinion concerning it. Notwithstanding the delay, however, he concluded that the appeal had to be decided since it had been fixed and listed for hearing and no application for adjournment had been made. Nor would it be right, he felt, "to put the parties to the expense of litigating the construction of clause 2(p) at first instance, with the prospect of a further appeal, when [the Court of Appeal had] heard full argument and reached a conclusion."

Observations

This appeal is a perfect example of the delay that is an almost inevitable result of allowing counsel and their clerks to control hearing dates. As Lord Justice Dillon stated in his judgment, the clerks look to the convenience of counsel first and that this is a common problem. American courts were faced with the same problem and responded by adopting a policy of active case management by the staff of the appellate court.

Given the fact that one of the parties is one of the best known stores in the world, it would have been thought that the critical remarks by the judges of the performance of counsel would have guaranteed the publication of the judgments in the case. It has not, in fact, been published anywhere, even in a newspaper.

The failure of the appellant to press for an early hearing in this appeal also suggests that there was no reason for the appeal of the interlocutory injunction. It would have made much more sense to have pressed for an early trial. Resolution of this dispute was thus delayed because counsel did not press for an early trial, took an unnecessary interlocutory appeal, and did not seek an early hearing of the appeal.

The arguments of counsel, aside from the opening sentence of the appellant, were typical of those the author observed. Counsel for the appellant had difficulty making his key point and got in trouble arguing minor points. Counsel for the respondent was repetitive.

It was apparent during the hearing on this appeal that an inordinate amount of time was wasted by the failure of counsel to give a list of the cases to be cited to the court to the ushers the day before to permit the ushers to collect the reports and mark the pages in advance of the hearing. These interruptions broke up the flow of the arguments. Again, this was common in most hearings.

The comments by one of the judges on the effect of the interlocutory appeal being heard by two judges on any appeal of the final judgment being heard by three judges was also significant. It suggested that there may be a difference in the precedential effect of the decision of a two judge panel on a three judge panel.

Appendix C   COURT OF APPEAL (CIVIL DIVISION)

Introduction to the Practice Direction
(By Lord Donaldson, Master of the Rolls)

The purpose of the Practice Direction which is being handed down this morning is to give advance notice of some important changes which the Civil Division of the Court of Appeal will be introducing with effect from 6th June 1989.

The principal changes relate to skeleton arguments, presentation of oral argument in court, and Court of Appeal listing.

Our objective is to reduce the amount of time spent in court whilst at the same time adhering to our long established tradition of oral argument in open court. Time spent in court is costly both to the nation and the parties. It is therefore vital that it is used economically and effectively.

The time lag between the date of lodging and the date of hearing of appeals is still far too long, particularly in the case of appeals against final orders made in the High Court. The average time lag in the case of such appeals (other than cases involving children and other urgent appeals) is still about 12 months. It is not right that a successful party to a High Court action, for instance a plaintiff who has been injured in a road or factory accident, should have to wait a year before knowing whether the award of damages in his or her favor is going to be upheld. This is particularly so bearing in mind the fact that the case is likely to have taken a considerable time to come to trial. Likewise, a defendant who has a decision against him or her which is erroneous, should not have to wait a year before having that judgement varied or set aside. Justice delayed is always unsatisfactory and it can amount to justice denied.

It is for those reasons that we have been giving thought to ways of reducing the amount of time spent in court and increasing the Court's "productivity" without detracting from the quality of our appellate system.

A working party was set up under the Chairmanship of Lord Justice Purchas. A number of proposals were made as a result of the deliberations of that working party and there were very helpful discussions with the representatives of the solicitors' and barristers' professions. The proposals included the establishment of a team of lawyers to assist the Civil Division, along the lines of the system of office lawyers which has obtained in the Criminal Division for some time. The need for such a team has been accepted by the Lord Chancellor and it is in the course of being established.

A very important element in the working party's strategy, which has been endorsed by all the judges of the Court, is that time spent in court will be shortened if the members of the court who are going to hear the appeal are able to do effective pre-reading. This can only be done if, well in advance of the hearing, the Court has details of the points which are going to be argued and the authorities which are going to be cited.

For that reason the keystone of the new system is that skeleton arguments will no longer be optional, but will be required for all civil appeals (other than appeals heard with exceptional urgency). So far as timing is concerned in all cases (other than those assigned to the Short Warned List, to which a different timetable will apply) skeleton arguments must be lodged not less than 4 weeks before the date on which the hearing is scheduled to begin.

Requiring the skeleton arguments to be lodged well before the appeal hearing has three main advantages. First and foremost, the Judges can do really effective pre-reading and thus save a considerable amount of time which would otherwise be spent reading aloud in court. Second, they can consider whether the time estimate is realistic, and, if not, the Court can direct that the necessary adjustments to the listing be made well in advance. Third, it brings forward the point of time at which the parties, particularly the appellant's side, have to make a firm decision whether or not to proceed to a hearing before the Court of Appeal, or whether to settle the case. Accelerating this point of decision should help to reduce the number of cases where the appeal is settled in a matter of hours, or even minutes, before the hearing is due to commence or where an appeal is pursued simply because a true appreciation of the prospects of success was only reached so late that a settlement could save little or no expense. Settlements of appeals the night before or at the door of the court usually result in a court day being wasted, because it is then too late to call another appeal on from the Short Warned List. This is a hardship to the parties to appeals waiting to be heard.

There is an important point which I want to make clear at this stage. When the practice of inviting counsel to put in skeleton arguments for the use of the Court of Appeal was first introduced about five years ago, word filtered back to us that some lawyers took the view that this was a first step towards adopting the system which is operated by the appellate courts in the United States of having very full arguments submitted in writing and then limiting oral argument in court to a very short period. That is not the case. I cannot emphasize too strongly that the English Court of Appeal remains firmly wedded to its long established tradition of oral argument in open court. For that reason, as the Practice Direction makes clear, skeleton arguments should be confined to identifying the points, not arguing them.

The Court recognizes that calling for skeleton arguments to be lodged four weeks before the hearing date will involve counsel preparing the appeal well in advance of the hearing and then inevitably doing further work by way of recapitulation shortly before the hearing. For that reason and with a view to ensuring that counsel are entitled to appropriate remuneration for any extra work involved, the Court is directing the Taxing Masters to tax the costs of preparing a skeleton argument separately from brief fees, but with due regard to the fact that more work may be involved in preparing the oral argument if the counsel presenting that argument has not been involved in the preparation of the skeleton.

The point was rightly made by the representatives of the two branches of the profession in our discussions about these new proposals that, if counsel are going to have to "get the case up" twice, that would make all concerned even more anxious to have counsel of their first choice to argue the appeal. We recognize that, and we are changing the arrangements relating to appeals which qualify for a fixture with a view to achieving greater certainty in relation to hearing dates. We are also giving directions designed to ensure that counsel's estimates of the length of hearing, which are a key factor in listing, are monitored and kept up to date.

I should make it clear, however, that it will still be necessary for the Court of Appeal to have a Short Warned List to which relatively short appeals will continue to be assigned and put "on call" from a specified date.

So that there are no misconceptions about our reasons for having a Short Warned List, I should perhaps say something about this. We do not maintain a Short Warned List on the basis of the notion, which may have obtained in earlier times, that the judge is such an important figure that not a moment of his time must be wasted and therefore there must always be cases on call to fill any gaps. In the modern Court of Appeal the Short Warned List is not based on the dignities of the judiciary. It is there to ensure that we make full use of the courtrooms and judicial resources at our disposal. However there is reason to hope that improved listing and increased flexibility consequent upon judges devoting more of their time to pre-reading in their rooms may reduce, even if it is unlikely to eliminate, the need for appeals to be included in this List.

We recognize that in the case of appeals which are put into the Short Warned List a party's counsel of first choice may not be available on the day for which the appeal is called on and that in such circumstances the brief will have to change hands. This is an inevitable consequence of putting cases into a Short Warned List, but we have to maintain one for the reasons I have given. We also recognize that, in such a situation, equity requires that each counsel should be properly remunerated for the part which he or she has played in the whole process of preparing and presenting the appeal. We believe that our direction to the Taxing Masters will achieve that result.

The Practice Direction sets out changes in the way in which oral argument is to be presented in future in cases where skeleton arguments have been lodged in advance and pre-reading has been done by the judges with the aid of the skeleton. For the benefit of those appearing in the case, and particularly their clients, it is important that the documents and authorities which have been pre-read should be identified, and the Presiding Lord Justice will do so at the commencement of the hearing. The rest of the directions dealing with oral argument are designed to achieve what we consider to be the proper and legitimate objective of ensuring that oral argument is devoted to making the relevant points, not working up to making them.

It is important that members of the legal profession should explain to their clients in advance of the appeal hearing what the Court of Appeal's practice is in relation to oral argument. Without such an explanation, the clients might jump to the mistaken conclusion that insufficient time has been allowed for their case to be put before the Court. If it is explained to them that the appeal bundles and the cases which bear upon the branches of the law concerned have been studied by the members of the Court of Appeal, together with skeleton arguments, it will not come as a shock to the parties to find that the Court then expects counsel to proceed to deal straightaway with the grounds of appeal.

These new arrangements represent the most fundamental change that has been made since October 1982, when the parts of the Supreme Court Act 1981 dealing with the Court of Appeal and the rules made in that connection came into force. When I introduced my Practice Statement in October 1982 explaining that new system, I said that we would need the co-operation of both branches of the profession. We have enjoyed that co-operation over the past six years, we have had it in the fullest measure in considering the changes which are now being introduced and I am sure that we shall continue to enjoy it in the future.

We recognize that so substantial a change in the practice of the Court is bound to give rise to teething troubles, but are confident that, with assistance from both branches of the profession, they can quickly be overcome. We also recognize that as a result of lessons learned in what might be described as the "running-in period", it may be desirable to introduce modifications. In this context, as in all others, we shall welcome constructive criticisms from both branches of the profession and from users generally.

PRACTICE DIRECTION

1. **Change Effective Date**

    The changes announced in this Practice Direction will apply to all appeals to the Civil Division of the Court of Appeal which have a hearing date commencing on or after 6th June 1989.

2. **Skeleton Arguments**

    With effect from that date skeleton arguments will be compulsory in the case of all appeals to the Civil Division of the Court of Appeal, except in the case of appeals which are heard as a matter of great urgency and any individual case where the Court otherwise directs. If counsel consider that a skeleton argument is unnecessary, application should be made to the Registrar for a special order.

3. **Content of skeleton arguments**

    The purpose of a skeleton argument is to identify not to argue the points. A skeleton argument should therefore be as succinct as possible. In the case of points of law, it should state the point and cite the principal authority or authorities in support, with references to the particular page(s) where the principle concerned is enunciated. In the case of questions of fact, the skeleton argument should state briefly the basis on which it is contended that the Court of Appeal can interfere with the finding of fact concerned, with cross-references to the passages in the transcript or notes of evidence which bear on the point.

In the case of respondents whose arguments will be simply that the judgment of the court below is correct for the reasons given, counsel for the respondent can send in a letter to that effect in lieu of a skeleton argument. Where, however, the respondent is going to rely on any authority or refer to any evidence which is not dealt with in the judgment of the court below, a respondent's skeleton argument must be lodged. The respondent's side must always lodge a skeleton argument in any case where there is a respondent's notice.

Skeleton arguments are *not* pleadings and, save in exceptional cases (see para. 8 below), need not answer the skeleton arguments of the other side.

4. **Chronology of events**

The appellant's skeleton argument must be accompanied by a written chronology of events relevant to the appeal. This must be a separate document in order that it can easily be consulted in conjunction with other papers.

5. **Specialist Law Reports**

There is no objection to counsel referring to specialist law reports, whether or not the decision is also reported in the official law reports, if doing so would assist the Court. However it must be appreciated that such reports may not be readily available to the judges and photostat copies should be provided of any such authorities relied upon in the skeleton argument.

Timetable for exchange and submission of skeleton arguments

6. **Appeals with fixed dates** In the case of appeals which are given any form of fixture (i.e. all appeals, other than appeals assigned to the Short Warned List and appeals which are heard as a matter of urgency) the skeleton arguments must be sent or delivered to the other side and three copies lodged with the Civil Appeals Office not less than four weeks before the date on which the hearing is due to commence.

7. **Short Warned List Cases** In the case of appeals assigned to the Short Warned List the skeleton arguments must be sent to the other side and three copies lodged with the Civil Appeals Office ten days before the date from which the Short Warned List appeal is "on call".

8. **Supplementary skeleton arguments** Either side may lodge a supplementary skeleton argument if exceptional circumstances give rise to a need for one. This will only occur if (a) one side raised a point which could not have been anticipated upon a reading of the notice of appeal or any respondent's notice and (b) it called for an answer e.g. confession and avoidance. Wherever a supplementary skeleton argument is called for, a copy of it must be sent to the other side and three copies lodged with the Civil Appeals Office at the earliest possible moment.

9. **Listing changes** Consequent upon the new arrangements for compulsory skeleton argu-

ments, some changes will be made to the Court of Appeal listing arrangements.

10. Fixtures The present system of giving fixtures to appeals estimated to last 5 days or more and a "flexible fixture" (i.e. a hearing date within a band) to appeals estimated at 4 days or less (see generally para. 59/1/10 of the Supreme Court Practice 1988) will be replaced by a single form of fixture.

In the case of all appeals (other than those assigned to the Short Warned List) which have a hearing due to commence on or after 6th June 1989 (whenever fixed) the present system of "banded dates" will be replaced by a single, form of flexible fixture which will apply to all such appeals, namely that the appeal will be booked to commence on a specified date, or on the next following sitting day.

If it does not prove to be possible for the court concerned to take the appeal on the specified date or on the following sitting day, and the Listing Office are unable to transfer the appeal to another court, the hearing date will have to be re-arranged.

The purpose of providing this new system is to assist both counsel and solicitors by providing greater certainty.

11. Short Warned List Unless the Court otherwise directs, three weeks' notice will be given of the entry of an appeal into the Short Warned List. This will allow time for the skeleton argument to be prepared, sent to the other side and lodged within the 10-day time limit prescribed above (see para.7).

The Court appreciates that, in the case of appeals assigned to the Short Warned List, counsel who has prepared the skeleton argument may not always be available on the date on which the appeal is called on, with the result that the brief will have to change hands. In order to ensure that the original counsel who prepared the skeleton argument is appropriately remunerated for that work, and that the brief fee is suitably adjusted to take account of the fact that the skeleton has already been done, a general instruction is being given to Taxing Masters to tax the cost of preparing skeleton arguments separately from brief fees in all appeals.

12. Time Estimates The system to be adopted in relation to counsel's certified time estimates of the length of the appeal hearing is that set out in the Practice Statement of 2 October 1987 [1987] 1 W.L.R. 1422; [1987] 3 All E.R. 434 (see also para. 59/1/9A in the current cumulative supplement to the Supreme Court Practice 1988). From 4th April 1989 it will be subject to this additional requirement, namely that a copy of the certified estimate must be placed and kept with counsel's papers. Each time counsel is asked to give any advice or to deal with anything in connection with the appeal he or she must look at the estimate and check whether it is still correct. It is particularly important that, when preparing the skeleton argument, counsel should check the certified time estimate to ensure that it is as realistic and accurate as possible. Efficient listing, which is in everyone's interests, is heavily dependent upon the accuracy of time estimates.

13. Oral hearing The following procedure will be adopted in the case of all appeals to the Civil Division, unless the Court announces in any individual case that some other course should be adopted:

(a) The Judges will already have read the notice of appeal, any respondent's notice, the judgment under appeal and the skeleton arguments. At the commencement of the hearing the Presiding Lord Justice will state what other documents and authorities have also been read.

(b) It will not normally be necessary to open the facts and, unless otherwise directed, counsel for the appellant will be expected to proceed immediately to the ground of appeal which is in the forefront of the appellant's case. Likewise, the respondent's counsel will be expected to proceed immediately with his or her submissions on the issues in the appeal without any preamble. In an exceptional case, such as where there is technical evidence which will need to be explained by counsel and to this extent some opening is necessary, the Presiding Lord Justice will notify counsel in advance of the hearing.

(c) When citing an authority which has been pre-read, counsel should not read the case at length, but go immediately to the passage in the judgment where the principle relied on in the skeleton argument is to be found.

(d) When dealing with issues of fact, the passages in the transcripts or notes of evidence relied upon will have been listed in the skeleton argument (see para. 3 above) and accordingly counsel should so far as possible avoid reading from them *in extenso*.

14. Duty of Solicitors and Counsel

It will be the duty of solicitors and counsel to ensure that their lay clients have had explained to them before the appeal hearing what the procedure will be and how the Court of Appeal now deals with oral argument. It is important that both appellants and respondents should be made aware of the new procedure, particularly the extent to which the Court relies on pre-reading, so that the parties do not infer that, because the appeal hearing has been shorter than has hitherto been customary, their case has not been just as fully considered.

1st March 1989

Addendum to Paragraph 5 of Practice Direction of 1st March 1989

The official law reports are to be preferred both by reason of their nature and their general availability. Accordingly where a decision is reported in that series of reports, the need to refer to specialist reports should be explained.

INDEX

A

ABA Appellate Judges Conference, 89
abuse of discretion, 36
admission to practice (solicitor), 64, 80, 81
admission to the bar (American lawyer), xvi, 58
advocacy, 60-64, 69-79, 86, 87, 95, 98, 101, 108, 118, 123, 126-133, 145, 206, 208, 216, 241, 246, 254
aggrieved, 17-18, 32-35, 47, 175, 196, 197, 220, 239
American Bar Association (ABA), xi, xiv, 82, 83, 89, 97, 160, 169, 250
annual review (Master of the Rolls), 9, 68, 120, 129, 150, 153-154, 170, 232
appeal, 1-49, 61-69, 77-110, 115-331
appealable order or judgment, 26
appeal as of right, 45, 46
    see also *right to appeal*
appeal of right, 229
    see also *right to appeal*
appellant, 3, 19-22, 31, 36, 51, 110, 119, 122, 142, 153, 160, 175-186, 192-215, 236, 256, 266, 271, 276-278, 282, 287-292, 297-298, 309-311, 316, 321, 326, 330
Appellate Committee, xiv, xxi, 5, 39, 62, 66, 129, 134, 195, 233, 255
Appellate Committee of the House of Lords, xiv, xxi, 5, 39, 62, 66, 129, 134, 195, 233, 255
appellate skills training, 88-89, 99
appellee, xxii, 3, 110, 142, 196-209, 215, 224, 258

appendix, 116, 158, 161, 195, 209

application, xxii, 10, 15, 17, 43, 44, 178, 179-184, 188, 193, 229, 232, 253, 262-271, 288, 325

assignment of errors, 2, 24, 25

B

bar, 44, 58, 59, 65, 70, 71, 75-81, 88, 89, 104, 107, 113, 123, 139, 169, 240, 246, 250

Bar Council, 61, 70, 71

   see also *General Council of the Bar*

barrister or counsel, xxii, 57-62, 63, 70-79, 86, 94, 96, 98, 105, 123-126, 130, 132, 133, 144, 145, 176, 240-241, 246-247, 254, 271

bill of exceptions, 2-6, 24, 25

Blom-Cooper, L. and G. Drewry, xii, 50, 134, 140, 149, 235

bond, 2, 3, 201

   see also *security*

brief, 24, 62, 63, 108, 109, 128-132, 141-143, 163-167, 188, 195, 206-218, 231, 322, 329

bundle, xxii, 149, 151, 181-189, 227-228, 230, 243, 256, 297

C

calendar, 214-215

call to the bar (barrister), xxii

case management, 160, 168, 230, 244, 316

case processing, 69, 184-188, 210-213, 230-232

caseload, xiii, 25, 30, 44, 149-161, 217, 243, 246, 251

chancellor, xiv, xvi, xxii, 1-6, 11, 12, 39, 45, 61, 64-65, 66, 67-69, 71-79, 105, 107, 149, 214

Chancery Division, 153, 175, 178, 184, 272, 274, 305-307, 312

Chief Judge (of a federal or state court of appeals), xiv, xxi, 19, 32, 67, 85

Chief Justice (of a supreme court), xxi

chronology of events, 132, 152, 184, 188, 326

Civil Appeals Office (Court of Appeal), xxii, 68, 69, 152, 153, 178-179, 180, 181-183, 184-186, 192, 224, 228, 230, 259, 265, 312, 327

clearly erroneous (standard of review), 36, 41

clerk, 60, 62, 67, 69, 74, 77, 84-85, 88, 91-92, 153, 157, 168, 178, 181, 196, 198, 207, 208, 210, 211, 213, 214, 215, 219, 225, 227, 228, 231, 255, 288, 309, 312

clerk's office, xxii, 168, 225, 231

common law, 1-4, 7, 10, 13, 15, 21, 23, 39, 41, 115, 118, 139, 314

Council of Legal Education, 58-60

counsel - see *barrister*

county court, 12, 14-15, 45, 57, 78, 79, 105, 177, 184, 187, 222, 240

Court of Appeal (Civil Division), xxi, xxii-xxiv, 3-19, 21, 38-39, 40-41, 43-45, 48, 51, 57, 61-62, 65-68, 77-79, 90-93, 101-103, 105-107, 117, 119, 121-130, 132-134, 136-137, 143, 149-154, 161-162, 168, 170-171, 173, 175-181, 183-185, 188-195, 220-225, 227-233, 239-243, 245, 247-248, 253, 256, 259-260, 265-267, 287, 295-296, 308, 319-331

Court of Appeal (Criminal Division), xii, 19-20, 251

Court of Appeal in Chancery, 3, 5, 6

Court of Chancery, 1, 3

court reporter, xiii

Court of Session, 21-22

    Inner House, xiv, 4, 21-22, 124, 259

    Outer House, 21

cross appeal, xxii, 180, 196, 200, 226, 266, 269

D

Daily Cause List, 185-188

defendant in error, 2

discretion, 4, 8, 14-15, 17, 18, 28, 34, 36, 40, 46, 47-48, 179, 181, 183, 202, 233, 297, 298-301, 308

disposition process, 188-193, 213-216, 232

Donaldson, Lord (Sir John Donaldson), xvii, xiv, 94, 96, 122, 129, 152, 289, 319

E

effectiveness, 123-133, 248, 250, 258

efficiency, 120-123, 135, 161-167, 250

en banc, 1, 26, 30-32, 157, 215, 217, 233

equity, 1-7, 12, 24, 38-39, 40, 50, 139, 323

error correction, 12-13, 28-30, 40-41, 112, 156, 239, 245, 249, 256, 260

error of fact, 9, 28, 36-37

error of law, 41

ex parte, 15, 17, 179, 183, 188, 228, 253

ex tempore judgment, 101-102, 106, 193, 195, 311

Exchequer Chamber, 2, 3-4

expedited appeal, 212

extension of time, 178-180, 182, 183, 188, 204, 220, 223-224, 228, 244, 255, 271

F

Family Division, 69, 76, 184

Federal Courts Study Committee, 45-46

Federal Rule of Appellate Procedure, 197-198, 203

file, xxii, 3, 105-106, 109-110, 119, 175-182, 188-190, 194-202, 205-216, 224, 228, 255, 260
final judgment, 32-33, 45-47, 160-163, 195-202, 239-240, 245, 249, 257, 285, 309-310, 317
final judgment rule, 33, 45-47, 249, 257
final order, 16, 17, 45, 253, 284
final order rule, 15-17
floater appeals, 152, 193

G

General Counsel of the Bar, 59, 61, 74, 76
see also *Bar Counsel*

H

hearing, xxii, 14-16, 18-19, 20-22, 39, 44, 51, 68, 83, 101-103, 116, 118-124, 126-132, 139, 149-155, 161-168, 176-177, 179-180, 183-195, 203, 215, 218, 228-232, 243-244, 247-248, 254, 256, 259, 261-262, 270-271, 272, 276-278, 282, 284, 287, 291, 293, 297, 301, 303, 308-310, 315-317, 319-323, 325, 327-331.
High Court, 3-5, 7, 11-12, 14-15, 19, 21, 38, 45, 57, 62, 64-67, 71, 77-79, 91, 93, 105, 153, 191, 222, 240-241, 273, 305, 319
historical development, xiii, 1, 23, 37, 297
House of Lords, xii, xxi, xxii, 3-6, 11-13, 15, 21, 39-40, 42, 44-45, 62, 66, 69, 77-78, 92, 104, 107, 119, 121, 123, 130, 133, 188, 193-195, 233, 234, 235, 255-256, 259, 276, 297

I

Inns of Court, 58-61, 74, 79, 88, 89, 105, 132

Inns of Court School of Law, 59-60, 79, 88-89, 132
interlocutory order, 14-16, 34, 46-47, 199, 254
intermediate appellate court, 3, 25, 30-32, 40, 84, 217-218, 233-234, 249-251, 257, 258
internal operating procedures, 230-232
issue of fact, 8, 274
issue of law, 12, 268

J

Jacob, Sir Jack, xii, 10, 44-45, 86, 121, 247
judges, 1-12, 17, 19-20, 21-22, 25-26, 28-32, 38-49, 57, 61, 65-69, 72, 78, 82-85, 89-93, 101-107, 110-112, 116-163, 167-171, 180-193, 205-209, 211-217, 227, 229, 231, 240-251, 253-258, 259-260, 266, 269-271, 276-282, 288-292, 294-300, 307-310, 316-317, 320, 323, 330
judgment (Court of Appeal), xxii
judgment (trial court), xxii
judgment entry, 225
Judicature Acts of 1873 and 1875, 5, 7, 12, 245
Judicial office (House of Lords), xxii
jurisdiction, 3-5, 7, 13-15, 20, 23, 25, 27, 30-34, 36-37, 39, 40, 43, 46, 79, 84, 85, 130, 152, 153, 175, 180, 196, 198-200, 201, 210-212, 216, 217-218, 222-223, 233, 239-240, 249, 250, 258, 294, 298, 300

K

King's Bench, 2, 3, 13, 33

L

law clerk, 84-85, 88, 91, 97, 98, 157, 205, 207, 208, 214, 215

law development, 10-13, 28-32, 40-42, 112, 156, 217, 218, 233, 239, 245, 249-251, 257, 258, 260

law lord
    see *Lord of Appeal in Ordinary*

Law Society, 64, 70, 74, 77, 105

leave to appeal, 14-17, 19, 20, 42-47, 152, 168, 179, 183, 188, 193, 194-195, 229, 233, 235, 246, 253-254, 256, 295

legal education, 57-64, 72-76, 77-78, 80-81, 86-89, 126, 240-241, 246, 254, 257

legal profession, 22, 45, 57, 62, 69-75, 80-81, 86-88, 101, 104, 110, 128, 132, 240, 247, 323

List of Forthcoming Appeals, 177, 181, 185-186

listing (or list), 127, 153, 176, 178, 179, 182, 184-185, 186, 187-188, 190, 222, 225, 231, 270, 317, 321, 322, 327

lodge, xxii, 178-186, 195, 326, 327

Lord Chancellor, xv, xxi, 5, 11, 39, 45, 56, 61, 65-69, 71, 72, 73-74, 76, 78-79, 96, 105, 107, 241, 320

Lord Chancellor's Department, 66, 67, 69, 94, 149, 235

Lord Chief Justice, xxi, 19, 65, 66, 69, 76

Lord Denning, 11, 96, 151-152

Lord of Appeal in Ordinary, xxi, 4, 67, 90, 91, 92, 104, 106, 137, 256

Lord Justice (Judge), xxii, 19, 38, 152, 330

M

mandate, xxii, 168, 198, 219, 232

Master of the Rolls, xxi, 3, 9, 11, 65, 66-67, 68, 69, 76, 91, 94, 96, 120-122, 127, 129, 136, 137, 150, 151, 152, 153-155, 162, 170, 174, 182, 186, 191, 227, 232, 261, 266, 269-270,

284, 289-291, 319
median, 158, 162-167, 171, 192, 243
motion or petition, xxii, 218

N

new issues, 37, 149
notice of appeal, 8, 25, 154, 176-180, 183, 197-201, 221-225, 327, 330
    service, 176, 177-178, 180, 199, 221, 224, 236, 307
    content, 176-177, 197-198, 200, 222, 255, 258
    filing, 109, 158, 161-163, 166, 171, 175, 197-199, 200, 204, 210, 221-223, 243, 255, 258, 264, 295
    lodging, 178, 180, 184-188, 275, 286

O

official shorthand writer, xxii
opinions or judgments, 104-108, 110-115, 118, 119, 133-139, 193-194, 196-197, 214, 216-217, 225
    published, 32, 85, 104-108, 112-115, 119, 135, 136-138, 242, 245, 255
    unpublished, 17, 107-108, 115-119, 127, 168, 242-243, 249, 254-255, 258
    transcripts, 106, 155, 228
oral advocacy, 101, 128
oral argument, xxii, 3, 85, 89, 103, 108-110, 116-118, 123, 125-126, 129-133, 146, 157, 167, 168, 187, 188, 207, 208, 210, 212, 213, 214-216, 231, 242, 243, 249, 319, 321, 323, 331
oral hearing, 15, 115, 116, 118, 119, 120-123, 126-133, 141, 152, 154-155, 168, 185, 188-189, 191-193, 194-195, 215, 228, 230-232, 243-244, 248, 254, 256, 259, 266-271, 276-

282, 285-292, 297-302, 309, 317, 331

oral tradition, 22, 90, 101-103, 115-130, 132, 135-136, 168, 190, 192, 230, 233, 242, 246, 259, 292

order, xxii, 7, 13-19, 26, 34, 43, 45, 46-47, 48, 52, 76, 175-190, 194-195, 199, 219-220, 226, 227, 232, 239-240, 253, 254, 255, 256, 261, 264, 265, 266, 270, 280, 284, 293, 300, 301, 305

Order 59, 9, 18, 43, 45, 51, 152, 176, 178, 220, 240

P

Parker, Judge John, 27-28

party or parties, 1, 2, 6, 8, 12-14, 17-19, 27-29, 33-35, 37, 44, 46-48, 57, 79, 85, 106, 109, 123, 128-129, 135-136, 139, 149, 151, 153-154, 158, 162, 169, 175-176, 177-179, 186, 188, 189, 191, 194-200, 203, 205, 206, 209-212, 214, 216-228, 245, 247, 254, 255-256, 260

per incuriam, 11, 292

plaintiff in error, 2

Pound, Roscoe, 24, 50, 52

Practice Direction, xv, 68, 122-123, 129-130, 132-133, 154-155, 171, 230, 248, 319-331

precedent, 10-12, 28-32, 41-42, 51, 72, 102, 104, 115, 129, 133, 136, 193, 245, 267, 297, 301

prereading, 121-122, 129-130, 131, 133, 168, 188, 190

printed case, 129, 188, 195

productivity, 118, 121-122, 149, 154, 155, 167, 170-171, 243, 247, 320

publication, 85, 104-108, 109, 112-115, 133, 136-139, 168, 185, 202, 214, 242, 243, 249, 255, 316

  opinions, 112-115, 168, 214, 249

  judgments, 104-108, 255, 316

pupillage, 58-60, 71, 77, 87, 126, 241, 246

Q

Queen's Bench Division, 4, 19, 66, 105, 175, 185, 187, 232, 284, 285, 286, 293

Queen's Counsel, 59, 61, 65, 66, 74, 77, 91, 124, 127, 130, 131, 191, 259, 282, 309

R

reconsideration, 205, 216-217, 229, 233, 258

record, xxii, 1, 2-3, 6, 12, 22, 32, 33, 35, 36, 69, 109, 116, 119, 123, 128, 134, 152, 158, 160, 161, 165-166, 186, 190, 196, 200, 202-205, 206, 209, 211, 212, 213, 214, 219, 221, 222, 225, 227-228, 231, 247

reform of legal profession, 70-79
    Green Paper, 71-75, 79, 94
    Benson Committee, 69-70
    Marre Committee, 70
    White Paper, 45, 75-77, 78-79

Registrar of Civil Appeals, 68, 91, 152, 153-154, 168, 241, 265

Registrar of Criminal Appeals, 20

re-hearing, 7, 9, 18, 39, 48, 176, 208, 217, 221, 239

relief pending appeal, 180-181, 183, 201-202, 205, 226-227, 255

reports, 69, 104-108, 112-115, 117, 119, 127, 136-137, 138, 195, 214, 242, 255, 258, 336, 331

reserved judgment, 105-107, 128, 136, 193, 267, 289

respondent, xxii, 15, 43, 175-177, 180-181, 182, 183, 186, 189, 190, 192, 195, 196, 222, 224, 226-227, 228, 266, 267, 271, 277, 282, 287, 288-289, 292, 297, 309, 310, 317, 326, 330, 331

respondent's notice, xxii, 180, 181, 190, 226, 265, 271, 308, 326, 330

reversible error, 18-19, 36-37, 48, 202-203, 207

right of audience, 22, 58, 61-62, 72-79, 101, 132, 240
right to appeal, 13-17, 25, 32-33, 43-47, 152, 169, 184, 194, 197, 239, 243, 253
  see also *appeal as of right* and *appeal of right*
Royal Courts of Justice, xiv, 69, 106, 188, 191, 222

S

Scarman Committee, 96, 129, 152
screening, 65, 85, 87, 90, 91, 157, 213
selection of judges, 65, 91, 101
settlement conference, 211, 231
Short Warned List, 187-188, 322, 328-329
skeleton argument, 129-130, 132, 152, 154-155, 176, 184, 188-189, 190, 226, 266, 275, 276, 277, 278, 286, 292, 296, 297, 308, 309, 320, 321, 323, 325-331
skills training, 59-60, 63, 81-82, 86-89, 132-133
solicitor, xxii, 57, 62-64, 70-71, 74-79, 86, 95, 96, 125, 130, 132, 176, 187, 189, 191, 220, 228, 240-241, 254, 256, 288
speech (House of Lords), xxii, 5
staff, 20, 57, 67-69, 72, 79, 84-85, 90, 91-93, 122, 138, 154, 156-160, 167-168, 171, 175, 184, 186, 189, 205, 211, 213, 214, 215, 224, 231-232, 240, 241-242, 243, 250, 254, 257, 260, 316
staff attorneys, 85, 98, 157, 211
standard of review, 18, 35-36, 40-41, 48, 271, 298-300
stare decisis, 10, 28, 29, 41
state court of appeal, xxi
state supreme court, xxi, 25, 26, 53, 156
statistics, 149-150, 155-156, 161-167, 170-171, 174, 192
structure and function, 4-37, 239-240, 253-254, 256-257
submission, 160, 162-166, 167, 189, 243

on briefs, 116, 213-214

after oral argument, 214-216

summary disposition, 157, 158, 212

Supreme Court Act 1981, 14, 51, 96, 152

Supreme Court of the United States, xxi, 23, 25, 26, 27, 30, 31, 39, 41, 81, 82, 97, 110, 112, 117-118, 121, 125, 146, 198, 218, 258

Supreme Court Rules Committee, 15, 16-17, 43, 45, 253, 254

T

Tate, Judge Albert, 29, 207-208

three judge panel, 169-170, 174, 205, 213, 229, 245, 253, 255, 309, 317

transcript of testimony, 22, 117, 133, 158, 160, 177, 256, 266-267, 268, 271

transcripts, 106, 117, 137, 150, 227, 228, 331

two judge panel, 173, 174, 317

V

Vice-Chancellor, 69, 76, 91

W

writ of error, 1-3, 5-7, 13, 14, 24-25, 37, 39

written tradition, xiii, 108-115, 116, 119-120, 130-133, 135-136, 229-230, 242, 249